The politics of fisheries in the European Union

Published in our
centenary year
❧ **2004** ☙
MANCHESTER
UNIVERSITY
PRESS

European Policy Research Unit Series

Series Editors: *Simon Bulmer, Peter Humphreys* and *Mick Moran*

The European Policy Research Unit Series aims to provide advanced text-books and thematic studies of key public policy issues in Europe. They concentrate, in particular, on comparing patterns of national policy content, but pay due attention to the European Union dimension. The thematic studies are guided by the character of the policy issue under examination.

The European Policy Research Unit (EPRU) was set up in 1989 within the University of Manchester's Department of Government to promote research on European politics and public policy. The series is part of EPRU's effort to facilitate intellectual exchange and substantive debate on the key policy issues confronting the European states and the European Union.

Titles in the series also include:

The politics of fisheries in the European Union

Christian Lequesne

Translated from the French by Cynthia Schoch and Jayne Pilling

Published with the support of the French Ministry of Culture–Centre National du Livre

Manchester University Press
Manchester and New York

distributed exclusively in the USA by Palgrave

Copyright © Presses de la Fondation Nationale des Sciences Politiques, Paris 2004

Published by Manchester University Press
Oxford Road, Manchester M13 9NR, UK
and Room 400, 175 Fifth Avenue, New York, NY 10010, USA
www.manchesteruniversitypress.co.uk

Distributed exclusively in the USA by
Palgrave, 175 Fifth Avenue, New York,
NY 10010, USA

Distributed exclusively in Canada by
UBC Press, University of British Columbia, 2029 West Mall,
Vancouver, BC, Canada V6T 1Z2

British Library Cataloguing-in-Publication Data
A catalogue record for this book is available from the British Library

Library of Congress Cataloging-in-Publication Data applied for

ISBN 0 7190 6770 7 *hardback*

This edition first published 2004

11 10 09 08 07 06 05 04   10 9 8 7 6 5 4 3 2 1

Typeset in Sabon
by Action Publishing Technology Ltd, Gloucester
Printed in Great Britain
by Biddles Ltd, King's Lynn

Contents

List of tables

Abbreviations

AC	autonomous community
ACFA	Advisory Committee on Fisheries and Aquaculture
ACFM	Advisory Committee on Fisheries Management
ACP	Africa–Caribbean–Pacific
AGLIA	Association du Grand Littoral Atlantique
AIPCEE/CEP	Association of Fish Industries of the EEC
ANACEF	National Association of Cephalopod Freezers
ARVI	Cooperative of fishing shipowners of the port of Vigo
CAEC	Court of Auditors of the European Communities
CAP	Common Agricultural Policy
CCF	Consultative Committee on Fisheries
CCFA	Consultative Committee on Fisheries and Aquaculture
CCT	common customs tariff
CECAF	Fishery Committee for the Eastern-Central Atlantic
CEFAS	Centre for Environment, Fisheries and Aquaculture Science
CFDT	Confédération Française Démocratique du Travail
CFI	Court of First Instance
CFP	Common Fisheries Policy
CGT	Confédération Générale du Travail
CJEC	Court of Justice of the European Communities
CNPMEM	Comité National des Pêches Maritimes et des Élevages Marins (National Committee of Maritime Fisheries and Mariculture)
COBRECAF	Compagnie Bretonne de Cargos Frigorifiques
COM	Common Organisation of Markets
COREPER	Permanent Representative Committee
CROSS	Centre régional opérationnel de surveillance et de sauvetage
CSO	Conseil supérieur d'orientation des politiques halieutique, aquacole et halioalimentaire

DATAR	Délégation à l'aménagement du territoire et à l'action territoriale (Delegation for Territorial Planning and Regional Action)
DG	Directorate General
DRAM	Direction régionale des affaires maritimes (Regional agency for Shipping and Maritime Affairs)
EAFE	European Association of Fisheries Economists
EAGGF	European Agricultural Guidance and Guarantee Fund
EAPO	European Association of Producers' Organisations
EC	European Community
ECA	European Court of Auditors
EEA	European Economic Area/Agreement
EEC	European Economic Community
EEZ	exclusive economic zone
ENGO	Environmental non-governmental organisation
ENIM	Établissement national des invalides de la marine
EPP	European People's Party
ERDF	European Regional Development Fund
ESF	European Social Fund
EU	European Union
FAO	United Nations Food and Agriculture Organisation
FCG	Fisheries Conservation Group
FEAP	Federation of European Aquaculture Producers
FEDOPA	Fédération des organisations de producteurs de la pêche artisanale (French producers' association)
FIFG	Financial Instrument for Fisheries Guidance
FIOM	Fonds d'intervention des organisations de marché
FPO	Fish Producers' Organisation
FROM	Fonds régional d'organisation des marchés (regional fund for the organisation of markets)
GATT	General Agreement on Tariffs and Trade
GDP	gross domestic product
GFCM	General Fisheries Council for the Mediterranean
GSP	generalised system of preferences
IBSFC	International Baltic Sea Fishery Commission
ICCAT	International Commission for the Conservation of Tunas
ICES	International Council for the Exploration of the Sea
ICJ	International Court of Justice
IEO	Instituto Español de Oceanografía (Spanish Oceanographic Institute)
IFREMER	Institut Français de Recherche pour l'Exploitation de la Mer (French Research Institute for the Exploitation of the Sea)
IOTC	Indian Ocean Tuna Commission

ISM	Instituto Social de la Marina
ITQ	individual transferable quota
MAFF	Ministry of Agriculture, Fisheries and Food
MAGP	multiannual guidance programme
MEP	Member of the European Parliament
MMPA	Marine Mammal Protection Act (1972)
NAFO	North-West Atlantic Fisheries Organisation
NEAFC	North-East Atlantic Fisheries Commission/Convention
NFFO	National Federation of Fishermen's Organisations
NGO	non-governmental organisation
OECD	Organisation for Economic Cooperation and Development
OFIMER	Office Interprofessionnel des Produits de la Mer
OJEC	*Official Journal of the European Communities*
OPOB	Organisation des producteurs de l'Ouest-Bretagne
PO	Producers' Organisation
PROMA	Organisation de producteurs du Morbihan-Loire-Atlantique
RFB	regional fishery bodies
RFO	Regional Fishery Organisation
SBF	Save Britain's Fish
SFC	Sea Fisheries' Committee
SFF	Scottish Fishermen's Federation
SFP	special fishing permit
SGP	System of Generalised Preferences
SNATC	Syndicat national des armateurs thoniers congélateurs (National Union of Freezer-Tuna-Boat Owners)
SNP	Scottish National Party
STECF	Scientific, Technical and Economic Committee for Fisheries
TAC	total allowable catches
UAPF	Union des armateurs à la pêche de France (Union of French Fishing Shipowners)
UCLAF	Unit for the Coordination of Fraud Prevention
UGT	Union General de Trabadores (General Workers' Union)
ULAM	Unité littorale des affaires maritimes
UNCTAD	United Nations Conference on Trade and Development
UNGA	United Nations General Assembly
WTO	World Trade Organisation
WWF	World Wide Fund for Nature

Acknowledgements

This book is the result of research conducted from 1997 to 2000 in Belgium, Spain, France and Great Britain as well as in Demark, the Netherlands and Morocco. It was published in French in 2001 by the Presses de Sciences Po. Its completion has been made possible by the support granted by the Fondation Nationale des Sciences Politiques. I am indebted to the Centre d'Etudes et de Recherches Internationales (CERI) in Paris which, for the past fifteen years, has offered me academic and logistic support. I wish to thank all of my colleagues – research and administrative staff alike – for their help in bringing this book together. Special gratitude goes to Linda Amrani for her administration of the project and organisation of the missions, to Sylvie Haas for making contacts in Spain, to Carmen Mitrea for the documentary research, to Cynthia Schoch and Jayne Pilling for translating the manuscript from French into English, and to Sibylle Poirier-Coutansais for compiling the index.

I particularly want to thank all those who agreed to read portions of the manuscript and contribute their critical comments. I am thinking especially of Loïc Antoine, at IFREMER (French Research Institute for the Exploitation of the Sea), Jean-René Couliou, at the Université de Bretagne Occidentale, Cyrille Guernalec, of the Comité National des Pêches Maritimes, Nicolas Jabko, at CERI, Dominique Levieil, Serge Beslier and Mireille Thom at the European Commission, and Emiliano Grossman and Sabine Saurugger at Sciences Po. The researchers in the seminar on policy-making at CEVIPOF (Centre d'Études de la Vie Politique Française) as well as Bruno Cautrès, in charge of the programme 'European Identity in Question' at CNRS, also enabled me to present my research in seminars that proved very helpful to me. By the same token, Marie-Claude Smouts, Helen Wallace and Peter Leslie, Denis Bailly and David Symes invited me to test several hypotheses underlying this work during meetings of the European Consortium for Political Research (Vienna, September 1998), the International Political Science Association (Brussels, December 1999) and the European Social Sciences Fisheries Network (Brest, September 1997; Copenhagen, April 1999) respectively. My thanks go to Helen and William Wallace, who offered me, in addition to their hospitality during my stays in London, an opportunity to draft the chapter on the Common Fisheries Policy for the fourth edition of their book *Policy-Making in the European Union*. I am also grateful to Simon Bulmer, who put me in contact with Manchester University Press.

This book could never have come about without the fishermen, fishery professionals, administrators and experts who for three years welcomed me in the privacy of their offices, on their boats, or simply a quiet spot on the docks or at an auction to talk about their job and also about Europe (see list in the Appendix). From these people, about whose codes and practices I knew nothing at the beginning of the research, I drew the material I was looking for to try to bring a Community policy 'to life'. My gratitude goes out to all of them.

Last but not least, this book owes much to Monique, Matthieu and Juliette Lequesne, who generously put up with my absences and my need for time to write. Their love and good sense of humour have been very supportive.

Introduction

Long confined to a limited circle of scholars, the study of the European Union (EU) has, since the 1980s, given rise to a growing number of studies in political science. The caricatural opposition between an intergovernmentalist school and a neofunctionalist school in intrepreting the EU belongs to a bygone era. As EU studies have multiplied, the cleavages have grown in complexity and diminished the often Draconian divisions between what existed within and among political science disciplines.[1] Political sociologists and public policy analysts working on the state have thoroughly invested the field of European integration, by looking into convergence phenomena of public action as it is affected by European rules and 'collision' processes between various state polities and the European polity.[2] As a result, numerous studies of the EU 'in action' have been conducted, taking as a starting point the formulation and implementation of Community policies. By underscoring the impact of the process of transnational recomposition on the modes of action employed by economic, political and social actors, these studies have gone beyond a purely inter-state approach to the EU and brought to light a new, polycentric polity, sometimes known as governance. This notion grew out of the need analysts felt to denominate the growing independence of sectors and groups in western societies that increasingly leads states to coordinate social subsystems instead of imposing mechanisms of imperative authority and vertical administration.[3] Although research on EU governance readily lends itself to the study of an EU in which the emergence of a single autonomous governing body or a clear-cut frontier between public and private actors is far from apparent, it has nevertheless become terribly routine. Much of it does little more than reiterate a series of observations on the constitution of a network of European actors through the convergence of public modes of action influenced by market norms, on expert debate as a stake in political compromise, or on the diversification of interest representation, without really testing these pertinent intuitions empirically.[4]

The option taken in this book is precisely to grasp the EU polity through the detailed study of a particular Community policy, the Common Fisheries Policy (CFP). The approach originates with the assumption that the meaning and the dynamics of European politics cannot be measured without first observing the practices of the actors involved in the processes, as well as their accounts of these practices.[5] Except as regards analyses approached from a political philosophy perspective, a political science study of the EU without making reference to its actors is in fact rather devoid of interest.[6] It even runs the risk of falling into the empty generalizations too often demonstrated, alas, in many macroscopic studies on European governance or the European public space. Of course, the point is not to oppose in vain abstract theories supposedly totally disconnected from EU reality and solidly constructed case studies that would be the sole means of illustrating them. Rather, it appears obvious that there can be no overall comprehension and conceptualisation of the EU without minute examination of the specific power arenas of which it is composed.[7]

Secondly, there is not one but *several* styles of research in which the political science study of the EU can be done. A perusal of the specialised literature shows the appeal of a style inspired by the North American academic tradition over numerous analysts working on the EU. Deriving mainly from constraints specific to the academic career of United States professors, this style is always poured from the same mould. It starts with a preliminary theoretical framework, the principal hypotheses of which are tested by one or two case studies that are never entirely field based, to reach the conclusion that the initial theory was the right one, discarding all the others.[8] The jubilant scientism of 'Hurrah, my theory is working!' is, however, far from representative of the only way for political scientists to investigate the EU. There are many others. One of them involves analytically reconstructing the processes by which Community policies have been devised and implemented with an aim to shed light on the major questions that any democratic polity poses, i.e. the process of legitimating decisions, representing interests, allocating and distributing resources, and so on. This approach, which can be qualified as *empiricist*, has repercussions on the way the demonstration is presented: analysis of the EU polity is in effect bound up in a sometimes very detailed narration of a given field, meaning that it appears in a purposely *implicit* manner. This manner of proceeding can give the impression that one has become an expert on the policy at hand and has forgotten the original aim of shedding light on the EU as a whole. A few years ago, Andy Smith and myself gauged this constraint by evoking the risk of 'starting from the bottom to work up, and getting sidetracked'.[9] And in writing this book I was indeed continually confronted with the problem of not losing sight of the EU in general while taking care also to address those with first-hand knowledge of the CFP.

In using the CFP to achieve an understanding of the EU polity, I have therefore been careful not to relegate the former to the rank of pretext. First listed on the European Community agenda in 1970, and not in 1983 as one often reads in reference to early resource conservation measures, the CFP is a Community policy that provides one of the most varied illustrations of European public action. It is a market organisation policy directly inspired from Common Agricultural Policy (CAP) mechanisms. It is a redistributive policy seeking to reduce inequalities among territories through the use of European structural funds. It is a regulatory policy which, like the environmental policy, sets standards for the use of a natural resource perceived as a common good. It is, last, a policy with regard to third countries that contributes to the emergence of an EU external policy. Since the work published in 1994 by a former Commission official, Mike Holden, no recent book with a political science background has been specifically devoted to the topic.[10] Yet its various facets make the CFP an inviting prism through which to explore the main questions raised by the study of the EU polity. This is the ambition of the chapters that follow. We will examine the conditions in which national policy-making has been shifted to the European level, the distribution of powers among multi-level institutions, the specific nature of a European interest representation and its interactions with national and local corporatism, budget allocation and redistribution of resources in a transnational polity, regulation and expertise as decision-making operational modes, the process of legitimation in a 'contested polity',[11] and last, the positioning of the EU as an actor on the world stage.

Employing a method chosen for prior work,[12] the primary source for this book has been semi-directive interviews. Conducted between 1997 and 2000 in Brussels and in five EU member countries – Spain, France, Great Britain, Denmark and the Netherlands – as well as Morocco, these interviews led us to speak with the actors involved in the CFP on a daily basis. These naturally include those who work in the fishery trade as well as European institution officials, but also politicians and national and regional officials, experts and scientists in oceanographic institutes, as well as representatives of non-governmental organisations (NGOs) (particularly environmental organisations). This research experience has provided the opportunity once again to test the pertinence of interviews as EU research material.[13] In gathering these testimonies, the inherent drawbacks linked to the representativeness of the social group studied were not neglected. Readers might object that the study concentrated on the problems the CFP poses for high-sea fishermen – industrials and artisans – rather than inshore fishermen. This is neither a deliberate choice nor omission, but rather an indication that this Community policy was primarily designed for fishermen whose vessels fish the 200-mile zone and the high seas.

Notes

1 See Ben Rosamond's useful and critical review, *Theories of Integration*, London, Macmillan, 2000; as well as Christian Lequesne and Andy Smith, 'Union européenne et science politique: où en est le débat théorique?', *Cultures et conflits*, 38, winter 1997, pp. 7–31.

2 See for instance Yves Mény, Pierre Muller and Jean-Louis Quermonne, *Politiques publiques en Europe*, Paris, L'Harmattan, 1995; Patrick Le Galès, 'Est maître des lieux celui qui les organise. How Rules Change when National and European Policy Domains Collide', in N. Fligstein, W. Sandholtz and A. Stone (eds), *The Institutionalisation of Europe*, Oxford, Oxford University Press, 2001.

3 See Renate Mayntz, *New Challenges to Governance Theory*, Chair Jean-Monnet, Florence, European University Institute, 1998; as well as Marie-Claude Smouts, 'Du bon usage de la gouvernance en relations internationales', *Revue internationale des sciences sociales*, 155, March 1998, pp. 95–108.

4 For instance, see Philippe C. Schmitter, 'Imagining the Future of the Euro-Polity with the Help of New Concepts', in Gary Marks I., *Governance in the European Union*, London, Sage, 1996, pp. 121–150.

5 See Claudio M. Radaelli, 'Logiques de pouvoirs et récits dans les pratiques de l'Union européenne', *Revue française de science politique*, 50 (2), April 2000, pp. 255–275.

6 See Jeremy J. Richardson, 'Actors-Based Models of National and EU Policy-Making', in Hussein Kassim and Anand Menon (eds), *The European Union and National Industrial Policy*, London, Routledge, 1996.

7 As can be seen in the comparative study by Helen Wallace and William Wallace (eds), *Policy-Making in the European Union*, Oxford, Oxford University Press, 2000.

8 See for instance Andrew Moravcsik, *The Choice for Europe: Social Purpose and State Power from Messina to Maastricht*, Ithaca and London, Cornell University Press, 1998; or Wayne Sandholtz and Alec Stone (eds), *European Integration and Supranational Governance*, Oxford, Oxford University Press, 1998.

9 Lequesne and Smith, 'Union européenne et science politique', p. 23.

10 Mike Holden, *The Common Fisheries Policy*, Oxford, Oxford Fishing News Books, 1994.

11 See Thomas Banchoff and Mitchell P. Smith (eds), *Legitimacy and the European Union. The Contested Polity*, London, Routledge, 1999.

12 Christian Lequesne, *Paris–Bruxelles. Comment se fait la politique européenne de la France*, Paris, Presses de Sciences Po, 1993.

13 Regarding interviews in political science, see Samy Cohen (ed.), *L'art d'interviewer les décideurs*, Paris, PUF, 1999.

1

When fishery becomes a European policy

In none of the thirteen EU coastal states did fishing contribute any more than 1 per cent of the gross domestic product in 2002. Fishery has nevertheless long figured on national public policy agendas in a solidly institutionalised manner. EU countries all had national fishery policies which were 'destabilised', starting in the 1970s, by the Common Fisheries Policy (CFP) developed in the European Community (EC). This Community policy was conceived and formulated as a centralised policy, such that the Court of Justice of the European Communities (CJEC) recognised it in 1976 as one of the rare policies that, like the Common Agricultural Policy and Trade Policy, came under the sole authority of the EC.[1]

This chapter focuses on the genesis and the main stages of development of the CFP since its inception. It first shows the role that fishery occupies in EU countries as an economic activity. It then proceeds to describe the institutional principles and aims of the CFP. Lastly, it shows how these result from a process of incremental EU agenda-setting, reflecting economic and institutional changes within the EU itself, its member states, and more generally on the international scene. In taking into consideration the latter factor, this work breaks away from policy-making or European governance approaches that too often disregard the EU's relationship to the rest of the world as they seek to understand the emergence of new forms of political regulation within it.

Fishery viewed as a sector
Like agriculture, fishing is an economic activity that brings into play diverse interests in EU countries. There is not one but many European fishing industries. To take the example of Spain, the boats, revenues and professional outlook of the Hondarribia coastal fishermen in the Basque country have nothing in common with those of the high-sea shipowners in Burela, Galicia who fish hake off the coast of Ireland. Their fate in turn has little in common with that of the Bermeo fleet-owners that go after

tropical tuna in freezer-trawlers in the southern Atlantic. This variety of activities results in a segmented economic landscape, a fragmentation that does not contradict the representation most professionals, administrators and scientists have of the 'fishery sector'. The sector is thought of as multi-faceted, with production from the sea being the common reference point for the various actors.

The problem of definitions

Structural differences exist in the means of production that actors in European fishery have integrated into their representation of the sector, naturally with variants that are discernible from one national context to another. A primary difference is one distinguishing long-range, distant-water or deep-sea fishing from middle-water fishing (also called high-sea fishing) and from coastal, or inshore, fishing.

Long-range fishing brings into play the largest vessels, those usually greater than 30 metres long. They travel outside of EU waters on voyages that generally last more than twenty days. High-sea fishing (or middle-water fishing) is done in medium-sized boats (from 20 to 30 metres) in EU waters for lengths of time ranging from four to twenty days. Coastal fishing, on the other hand, is done with the smallest vessels on trips that do not usually exceed four days.

Another structural difference distinguishes between large-scale fishing and small-scale fishing. The former involves the activity of large vessels belonging either to a commercial fishing company or a shipowner who is not on board. Large-scale fishing crews are usually remunerated with a minimum guaranteed wage in most European countries.[2] On the other hand, small-scale fishing is done on boats belonging to natural persons usually on board as skipper or even as engineer. In most EU member countries, the form of remuneration practiced is highly specific with regard to that of other professions. The system is 'by the share', in which the proceeds of each trip are divided up between the shipowner and crewmembers according to the catch and sales.

Within the EU, small-scale fishing does not cover only coastal fishing. The netters of Penzance, in southwest England, the pelagic trawlers of Lorient in Brittany and the liners of Hondarribia in Spanish Basque country who, until 2001, left the harbour for three weeks to fish albacore tuna in the Bay of Biscay on boats no longer than 25 metres belonged to the small-scale sector. The distinction between large-scale fishing and small-scale fishing is important in order to understand the types of interest organisation and political mobilisation that fisheries questions induce on the national and European levels. The diversity of the sector cannot, however, be truly appreciated through this distinction alone. Each major type of fishing activity is also broken down into a variety of occupations that differ according to the fishing methods and species fished, implying specific types of organisation: pelagic trawlers, demersal trawlers, netters, longliners, potters, etc. The reference to an occupation also depends on the fishing areas frequented, as illustrated in accounts by the fishermen themselves. In a fine study on the organisation of sea fishing in southern Brittany, Jean-René Couliou points out that Douarnenez once knew a period of those referred to as the 'Mauritanians', in other words, fishermen who trapped spiny lobster off the coast of Mauritania. When Lorient registered high hake catches in the 1960s, on the wharf of this Morbihan port they talked about the 'Iberian trade'. In Brittany, coalfish and blueling fishing in British waters is still referred to as the 'North trade' as opposed to the 'South trade', which corresponds to fishing activities practised below the latitude of southern Ireland.[3]

Although not within the scope of this book, aquaculture, meaning fish and shellfish farming, is another production activity that is now an integral part of the marine fisheries sector. Aquaculture, which has been on the rise since the late 1970s in the EU, also relies on very different production methods ranging from small-scale crustaceans, such as oyster farming in the Marennes-Oléron basin in France, to industrial salmon farming off the coast of Scotland and Ireland organised by major industrial groups such as Golden Sea Produce, a subsidiary of the Norwegian food and beverage conglomerate Hydro Seafood. Aquaculture is an activity that scientists have contributed to legitimating within the EU by presenting it as an alternative to the problem of resource depletion. It is nevertheless subject to intense world competition. In the sector of salmon farming, Chilean aquaculture industries, for instance, more than doubled their production between 1994 and 1999, taking advantage of cheap labour and easy access to fishmeal. They have thus earned a solid reputation of being highly competitive on the world markets to the detriment of European countries.

Fleets and jobs
There are approximately 92,000 fishing vessels in the EU, 80 per cent of which are active in the small-scale sector. Greece has the largest fleet (19,992 boats in 2001), followed by Italy, Spain and Portugal (Table 1.1). In terms of tonnage and horsepower, the Spanish fleet, however, ranks first with 532,000 tonnes in 2001, or double that of the United Kingdom, which holds second place with 258,000 tonnes. Since the creation of the CFP in 1970, there has been a general tendency in the EU to reduce the number of long-range fishing vessels due to access restrictions that many third countries impose in their waters to preserve their resource base, whereas the proportion of boats used for inshore fishing and high-sea fishing has increased.

Table 1.1 Number of fishing vessels in the EU (1993–2001)

	1993 01/01/94	1994 01/01/95	1995 01/01/96	1996 01/01/97	1997 01/01/98	1998 01/01/99	1999	2000	2001
Belgium	185	170	156	156	148	142	128	127	130
Denmark	3,308	5,292	5,165	5,091	4,648	4,373	4,223	4,149	4,058
Germany	2,480	2,454	2,406	2,382	2,373	2,310	2,313	2,314	2,281
Greece	20,420	20,444	20,328	20,334	20,243	20,445	19,818	19,972	19,992
Spain	19,013	19,010	18,478	18,351	17,972	17,521	17,312	16,680	15,477
Finland		3,798	3,881	4,010	3,979	3,882	3,763	3,661	3,610
France	7,021	6,829	6,593	6,496	8,836	8,537	8,310	8,191	7,928
Ireland	1,435	1,417	1,366	1,355	1,246	1,182	1,212	1,193	1,195
Italy	16,692	16,484	16,352	16,353	16,325	18,934	18,385	17,503	16,546
The Netherlands	1,610	993	1,009	1,009	1,040	1,053	1,073	1,076	1,074
Portugal	13,133	12,604	12,306	12,183	11,579	11,171	10,869	10,718	10,691
Sweden		2,323	2,514	2,481	2,481	2,123	1,899	1,943	1,950
UK	11,344	10,530	9,767	8,482	8,658	8,433	8,526	7,666	7,540
Europe of the Fifteen	96,641	102,348	10,0321	98,683	99,528	100,106	97,300	98,163	92,472

Sources: European Commission, Directorate General XIV, *Facts and Figures*, September 1999 and *Fisheries Yearbook 2002*

Statistics are seriously lacking for fishery as an economic activity in most EU member countries. It is therefore difficult to assess the number of working fishermen with any real precision. On the basis of data collected by governments and national organisations of fishermen, the European Commission nevertheless estimated in 2001 that there were approximately 250,000 fishermen in the thirteen coastal European states, or 0.2 per cent of the EU working population, and that this number had decreased by 10 per cent compared to 1990. More than farmers, fishermen are hence an occupational group whose capacity for mobilisation far exceeds the numerical proportion they represent in the working population (Table 1.2).

Its capacity for political mobilisation is explained by the fact that fishery is an activity with a high territorial concentration sometimes generating a significant assortment of jobs in coastal regions where access to the labour market is otherwise limited. Of the working population in the autonomous community of Galicia, Spain, 12 per cent were thus directly or indirectly involved in fishery or supplying goods and services to the fisheries sector in 1998. In certain Galician ports such as Ribeira, Canido and Cangas, the numbers can be as high as 30 per cent of the working population. Though not as high as in Galicia, local fishery-related jobs also reach significant proportions in certain ports in the Highlands region of Scotland: 12.5 per cent of the jobs in the ports of Lerwick and Scalloway.[4] In these coastal micro-zones, dependence on the activity often contributes to maintaining a guild-type of interest organisation that in fact draws its legitimacy in reference to a sea-faring history. In the event of economic perturbations, these interests are able to generate anti-government protest that is backed by local corporations. In 1993 and 1994, a sudden collapse in the price of fish in France brought the Brittany fishermen and their families to mobilise and form a *comité de survie* (survival committee) that, at least in its early stages, enjoyed the support of the coastal inhabitants despite breaches of the peace.[5]

Production and fishing areas
In 2000, EU fishermen took 7.2 million tonnes of fish and shellfish. The countries of the European Economic Area (EEA: the EU as well as Iceland and Norway) thus ranked second in the world for exploitation of fishery resources after China and before the major Latin American and Asian producer countries: Peru, Chile and Japan. In the EU, Denmark has the highest production rate with over 1.5 million tonnes in 2000, corresponding to approximately 21 per cent of the total EU catch (see Table 1.3). This rank can be attributed to the activity of an industrial fleet operating mainly out of the port of Esberg, Jutland, and which has specialised in the fishing of species meant for oil and fish-meal manufacture. Spain holds

Table 1.2 Jobs directly related to the fishery sector (1992–2000)

	1992	1993	1994	1995	1996	1997	1998	1999	2000
Belgium	762	720	652	624	600	579	564	544	N.A.
Denmark	7,121	6,380	6,256	8,061	7,579	7,130	6,999	6,711	6,564
Germany	4,377	4,142	4,209	4,646	4,450	4,422	4,335	4,363	4,358
Greece	20,881	31,549	32,704	22,290	22,192	13,379	18,007	19,620	19,847
Spain	94,246	89,355	87,967	84,877	84,902	N.A.	N.A.	N.A.	N.A.
Finland	5,918	6,116	5,588	6,207	6,373	6,180	5,928	5,718	5,689
France	29,588	28,306	27,598	26,879	26,522	21,162	21,018	N.A.	N.A.
Ireland	7,700	7,700	7,700	7,500	7,500	3,269	8,476	N.A.	N.A.
Italy	45,620	45,000	45,000	45,000	48,238	40,224	N.A.	N.A.	48,770
The Netherlands	4,881	4,910	3,762	3,756	3,810	3,711	3,749	N.A.	N.A.
Portugal	36,337	34,454	31,721	30,937	28,458	27,347	27,197	26,680	25,021
Sweden	N.A.	3,000	3,500	3,287	N.A.	N.A.	N.A.	2,880	2783
United Kingdom	20,678	21,351	21,874	19,921	19,044	18,604	N.A.	N.A.	N.A.
Europe of the Fifteen		285,483	280,829	288,305	[258,572]	[250,220]			

Sources: European Commission, Directorate General XIV, *Facts and Figures*, September 1999 and *Fisheries Yearbook 2002*

second place with 18 per cent among the EU production, mainly intended for human consumption, followed by France, the United Kingdom, the Netherlands and Italy. If the negative outcome of the 28 November 1994 referendum had not obliged the Norwegian government to abandon EU membership, this picture would have been different on 1 January 1995. Norway would indeed have taken the lead among EU-producer countries, in front of Denmark and Spain (see Table 1.3).

In inventorying the species caught by fishermen, scientific experts usually take into account two criteria: their biological classification and their habitat. In 1995, two categories of fish – codfish, hake and halibut; and herring, sardines and anchovies – amounted to 42 per cent of the fish caught by countries in the EEA. This means quite simply that the fishery effort in the EU is concentrated on a limited number of marketable species, a fact that has largely contributed to putting the question of resource conservation high on the agenda of topics debated by the CFP. National variations exist nevertheless in the composition of catches made by the fleets, due to differences not only in the frequentation of fishing areas but also in local consumption habits. Thus, two flat fishes, sole and halibut, account for 50 per cent of the catches made by Belgian fishermen in the North Sea and the Atlantic. Similarly, only fishermen in the southern countries of the EU – including France – catch tuna intended for the canning industry.

Turning to fishing areas, 86 per cent of the catch in 2000 took place in the north-east Atlantic, in other words in a triangle linking the Azores, Iceland and the north of Norway. The north-east Atlantic has therefore always been a preferred field of experimentation for Community resource conservation policy, unlike the Mediterranean, which until 1994, escaped any common regulatory measure. Conversely, in thirty years, there has been a significant decrease in catches by EU fishing vessels in the north-west Atlantic: 0.7 per cent of the total in 2000 compared to 8.1 per cent in 1970. This is due to a decline in European deep-sea fishing (for instance Spanish Basque and Portuguese cod fishing, which have now diminished considerably) as a result of restrictive access policies decided since the 1980s by countries such as Canada and Greenland to protect stocks (Table 1.4).[6]

Consumption and trade dependence
According to the 1995 FAO (UN Food and Agriculture Organisation) report on food supplies, the apparent consumption of fishery products in the EU was 22 kg per year and per inhabitant. This figure is higher than the world average (13 kg), though considerably lower than Japanese consumption (68 kg) and Icelandic consumption (93 kg). EU countries have significant consumption discrepancies due to different eating habits,

Table 1.3 Catch volume of fishing product (in tonnes) in the EU (1992–2000)

	1992	1993	1994	1995	1996	1997	1998	1999	2000
Belgium	37,129	6,111	4,259	35,628	30,839	30,508	31,682	91,473	31,440
Denmark	1,953,819	1,492,290	1,843,735	1,998,907	1,681,186	1,826,854	1,599,698	1,447,582	1,577,689
Germany	217,104	253,044	228,251	238,817	236,565	259,785	333,646	312,488	265,136
Greece	160,661	168,652	191,826	167,338	163,647	171,031	168,517	198,257	179,171
Spain	1,099,669	1,110,118	1,179,669	1,214,049	1,128,770	1,109,984	1,580,647	1,512,112	1,310,593
Finland	131,775	136,307	152,322	155,515	165,030	166,099	171,661	169,969	171,880
France	658,995	640,077	645,813	675,612	632,940	571,652	861,871	940,667	958,236
Ireland	278,721	321,626	331,389	437,102	368,044	329,802	367,114	327,478	334,172
Italy	457,911	460,607	479,761	488,543	427,787	350,547	526,421	504,528	518,480
Netherlands	431,732	461,641	419,927	438,110	410,807	461,016	656,721	623,400	571,145
Austria	479	420	388	404	450	465	3,363	9,502	3,706
Portugal	296,059	291,010	265,396	262,264	261,341	221,683	231,505	216,394	195,984
Sweden	307,548	341,901	386,821	404,595	370,893	357,415	416,390	357,380	343,371
The UK	828,247	877,703	897,562	913,604	869,800	896,361	1,059,641	992,567	898,779
Europe of Fifteen	6,859,849	6,591,507	7,057,119	7,430,488	6,748,099	6,753,202	8,008,777	7,627,728	7,267,174

Sources: European Commission, Directorate-General XIV, *Facts and Figures*, September 1999 and *Fisheries Yearbook 2002*

Table 1.4 Catches (in tonnes) in the EEA by fishing area (1970, 1995 and 2000)

	1970		1995		2000	
	Catches	% of total catch	Catches	% of total catch	Catches	% of total catch
North-west Atlantic	858,800	8.1	52,876	0.5	76,886	0.7
North-east Atlantic	8,318,503	78.7	9,528,900	84.9	9,292,064	86.4
Western Central Atlantic	0	0	1,948	0	0	0
Eastern Central Atlantic	524,350	5.0	437,347	3.9	389,526	3.6
Mediterranean and Black Sea	520,263	4.9	686,297	6.1	568,125	5.2
South-west Atlantic	0	0	113,719	1.0	83,038	0.7
South-east Atlantic	267,400	2.5	30,503	0.3	31,133	0.2
Indian Ocean, Antarctica	0	0	4,173	0	0	0
Western Indian Ocean	0	0	240,034	2.1	149,149	1.3
Inland waters	82,964	0.8	126,723	1.1	86,230	0.8
Total EEA catches	10,572,281	100	11,222,520	100	10,747,244	100

Sources: Eurostat, *La pêche européenne en chiffres*, Luxembourg, OPOCE, 1998 and *Fisheries Yearbook 2002*

the main fish and shellfish eaters being the Portuguese (57 kg), followed by the Spanish (39 kg). The countries which, on the other hand, have the lowest consumption are Austria (10 kg) – the only landlocked EU country together with Luxembourg – Germany (12 kg) and, rather oddly, given their production, the Netherlands (12 kg). Since the 1970s, the European processing industry, which includes major multinational corporations such as Unilever, Pescanova and Trinity, has adapted to new consumption patterns. The marketing of frozen and processed marine products has in fact risen considerably.

The trade deficit of EU countries in fishery products is nevertheless recurrent (see Table 1.5). It has multiplied nearly thirteen times in thirty years, rising from 735,430 ecus in 1970 to 10,210,200 euros in 2000.[7] In 2000, only Denmark, the Netherlands and Ireland experienced a positive trade balance. Intra-Community trade was responsible for a large portion of these exchanges, which were particularly exposed to variations in exchange rates until the euro came into being. In 2000, more than two-thirds of French exports were intended for EU country markets, particularly Italy and Spain, where fresh fish has a high market value and good commercial outlets. Similarly, one-third of French imports come from EU countries, particularly Denmark and the United Kingdom. But EU fish wholesale traders and processors also import large volumes of marine products from third countries, particularly South America and Asia, because prices are competitive and customs duties are generally low, the latter having been consolidated in the 1960s in the General Agreements on Tariffs and Trade (GATT). Imports from third-country markets involve not only frozen products but also fresh products. It takes twenty-four hours to ship hake fished off the coast of Chile via cargo plane from Santiago, Chile, to Vitoria, in Spanish Basque country, placing it in direct competition with Galician hake fishmongers' stalls in Bilbao and Madrid. Jaime Tejedor Uranga, president of the fishery brotherhoods of the Basque province of Guipuzcoa, humorously described the Vitoria airport as the Basque country's main fishing port.[8] For this reason, the level of protection that should be ensured at EU borders is a recurrent debate among fishermen, processors and European political leaders (see Chapter 7). This debate often causes governments to face totally contradictory professional interests at the domestic level, because, apart from Germany, the main EU countries importing fishery products are also the main producers.

Principles and main areas of the Common Fisheries Policy

In 1957, article 38 (now article 32) of the Treaty of Rome establishing the European Economic Community (EEC) stipulated that the common market rules would apply to fishery products as they did for agricultural

Table 1.5 Total foreign trade of EU countries in fishery products (in 1,000 Ecus/Euros) (1970, 1995 and 2000)

	1970			1995			2000		
	Imports	Exports	Balance	Imports	Exports	Balance	Imports	Exports	Balance
Belgium–Luxembourg	84,467	17,724	−66,743	796,770	283,708	−513,062	1,214,952	570,831	−644,121
Denmark	46,045	162,033	115,988	1,215,572	2,050,241	834,670	1,942,067	2,842,463	900,396
Germany	259,032	62,490	−196,542	1,928,019	644,604	−1,283,416	2,560,486	1,126,043	−1,434,442
Austria	28,087	829	−27,258	144,049	13,310	−130,739	179,275	9,391	−169,884
Greece	12,235	3,814	−8,421	176,564	135,879	−40,684	322,983	252,743	−70,240
Spain	45,543	93,414	47,872	2,343,833	936,413	−1,407,419	3,830,794	1,857,120	−1,973,674
Finland	20,292	429	−19,862	86,738	17,150	−69,588	131,564	17,498	−114,066
France	199,438	36,188	−163,250	2,468,560	766,466	−1,701,794	3,328,602	1,230,771	−2,097,831
Ireland	8,360	11,491	3,130	69,131	264,424	195,293	123,672	382,422	208,750
Italy	156,132	11,875	−144,257	1,894,468	272,556	−1,621,912	2,812,034	421,524	−2,390,511
The Netherlands	91,209	109,328	18,118	942,254	1,179,747	237,492	1,872,455	1,897,479	325,025
Portugal	31,662	45,624	13,962	602,775	222,272	−380,503	963,123	319,310	−643,814
Sweden	96,633	22,240	−74,393	414,611	195,925	−218,685	771,191	510,927	−260,283
UK	287,649	53,875	−233,773	1,496,495	865,600	−630,895	2,381,537	1,180,131	−120,408
Europe of the Fifteen	1,366,783	631,353	−735,430	14,579,539	7,848,296	−6,731,243	23,149,685	12,939,485	−10,210,200

Sources: Eurostat, *La pêche européenne en chiffres*, Luxembourg, OPOCE, 1998 and *Fisheries Yearbook* 2002

products. The original Community rules (2141/70 and 2142/70) dealing with the creation of specific measures for fisheries were not, however, adopted by the European Agriculture ministers until 1970.[9] They first aimed to set up a common organisation for the market for fishery products on the pre-existing model of the fruit and vegetable sector, then to set up structural actions financed by the Community budget in order to modernise production facilities, and finally, to implement, under certain conditions, the Community principle of free access for every fishing vessel flying the flag of a member state in the waters of another member state.

An additional step was made in January 1983 when rule 170/83 was adopted, establishing a Community system for the conservation and management of fishery resources.[10] This cornerstone text of the CFP has not undergone any fundamental reform since. Following an assessment report drawn up in 1991 by the Commission's Directorate General (DG) for Fisheries,[11] regulation 3760/92, adopted by the Council in December 1992, extended the rules of access for fishing vessels through 31 December 2002 while initiating a more ambitious policy to restrict fishery, particularly by introducing fishing licences.[12] The CFP, not unaffected by the peculiar relationship the EU has with time, thus continues to evolve and reform.[13] December 1992 regulation 3760/92 stipulated that on the basis of a Commission proposal, European fishery ministers had to decide by 31 December 2002 at the latest, any adjustments to be made in a number of areas, including the rules of access to fishing areas. In the Commission and the European Parliament, in fishery administrations and national professional organisations, implementation of the CFP was thus carried out with this constant reference to the 2002 reform, which was decided, after very difficult negotiations, in December 2002.

The CFP in fact involves action in four areas: resource conservation policy, structural policy, common organisation of the market and a policy of agreements with third countries allowing access to fishing areas. These four aspects will be described briefly, bearing in mind that each of them will be analysed in detail throughout the book.

Resource conservation policy
This policy is exemplified in the annual setting by European Fishery ministers of maximum quantities of a species that fishermen in each EU country can catch in order to limit the estimated risk of stock overexploitation. These maximum quantities, also known as total allowable catches (TAC), are divided up into fishing rights among member states during an annual negotiation that intricately links scientific and political considerations. The share that each member country obtains constitutes a national quota. In addition to TACs and quotas, a body of Community regulations has been added since the 1980s stipulating stringent technical standards for net mesh size, the size of catches and vessel power.

European fishermen often view these specific rules, devised by the Commission Fishery DG but approved as regulations by Fishery ministers, as a symbol of EU bureaucratic invasion into their activity. Although it would be entirely incorrect to assert that the CFP is exclusively based on a resource conservation policy, since the 1980s, this aspect has nevertheless become the dominant regulatory activity in response to the global issue of stock depletion.

Structural policy

Redistributional measures have aimed since 1970 to enhance modernisation of the Community fishery sector through structural funding to the territories. Fishery-related structural actions led to the creation in 1994 of a specific fund, the Financial Instrument for Fisheries Guidance (FIFG) whose grants finance a good share of the programmes. The share of FIFG in the Community budget is in no way comparable to that of the European Agricultural Guidance and Guarantee Fund (EAGGF) or the European Regional Development Fund (ERDF). It was hence easily renewed when the Berlin European Council laid out the 2000–2006 financial priorities in March 1999 (Agenda 2000). According to some estimates, structural fund subsidies have indirectly encouraged overexploitation of the resource since the 1970s by contributing to an increase in Community fleet capacity.[14] Consequently, at the initiative of the Commission's DG Fish, EU structural policy in the fishery sector became more linked to resource conservation policy as of 1983. Since that date, multiannual guidance programmes (MAGPs) developed by the Commission DG Fish set fleet reduction objectives for each member state and each type of occupation that must be achieved before aid can be granted for permanent cessation of fishing activities or retraining schemes. As a result, EU structural policy appears less legitimate in the eyes of European fishermen than it did in the early 1970s, since they view it as a yet another tool in the hands of the Commission aiming to cut back on their activity bit by bit.

Common organisation of the markets

Directly modelled on the Common Agricultural Policy (CAP), the Common Organisation of Markets (COM) provides for the purchase of fresh and frozen fishery products that are taken off the market when they reach a minimum price that is set by the Commission. Again following the CAP model, national administrations do not manage product withdrawals. This is handled by national producers' organisations (POs) formed with the approval and often the financial support of the EU. Depending on the product withdrawn from the market, the fishermen belonging to the PO receive an indemnity from the PO, in turn compensated by the EU budget. Limited to occasional production surpluses, the products withdrawn are usually destroyed but can sometimes be put back on the market at a later date or sold to manufacture animal-meal. The COM is thus based on a distributional rationale. Despite benefits that their own fishermen may draw from it, the administrations of net-contributing countries to the Community budget such as Germany, Great Britain and the Netherlands have often contested the COM, viewing it as costly and interventionist.

Agreements with third countries

Faced with overall resource overexploitation and the gradual nationalisa-tion of marine space recognised by international maritime law, European governments transferred to the EC the power to conduct foreign policy in the fishery sector in 1976. This policy has three aspects: trade in fishery products with third countries, multilateral agreements for the conserva-tion and division of stocks in the high seas, and above all, bilateral agreements with third countries aiming to allow access of Community vessels to fish stocks.

   In 2000, the activity of 1,300 vessels and 20 to 25 per cent of fishery products consumed in the EU was conditioned by these bilateral agree-ments. Negotiated by the Commission in various forms, they guarantee access rights to EU vessels in third-country waters in exchange for recip-rocal rights or financial compensation. As we will see in Chapter 7, these bilateral agreements are the source of much debate in the EU, as regards both their cost to the EU budget and their role in diminishing the resource.

Putting Community policy on the agenda

To understand the process by which the CFP has appeared on the agenda since 1970, three factors must be considered: the successive EU enlarge-ment processes, the global debate on resource overexploitation and the gradual assertion of the world's coastal countries of their increased sover-eignty over ocean resources, legitimated by the international law of the sea.

The enlargement processes

It was in June 1966 that a small team of officials forming the fisheries unit within the Commission's DG-Agriculture drew up the first document addressed to the six EC governments. It was entitled *Basic Principles for a Common Policy in the Fisheries Sector*. This was an ambitious docu-ment, drafted principally owing to a French official at the fisheries administration temporarily assigned to the Commission, Raymond Simonnet, calling for the establishment of common actions stemming from the principle of non-discrimination in four areas: structural policy, market policy, trade policy and social policy.[15] With the exception of the last segment, these basic areas were formalised by the members of the Commission in the form of two proposed regulations submitted to the governments of the six EC countries in June 1968. The first had to do with the organisation of a common market for fishery products and the development of a trade policy; the second provided for a policy of aid schemes to modernise economic structures and a definition of principles of free access to fishing areas. In a polity where putting items on the agenda is both an open and fluid process, it is often difficult to identify the actors that convey the ideas and interests leading to a Commission proposal.[16] In what was still the Europe of the Six, French fishermen's organisations seem to have had a considerable influence on the process. Taking as a reference the price and structure support granted since 1962 to farmers by CAP, they envisaged similar mechanisms in the fishery sector as compensation for the competition induced by the entry into force of the Common Customs Tariff (CCT).[17] In the late 1960s, a Community policy of markets and economic structures seemed much more important to French fleet-owners than a European regulation on resource conservation. But these French demands also matched the Commission's own ambitions, particularly those of Dutch Commissioner Sicco Mansholt and the team of officials seconding him. Well before there was any question of applying the principle of subsidiarity, Commission members and officials often behaved as policy entrepreneurs in search of new powers.[18] As Raymond Simonnet pointed out, 'our state of mind in Brussels was mainly to get states to give way in the development of a new policy.'[19]

Any significant progress in proposals to the Commission was blocked for two years in the Council of Ministers by the practice of the Luxembourg Compromise, which requires a systematic quest for consensus. The German government was not at all in favour of a common organisation of the markets that could possibly put a damper on its dynamic processing industry. As main contributor to the Community budget, nor did it want to support its competitors through a structural policy. As for the Belgian, Italian and Dutch governments, they did not really believe they had anything to gain from a common fisheries policy and were highly apprehensive as to the cost of such an operation.

Beginning in 1969, applications for membership from Denmark, Ireland, Norway and the United Kingdom totally changed the terms of the negotiation. The perspective of multiplying fishery production fourfold and the potential institution by the applicant countries of an exclusive economic zone (EEZ) extending to the 200-mile zone sparked a new debate among EU fishery organisations regarding the wisdom of a common fishery policy. It gave Sicco Mansholt and his network of experts a political argument to reactivate their proposals, as illustrated in this declaration by the Commissioner: 'Applicant countries have a fishery policy; in its dealings with them, the Community must have its own.'[20] In

France, the issue of access to the resource worried many high-sea fishermen from Boulogne, Brittany and Normandy who in 1970 made no less than 65 per cent of their catch of fresh fish in what was to become the British EEZ and 20 per cent in the Norwegian and Faroe Islands' EEZ.[21] German and Dutch high-sea fishermen also began to ponder the advantages of access to the future EEZ of the applicant countries, particularly the United Kingdom and Norway. In exchange for the French and Italian governments' renouncing the systematic financing of all fish product withdrawals by the EAGGF, in June 1970 the German and Dutch governments finally accepted a compromise at the Council of Ministers. Regulations 2141/70 and 2142/70 were thus adopted, laying down the foundations of the CFP as regards not only markets and structures, but also free access. The Commission in fact put considerable emphasis on making the principle of free access a part of the *aquis communautaire* before embarking on accession negotiations.[22]

Knowing that their waters were extremely coveted by the fishermen of the six EC countries, the governments of the four applicant countries immediately considered the principle of free access as a *fait accompli* policy right from the start. When the chapter on fisheries was examined in 1971, everyone demanded exemptions from this principle for their fishing areas. It was in the United Kingdom and Norway that debates were the most heated, both in the national parliaments and professional organisations. Although the British Prime Minister, Edward Heath, seemed 'determined not to allow the fisheries problem to block the conclusion of the Accession Treaty',[23] the minister in charge of enlargement, Geoffrey Rippon, regularly insisted in negotiations on the unacceptability of free access given the extent of British waters. In Norway, the perspective of free access for Community vessels to fish stocks was also a theme exploited by political parties opposed to enlargement that fuelled the negative vote in the membership referendum of September 1972.[24] Having by then become incorporated into the *acquis communautaire*, the application of common market rules to fisheries was written into the acts of accession of Denmark, Ireland, Norway and the United Kingdom.

Beginning in 1977, the prospect of another enlargement to include Greece, Spain and Portugal constituted a new vehicle for change to the CFP. Europe of the Nine fishermen were faced with a doubling of numbers, a 65 per cent increase in fleet tonnage and a 45 per cent rise in the production of fish and shellfish. Spanish fishermen were their main concern. In the early 1980s, they had the fourth largest fleet in the world, after the USSR, Japan and the EC, and took two-thirds of their production outside of national waters. The acts of accession signed in 1985 allocated fishing quotas to Spain and Portugal in Atlantic waters starting from 1 January 1986. Given the insistence of the British, French and Irish fishing industries, the respective governments nevertheless secured resource access limitations on Spanish and Portuguese vessels until the end of 2002, in other words a seventeen-year transitional system, unequalled in the history of EC enlargement. Only three hundred Spanish vessels are allowed to fish in Community waters. Furthermore, Spanish and Portuguese fishermen are partly barred from the Irish Sea, extremely coveted for its hake, as well as the North Sea. Enlargement to the Iberian countries was nevertheless an opportunity for the Commission to activate work on reinforcing ties between structural aid policy and resource conservation policy. The adoption of the first MGP by the Council of Fisheries Ministers in 1983 corresponded to the intention of DG Fish officials to ensure that restructuring aids did not increase fleet capacity. This position was reinforced by the adoption of MGP II, which, beginning in 1987, no longer called for a freeze but a reduction in fleet tonnage and power. Enlargement to Spain and Portugal contributed, lastly, to stimulating the external dimension of the CFP by obliging the EC to take over the obligations – including budgetary ones – contained in many agreements regarding access to fishing areas that bound the new member states to third countries, or even to negotiate new ones. To take but two examples, the interests of the Spanish high-sea fleet weighed preponderantly in the EC signature of agreements with both Morocco and Argentina.

In effect as of 1 January 1995, the third enlargement of the EU to Austria, Finland and Sweden had fewer repercussions on the CFP than the two previous ones, given the moderate role that fishery occupied in the economy of the two Scandinavian countries involved. The situation would have been considerably different had not a majority of Norwegians once again rejected their country's membership to the EU by 52.4 per cent of the vote in November 1994. The arrival of Norway would have certainly raised debates calling for a less restrictive CFP for fishermen than Norwegian policy has in such essential areas as conservation of the resource base and monitoring. To take just one example, since 1983 it has been forbidden to discard unmarketed fish into the sea in Norway. Unlike their EU counterparts, Norwegian fishermen are thus obliged to unload all of their by-catch, which is counted and deducted from the annual quotas allocated to each vessel.[25] This regulatory measure, which allows a more accurate assessment of stocks, is still considered unacceptable by most EU fishermen's organisations.[26]

At the dawn of the twenty-first century, the CFP cannot escape the prospect of new reform made necessary by the fourth enlargement of the EU, although fishery does not represent a vital sector for the national economy in any of the central and eastern European applicant countries (including Poland where it employs 40,000 people). The policy of trimming down the fishing industry conducted by the EU since 1983 will nevertheless affect the Polish, Estonian and Slovenian fishermen, whom the Commission has already asked to decommission the least competitive elements of their fleets.[27] This will lead to Community-financed restructuring plans. Consequently, as for the previous enlargements, the terms of redistribution among European fishermen will have to be renegotiated.

The debate over resource depletion

At the end of the 1960s, the decline of several fisheries, such as cod in Greenland and herring in the Atlantic, due to a decline in the stocks that support these species is a second factor that helped to put a CFP on the EU agenda. Stock depletion is not an unknown phenomenon. In the early twentieth century, herring off the Scandinavian coasts and sardines off the coast of Brittany went through periods of short supply, causing a spate of sometimes very violent social movements. But stopgap measures were almost always found by the fishermen themselves, or by governments, 'not so much by reducing the structural causes but more by exploring new opportunities, or else through aids'.[28] In the 1960s, stock depletion began to occur in a different economic context marked by the expansion of industrial fishing not only in western countries but also in Japan, the USSR and eastern European countries, as well as emerging Asian countries such as Korea and Thailand in Asia, and Cuba and Chile. The escalation of industrial fishing fuelled an international debate on the wide-scale depletion of fish resources, first in the restricted circle of experts, then among governments. The governments were not devoid of international institutions to regulate overfishing. At the end of the Second World War, intergovernmental agreements multiplied, creating regional fishery organisations (RFOs) aimed to improve knowledge and management of the stocks. For EU member States, the largest of these institutions is the North-East Atlantic Fisheries Commission (NEAFC), created in 1959. But RFO recommendations on catches or fishing techniques were often not adapted to producing an actual decrease in overfishing, since their implementation remained optional on a national level. In reaction to this deficiency in implementation, Commission officials grouped together as of 1977 in the Directorate General of Fisheries headed by Irish diplomat Eamonn Gallagher, and considered a Community policy of resource conservation. In an August 1976 internal memo, one of the architects of the CFP on the Commission, Louis Mordrel, underlined the failings of the NEAFC in enforcing TACs. The reasons for this, specified the Community official,

> had to be sought in the very nature of these commissions, which only have advisory powers and in the consequence that partially results from attempting the utmost to obtain political agreements, to the detriment of opinions formulated by scientists [...]. In this respect, the Community seems a much better adapted framework than are fishery boards to resolve the problems posed in the context of the 200-mile zone. The Community in fact has the

political means to make the difficult but inevitable decisions necessary and especially to enforce them.[29]

The idea championed by Louis Mordrel was thus that the Commission's expertise, backed by a binding legal system for both states and social actors, would make the EC the first international institution capable of guaranteeing an effective system of resource conservation. Meeting at The Hague on 3 November 1976, the European Foreign Ministers adopted a resolution that included two essential commitments for the future of the CFP. The first is the extension of the limit of national fishing areas to 200 miles starting 1 January 1977 in the North Sea and the Atlantic Ocean. The second commitment, a corollary to the former, was the delegation of the power to the EC to conclude fishery agreements with third countries.[30] The Commission also proposed the adoption of criteria by which to set up a Community TAC system divided into national quotas to manage the most common species. But most governments were not yet ready to accept this project.[31] In May 1980, the Foreign Ministers adopted three criteria to divide TACs into national quotas which founded the principle known as 'relative stability': traditional fishing activities, the specific needs of fishermen operating in regions with few employment opportunities outside of fishing and related industries;[32] and the loss of fishery potential in third-country waters after the institution of the EEZs. Backed by DG-Fisheries officials, the movement that was taking shape in favour of a resource conservation policy nevertheless had to wait until regulation 170/83 was adopted for a Community system of TACs and quotas to be formally established.

Riparian rights win out
The decline in yield due to overexploitation of fishery stocks in the 1970s sparked another worldwide debate that helped put a fishery policy on the EU agenda. It involved a demand expressed by the major seafaring states to do away with the principle of the sea *res nullius*, a legacy of former public international law, so as to strengthen their respective control over marine areas and resources. This trend, which began in the 1950s in several Latin American countries, eventually spread to Europe. In 1971, the Icelandic government unilaterally proclaimed its exclusive sovereignty over a zone extending 50 miles from its shores, abruptly banning British and German cod fishermen who fished its continental shelf. Despite complaints that the German and British governments brought before the International Court of Justice (ICJ), the Icelandic government again decided in 1975 to extend its fishing area, this time to 200 nautical miles. Shortly afterward, the Norwegian and Canadian governments followed suit.[33] While the third UN Conference on the Law of the Sea opened in 1973, in an atmosphere of 'maritime nationalism' that substantiated states' extension of the EEZ to 200 miles, the decisions made by Iceland,

Norway and Canada had a major political impact on the EC governments, particularly on new members. British fishermen, who were used to operating in Norwegian and Icelandic seas, strongly protested against their exclusion by the 200-mile rule. Fishing being one of the rare professional activities in Europe where conflicts of interests still give rise to shows of force between states, between November 1975 and June 1976, the British government did not hesitate to provide Royal Navy escorts for English and Scottish boats fishing in Icelandic waters. British and Irish professionals did not, however, request a return to the universal conception of marine exploitation. Focused on obtaining derogations from the principle of free access in the framework of the EC, their organisations – such as the British Fishing Federation – argued instead for a renationalisation of coastal waters. In Brussels, British Commission members Sir Christopher Soames and George Thomson, and Irish Commission member Patrick Hillery, supported their industry's demand and suggested establishing a 50-mile coastal waters zone to be exclusive sovereign preserve of each nation's fishermen. The Commission dismissed the project by ten votes against three in September 1976.[34] Eager to conform with the international law of the sea, the Commission in fact believed that the coastal waters designated as the exclusive preserve of a single coastal state should be set at 12 miles while reserving 'historic rights' for vessels of other member states that had frequented it previously. Although, as was pointed out above, the Foreign Ministers decided together in a meeting in The Hague in October 1976 to extend the limits of the national fishing areas to 200 miles, they did not agree to establishing a 12-mile zone for coastal waters. The British and Irish ministers in fact felt that this measure would result in insufficient protection for their fishermen, whereas others – German and Dutch – considered it on the contrary prejudicial to the principle of free access. Once again, it was not until Regulation 170/83 was adopted in January 1983, that the 12-mile system was also accepted as a legitimate derogation to the principle of free access. A majority of European national professional organisations declared themselves in favour of maintaining this Regulation, renewed until 31 December 2002, after this date. Some Spanish high-sea fishermen have nevertheless declared themselves in favour of abandoning it at the next reform of the CFP to gain total access to the waters of other member states. On the other hand, English and Irish industrial organisations, faithful to a long-standing demand, maintain the idea of extending the coastal trip beyond 12 miles.[35] In 1999, a European Parliament resolution in fact backed this proposal, which, if it were adopted, would encourage an indirect renationalisation of the CFP.

Placing the CFP on the EU agenda was an incremental process in which the successive enlargements, the world debates over fishery resource depletion and the renationalisation of marine space have each exercised their share of influence. The mobilisation of social actors, fishermen in this case, petitioning their respective governments does not in itself explain the genesis and evolution of the CFP since 1970. Experts, in particular Commission officials, have also contributed to institutional creation and change of the CFP. Their entrepreneurship preceded inter-governmental compromises within the Council of Ministers, without whom, however, no essential decision could have been made.[36]

Notes

1 Judgment of the Court of 14 July 1976 *Kramer/Public Ministry* (joined cases C-3/76, C-4/76 and C-6/76).
2 In France, when crews are remunerated by the share in addition to a minimum guaranteed wage, the activity is referred to as 'semi-industrial'. This is the case for fishermen working for certain fishing companies in Lorient, Concarneau and Boulogne.
3 Jean-René Couliou, *La pêche bretonne. Les ports de Bretagne sud face à leur avenir*, Rennes, Presses Universitaires de Rennes, 1997, p. 434.
4 European Parliament, *The Regionalisation of the Common Fisheries Policy: Impact on Structural Policy and Multiannual Guidance Programmes in Relation to Agenda 2000*, Brussels, Directorate for Research, 1999.
5 Couliou, *La pêche bretonne*.
6 Territory under Danish administration, Greenland decided to withdraw from the EC in 1985, with the aim mainly of recovering its independence/autonomy in managing its fishing area.
7 These figures include intra-EU trade.
8 Interview, San Sebastian, 26 July 1999.
9 *OJEC*, L 236, 27 October 1970.
10 *OJEC*, L 24, 27 January 1983.
11 European Commission, *Rapport au Conseil et au Parlement sur la politique commune de la pêche*, SEC (91) 2288, 1991.
12 *OJEC*, L 389, 31 December 1992.
13 Marc Abélès, *En attente d'Europe*, Paris, Hachette, 1996.
14 Brian O'Riordan, 'La pêche au-delà des eaux communautaires. Qui paye et qui bénéficie?', *El Anzuelo*, 3, 1999, p. 4.
15 Jacques Huret, *Le livre de bord*, Paris, UAPF, 1990.
16 See Guy B. Peters, 'Agenda Setting in the European Community', *Journal of European Public Policy*, 1 (1), June 1994, pp. 9–26.
17 Michael Leigh, *European Integration and the Common Fisheries Policy*, London, Croom Helm, 1983; see also Huret, *Le livre de bord*.
18 Laura Cram, *Policy-Making in the European Union: Conceptual Lenses and the Integration Process*, London, Routledge, 1997.
19 Interview with Raymond Simonnet, Brussels, 21 October 1999.
20 Interview in *Figaro*, 1 July 1970.
21 Huret, *Le livre de bord*, p. 17.
22 Interview with Raymond Simonnet, Brussels, 21 October 1999.
23 Michael Shackleton, *The Politics of Fishing in Britain and France*, Gower,

Aldershot, 1986, p. 99.

24 On the CFP and the first enlargement of the EC, see Leigh, *European Integration*.

25 FAO, *The State of World Fisheries and Aquaculture1998*, Rome, FAO, 1999.

26 European Commission, *La politique commune de la pêche après 2002. Analyse des réponses au questionnaire*, Brussels, DG XIV, internal document, 1999.

27 See the accession progress reports published by the European Commission in November 1998 (www.europa-eu.int).

28 Jean-Paul Troadec (ed.), *L'homme et les ressources halieutiques. Essai sur l'usage d'une ressource renouvelable*, Paris, Presses de l'IFREMER, 1989, pp. 25–26.

29 Memo of 2 August 1976 on the adaptation of the Common Fishery Policy, Brussels, Commission of the European Cummunities, Directorate General of Agriculture (Louis Mordrel, personal files).

30 European Commission, *Bulletin of the European Communities*, 10, 1976, p. 24.

31 Gwenaële Proutière-Maulion, *La politique communautaire de réduction de l'effort de pêche*, Paris, L'Harmattan, 1998, p. 82.

32 This second criteria, accompanied by a special provision, is known by the term 'The Hague Preferences'.

33 Jean-Pierre Beurier, 'Le droit international des pêches maritimes', *Droits maritimes*, vol. III, Lyon, Éditions Juris, 1998, pp. 13–66.

34 Leigh, *European Integration*, p. 72.

35 European Commission, *Bulletin of the European Communities*, p. 72.

36 Andrew Moravcsik, *The Choice for Europe*, Ithaca and London, Cornell University Press, 1998.

2

Actors and institutions: multi-level politics in action

As opposed to analysts who view the EU as the product solely of bargaining among states, I prefer to see it as a political configuration in which the exercise of power is shared among state actors and non-state actors operating at different levels. Precise identification of these actors, as well as their resources, their institutional practices and their ideas, is necessary to understand just how the processes of policy-making and polity-building come together within the EU.[1]

In choosing to dwell on the actors of the CFP, the analysis makes no claim to exhaustivity. Essentially, this chapter intends to address two questions. The first has to do with the distribution of power among the supranational, national and local politico-administrative institutions within the European polity. If these authorities can no longer be apprehended from the standpoint of the notion of centre, have other forms of hierarchy come into play? The second question deals with the interconnections between the interest representation of national and local actors and the encompassing EU polity.

Shared political–administrative institutions

Like many Community policies, the formulation and implementation of the CFP has involved the participation of politico-administrative institutions whose power is constituted and legitimated at multiple territorial and spatial levels: the EU, the state and the sub-national region. Though fisheries regulation in the EU may appear to be an instance of multi-level politics, there is no evidence that the power of states automatically decreases in the face of a supposed collusion between supranational institutions and local institutions.[2]

Fisheries through the prism of state institutions
In 2002, government monitoring of fisheries was handled in most EU countries by a fisheries administration under the Ministry of Agriculture.

Fisheries and agriculture are associated for functional reasons to be found in similar market, consumption and product-processing issues. In certain EU countries where fishery has a distinct relationship with the definition of national interest, such as in Great Britain and Portugal, a Secretary of State for Fisheries stands in for the Agriculture Minister in EU Council negotiations and as representative to national professional bodies.

Of the thirteen coastal EU countries, Ireland and to a certain extent France depart from the rule that fisheries comes under the Ministry of Agriculture alone. Ireland has had a Minister for the Marine and Natural Resources since 1987. In an insular context, this attests to the government's decision to display an independent marine policy interlinked with environmental policy. Following François Mitterrand's first election to the French presidency in May 1981, a Marine Ministry was also created in France in response to a demand – recurrent since the advent of Gaullism – from elected officials in coastal departments and French maritime occupations to assert more overtly a national maritime policy.[3] The new ministerial portfolio was handed to Louis Le Pensec, a socialist deputy from Brittany, who rose to the challenge – in many respects a complicated one – of bringing under his wing the various maritime activities that had previously come under the Transport or Infrastructure Ministry: the merchant marine, fisheries, port administration, shipbuilding, seamen's social welfare and research.[4] In March 1983, a government reshuffle, however, relegated the new Maritime Minister to the rank of Secretariat of State under the Transport Ministry. Fisheries was then brought under the responsibilities attributed to State Secretary for Maritime Affairs, a post always filled from among elected officials from coastal regions (Boulogne mayor Guy Lengagne, Breton MPs Charles Josselin and Ambroise Guellec) but the real influence of which was actually limited in the various governments. This explains why the decision taken in 1993 to bring fisheries under the Agriculture Ministry was greeted so favourably by the French fishing industry. However, a certain number of issues, such as occupational training, social welfare and safety remained under the authority of the French Fisheries and Seamen Directorate under the Ministry of Infrastructure, Transport and Housing. The State Secretary for Maritime Affairs vanished from the government's organisation chart. There is nevertheless a Secretariat-General for Maritime Affairs that reports directly to the Prime Minister's office. This agency, headed by a senior civil servant from the prefectural corps, has, however, never exercised authority over the French Fisheries and Aquaculture Administration or the Fisheries and Seamen Directorate. It was principally designed as a political symbol aiming to demonstrate the state's interest in the sea among French maritime occupations often persuaded that their government had abandoned the idea of having a maritime policy.[5] This criticism is partially justified by the fact that the mental image of French political elites is indeed more characterised by a rather continental representation of France within Europe. The historical bases for this 'land-bound' representation, which differentiates the situation in France from that of Spain or the United Kingdom, were best analysed by the historian Fernand Braudel.[6]

Within national parliaments, fishery is a subject that rarely divides Agriculture ministries and fishery administration along very sharp party lines. On the contrary, it is often the topic of a national consensus capable of mobilising elected officials of coastal regions, whatever their political allegiance. This fact is observable not only in the British House of Commons, but in the French National Assembly as well. To take an example, the adoption process for the 'framework law on maritime fisheries and marine aquaculture', intended to provide a legal framework for fishing occupations in France, occurred in 1997 in a context of parliamentary majority changeover. The Assembly only very marginally influenced the content of the law, which had been negotiated mainly by the previous majority's Agriculture minister and the professional organisations.[7]

Moreover, the regulatory nature of the CFP removed part of the power of national parliaments to pass legislation to the benefit of national governments and administrations. Parliamentary representatives in EU countries – particularly those from coastal voting districts – are hence prompted to query national ministers and administrations regularly on the development of a Community policy which, except for in Denmark, escapes all form of a priori control. Throughout the year 1999, the prospect of the expiration of the fishing agreement between the EU and Morocco, the economic implications of which were essential for the Andalusian, Canary and Galician fleet-owners, naturally led the Spanish MPs and senators to question the Aznar government regarding the policy the EU intended to conduct in this area of exclusive jurisdiction. The favourable image that fishermen generally enjoy in the eyes of national public opinion, some form of solidarity being felt to be owed toward a dangerous profession, sometimes encourages political movements opposed to the EU to use the CFP to fuel more general anti-EU rhetoric. The intensity with which Tory Eurosceptics in the House of Commons denounced, in 1997, on the eve of legislative elections and the signing of the Amsterdam Treaty, the Community rules that allow Spanish and Dutch fleet-owners to purchase vessels and use British quotas illustrates the way that the CFP can be exploited in order to criticise European integration. This is true to such an extent that the Conservative Manifesto presented by John Major in the May 1997 legislative elections, included a call to stop quota-hopping among the priority measures intended to protect the economic sovereignty of the United Kingdom against EU intrusion (see Chapter 5).[8] The way in which most of the same Eurosceptic

MPs abandoned the crusade against quota-hopping in the House of Commons once they were re-elected further illustrates how the CFP could be manipulated as a more general anti-European rhetorical device.[9] It is nevertheless rare that a government or minister of an EU country is threatened by its national parliament over issues of fishery management. This did occur, however, in the Netherlands in September 1990. Minister Braks was forced to hand in his resignation to the Prime Minister after a parliamentary investigation revealed that his administration had done a poor job of monitoring his fishermen's use of quotas and allowed fraud to develop.[10]

Fishery administrations within Agriculture ministries are not always steered by administrators who are experts on fishery issues. In Great Britain, the civil servants in the Fishery Department are generalists from the Ministry of Agriculture, Fisheries and Food (MAFF)[11] who change departments every three years. In France, the director of the Pêches maritimes et de l'Aquaculture at the ministry, like many high-ranking civil servants in his entourage, are often recruited among mid- and senior-level civil servants from the Agriculture Ministry.

Moreover, one of the characteristics of fishery departments is that they rarely have decentralised administrations in charge of implementing state policy in the field. In Great Britain and in Spain, local presence of central fishery administrations is limited to a small corps of inspectors. For the rest, responsibility for the implementation of the CFP either falls to other central administrations (navy, customs, finance), regional administrations or regulatory bodies (such as the Sea Fish Industry Authority in Great Britain). In this regard, fishery administrations are national administrations with slender budgets and meagre administrative resources. France is nevertheless an exception for reasons that have to do with its state history.

The legacy of an edict issued by Colbert in 1668, the law of 3 Brumaire Year IV (25 October 1795) gave birth to a dedicated administration in France: the Administration de l'inscription maritime (Maritime Registry Administration).[12] Its original mission was to make sure that a regular census of seamen – fishermen and commercial sailors – was conducted to serve in the event of conflict involving the navy. In 1902, a corps of Inscription maritime administrators was created and entrusted with this same assignment (which explains its military status) in addition to civilian duties exercised in territorial districts known as *quartiers maritimes*: to regulate navigation and fishing activities and look after the seamen's social welfare. Although the law of 1965 ending the mandatory enrolment of seamen in the national navy severed the new fisheries administration[13] of its 'recruitment sergeant' mission (without, however, abolishing its military status), it remains largely responsible for policing the sea in the broad sense. Organised like other state agencies into regional and departmental offices, the French fisheries administration, which comes under the

Ministry of Infrastructure, Transport and Housing, not only monitors compliance with rules but also social functions embodied by a medical service, the approval of work contracts, mediation of conflicts between a shipowner and his crew, etc. Exemplifying French state paternalism in a rather old-fashioned way by protecting and sanctioning seamen, the fisheries administration is the main local liaison for the ministries in implementing the CFP (possible closing of a fish quota, application of structural funds, inspections at sea and on land, sailor training, etc.). This local presence of a state administration does not, however, always guarantee more effective CFP implementation. In keeping with negotiation practices between prefects and local officials (*notables*) analysed by sociologists of French decentralisation,[14] fisheries administrators often bend the rules with fishermen. The report made in 1993 by a civil servant in training in a *quartier maritime* on the Atlantic coast concluded 'the administrator often poses as champion of the fishermen's interests, since statements of violations of the law often come to nothing'. The presence of a state sea administration in French ports, which more than anything fears a deterioration of the social climate among fishermen, can even be considered in France as a factor that encourages flexibility rather than strict enforcement of Community rules.

Within Agriculture ministries, fishery administrations are nevertheless 'small worlds' that have their own sources of expertise to respond to proposals by the European Commission regarding the various aspects of the CFP: markets, trade, structural policies and conservation of fish stocks. Expertise is usually produced by specialized agencies incorporated into the ministry. In France, the Office interprofessionnel des produits de la mer (OFIMER), which in 1998 replaced the Fonds d'intervention des organisations de marché (FIOM), supplies the French fisheries administration with statistics on fishery production, marketing and promotion. For resource conservation, the institutional links that fishery administrations have with national oceanographic research institutes are also privileged sources of information. In France, the Minister of Agriculture and Fishery shares with the Infrastructure and Research Ministries the task of overseeing the Institut français de recherche pour l'exploitation de la mer (IFREMER), created in 1984 by bringing together previously extant bodies. In Great Britain, the Centre for Environment, Fisheries and Aquaculture Science (CEFAS), founded in 1902, and in Spain, the Instituto español de oceanografía (IEO), created in 1914, are other research agencies incorporated into the Agriculture ministries. Their research teams work on fish stocks with the aim of helping governments to take appropriate measures to regulate the resource base. The straddling of fishery researchers between science and public action has certain effects on their scientific attitudes. If the internationalisation of expertise since the end of the Second World War has indeed fostered independence of fishery experts with regard to their governments (see pp. 00), they never-theless remain subjected to forms of allegiance that are sometimes expressed in terms of national interest. In 1997, the director of living resources at IFREMER, also the incumbent president of the ICES, spoke of his 'staunch republican-mindedness which would not allow him to forget that the work of the ICES has economic consequences on the French fishing industry.[15] His British counterpart, CEFAS deputy direc-tor, emphasised the need to 'be knowledgeable about science but also about the economic context that frames each fishery in the country'.[16] Such propinquity of scientific expertise and politico-administrative power can sometimes be a factor of conservatism in that scientists become dependent on the contextual priorities set by governments.[17]

Various degrees of sub-national government involvement

Sub-national governments comprise another administrative level of the CFP in the EU member states.[18] The powers of sub-national governments, however, vary considerably from one state context to another and are not necessary a reflection of other political mobilisations that can be observed in the territories. Furthermore, the involvement of sub-national govern-ments is different in Spain, France and Great Britain, depending on whether it is the formulation phase or the implementation phase of the CFP that is under scrutiny.

Be it at the regional, departmental or local level, the regulatory and distributional effects of the CFP in France provoke a variety of forms of political mobilisation that crystallise around local elected officials, indus-trial and chamber of commerce representatives, scientists and academics. Locally rooted mobilisations are sometimes reactive and demonstrative, like those in February 1993 following the creation of the *comité de survie* in south Brittany by fishermen protesting against competition from low-cost third-country imports.[19] These effects can also be in the form of production of expertise. In 1998, right-wing elected officials from the regional councils of Pays de la Loire, Poitou-Charentes and Aquitaine, gathered in the Association du grand littoral Atlantique (AGLIA) and decided to sponsor the creation of a Fishery Watch (Observatoire des pêches), with the support of the Institut maritime et aquacole in Biarritz and the University of Nantes. The aim was clearly to contribute an alter-native interpretation to the European Commission's view of problems specifically plaguing regional fishermen in the Bay of Biscay. Lastly, mobilisation sometimes leads to institutionalising a social demand into an organised interest group. The best example is the PESCA–Cornouaille association in Finistère, Brittany, created around the local Le Guilvinec fishery committee. Its aim is to reassert the importance of EU financial support for the development of the area around Quimper, and more specifically the Pont-l'Abbé region (see Chapter 4).

In France, European structural funds for the fishing industry are never-theless primarily administered under the responsibility of centralised state officials, particularly the regional prefects and regional Fishery Administration authorities (Directions régionales des affaires maritimes: DRAM). The same holds true for inspections, both on land and at sea, of fleet-decommissioning schemes or the compatibility of ship-owning companies' investment plans with the European MAGPs. So it is with government representatives that individuals in the fishing industry, chamber of commerce officials and mayors of French port towns prima-rily continue to negotiate the conditions of a territorially specific implementation of the CFP. However, fishing, particularly on a small scale, far from escapes local government control, since the 1982–83 decentralisation laws stipulated that regions were to fund the renewal and modernisation of the coastal fleet. French regions also intervene, some-times via association activities, in favour of a semi-industrial fishery.[20] For instance, in December 1999, the regional council of Brittany disbursed 7.3 million fr. out of its budget to finance various investments (putting new vessels into service and improvement of port facilities) in the Pont-l'Abbé area. These funds may have been earmarked for the area that is the most dependent on fishing in Brittany, but it is also the area in which the fishermen demonstrate a strong capacity for political mobilisation against both national and regional political authorities. Subsidies to the regions, even the departments can, in fact, be designed to supplement EU financial aids that do not, moreover, escape regional and departmental elected offi-cials associated with the definition of regional EU policy in the context of an institutionalised partnership. In 1998, the Aquitaine regional council thus granted a 33 per cent bonus over the premiums paid by the EU and the French government to any shipowner who agreed to submit a vessel between 12–25 metres long to the national decommissioning scheme in compliance with the MAGP.[21]

Unlike France, the sub-national governments of some other EU coun-tries have formal powers to implement the CFP. In Spain, the Constitution of 27 December 1978 granted its Autonomous Communities (ACs) the exclusive authority to regulate maritime fishing in its inland waters – in other words in the area located within the baselines – as well as shellfish culture and aquaculture. In the 1980s, the Catalan, Basque and Galician autonomous parliaments passed regional laws defining their intervention in fisheries in conformity with the Constitution and their autonomous status. An illustration of the both pragmatic and conflictual process of autonomous state-building, the central Spanish government systemati-cally challenged these regional fishery laws before the Constitutional Court and sometimes even the decrees to enforce these laws on the pretence that they did not respect the limits of jurisdiction outlined in the Constitution. Adopted in 1992 by a large majority of the regional parlia-

ment, the Galician law on fisheries thus reserved the autonomous government the right to execute a number of measures, in addition to those in
areas of exclusive authority provided by the Constitution, that came
under the central administration, such as distribution of fishing licences,
permits to build vessels or measures concerning sea-rescue. Since it was
not invalidated by the constitutional judges within five months following
the filing of an appeal by the central government, this Galician fishery law
came into force in 1993.[22] As a result, the autonomous government itself
enforces a number of norms contained in Community law.

In Galicia, fishing constitutes a major theme in the political platform of
the Xunta de Galicia which since 1989, has been presided over by Manuel
Fraga Iribarne, a former Franco minister and national figure of the
Partido Popular, backed by a conservative electorate and a clientelistic
party 'divided into strongly territory-based areas of influence corresponding to various local internal groups'.[23] Both Manuel Fraga Iribarne and
the Galician fishery ministers never miss an opportunity to emphasise that
the tonnage of Galicia's fleet alone exceeds that of the British or French
fleets and that it is mainly active in Community and international waters.
They present themselves to the Galician fishermen as their spokespersons
not only in relation to the central government, which maintains certain
areas of authority (for instance in matters of inspection and management
of the MAGP),[24] but also in relation to the European Commission. This
spokesperson role can also be seen among officials in the Galician
Fisheries Ministry, which has a much larger staff than most national
fishery administrations in EU countries. It goes together with a regionalist rhetoric claiming full execution of the CFP in Galician territory and,
even more, with a demand that they be systematically consulted on the
formulation of positions negotiated by the central government in the EU
Fishery Council.[25]

In Great Britain, involvement at the sub-national level in CFP implementation pre-dates the entry into force of devolution in 1999. In England and
Wales, the fishery administration in the 0–6 mile area comes under the
jurisdiction of the twelve Sea Fisheries Committees (SFC). These emana-
tions of local governments are in charge of implementing a policy that
remains formally under the state's jurisdiction. Created in 1890, the
Cornwall Sea Fisheries Committee thus oversees all fishing activities in
inshore waters associated with the county of Cornwall. To do so, SFC
establishes by-laws containing measures for resource management and use
of fishing vessels. These local by-laws are submitted to MAFF, which
grants them delegation from the government. In most cases, delegation is a
mere formality because the measures proposed at the local level are more
stringent than those contained in the Community and national texts.[26]

In Scotland, implementation of most aspects of the CFP was also decentralised as soon as the United Kingdom joined the EU in 1973. Over two

decades before the creation of a Scottish Parliament, concrete measures relating to application of the CFP, such as allocation of quotas to producer organisations or the arranging of inspections (on land and at sea), were already managed by the Agriculture and Fishery Minister at the Scottish Office in Edinburgh. Since fishery was one of the functions devolved to the new Scottish Parliament by the Scotland Act, it is now civil servants from the Scottish Executive Rural Affairs Department that have taken over the functions previously performed by the Scottish Office.[27] As in most other sectors, two concordats signed between MAFF and the new Scottish Executive – one general in nature, the other specific to fishery – established a cooperative division of responsibilities between London and Edinburgh to implement and enforce legislation.[28] In the field of fisheries, the formal transfer of authority to the new Scottish Government merely reinforced the territorial relationship that the Scottish fishing industry already had with the politico-administrative authority at the time of the Scottish Office, thereby allowing it to use the Scottish Parliament to better control the administration.[29]

But the true political stake for sub-national governments is to be involved in the development of Community policies within the EU Council of Ministers in which central governments remain to a large extent in control of the situation. In this respect, the situations of each country once again differ considerably, as can be seen in the examples of Scotland and Galicia.

Well before devolution, the Fishery and Agriculture Minister of the Scottish Office sat beside the British Minister of State for Fishery in the EU Council of Ministers.[30] In accordance with an administrative custom, a Scottish Office official also alternated with a MAFF counterpart in occupying the position of fishery advisor in the United Kingdom permanent representation to the EU. Great Britain's positions in preparation for the Fisheries Councils were in fact drafted in London by MAFF in coordination with the Scottish Office. With devolution arose the question of the new Scottish Rural Affairs Minister's involvement in preparing British positions at EU Councils, keeping in mind that fisheries is one of the functions devolved to the Scottish Parliament by the Scotland Act, but that European negotiations also remain a 'reserved matter' for the British government.[31] The two concordats signed between MAFF and the Scottish Executive, as well as that of the coordination of questions relating to the European Union, help to answer this question from a formal standpoint: the preparation and defence of British positions at the EU Council of Ministers and subordinate committees remain the responsibility of the central ministers, but in close association with the Scottish Executive when they have to do with devolved matters such as fisheries. The central and regional administrations are hence bound to cooperate. Their possible divergences are subjected to the arbitration of a new common ministerial commission formed by central, Scottish, Welsh and North-Irish ministers. Labour Party majorities in both the House of Commons and the Scottish Parliament[32] limit potential for conflict in the current political situation. But what would happen if a majority from the regionalist Scottish National Party (SNP) were to control the Scottish Parliament?

In Spain, the autonomous governments do not formally participate in EU Council negotiations.[33] AC Ministers, Members of Parliament and fisheries officials must therefore cultivate their political exchanges with the central government in order to assert their interests with regard to the CFP. This is done with greater ease in the case of Galicia since the majority party in Santiago de Compostela is the same party in power in Madrid. Moreover, since 1994 there has been a Sector Conference on Fishery that enables the 'central' Minister of Agriculture, Fishery and Food to convene all Fishery Ministers twice yearly to inform them of the major issues on the EU agenda. But the autonomous governments also have political resources that allow them to pitch their interests directly within the European political arena. In this case, the EU tends to further reduce the usual distinction between the interest of autonomous governments and the representation of various territory-based 'private' interests. The channels of sub-national representation are many. Beyond the task of representation that the Galicia office in Brussels fulfils, a true 'territorialized political exchange'[34] has been established between Galician elected officials, local fishing industry representatives (such as those from the influential Vigo Fleet-Owners' Cooperative) and the Partido Popular MEPs (Members of the European Parliament) from Galicia. It is not by chance that Carmen Fraga Estévez, the daughter of the President of Xunta de Galicia, then Daniel Varela Suanzes-Carpegna, a deputy from Lugo, have for many years presided over the Fishery Commission in the European Parliament. These positions of power at a European level help the Galician fishing industry to assert its interests directly in the EU. To illustrate this, the CFP report after the 2002 reform, presented to the European Parliament by Carmen Fraga Estévez in 1997, strongly reflected the interests of the Galician high-sea fishermen in favour of increased freedom of access of fishing vessels to EU waters.[35] Community conflict-resolution procedures are another resource that allows infra-national governments to become more involved in CFP formulation. In July 1996, the Xunta de Galicia gained from the EU Court of First Instance (CFI) the right to intervene alongside Galician fleet- owners in the lawsuit that the latter had filed with the EU Council to annul a ruling that reduced the black-halibut quota in international waters off the coast of Greenland, following strong pressure from the Canadian government. This was the first time that an infra-national government, having demonstrated an economic and social interest, had such a prerogative recognised by

Community judges. In 1998, Galicia's detour via Luxembourg enabled the ACs to negotiate a general resolution with the central government authorising them to ask the state to intervene on their behalf with the CJEC when a Community action threatened their jurisdiction.[36] Lastly, participation in interregional forms of collective action, such as the Conference of Peripheral Maritime Regions founded in 1973, or the Atlantic Arc Commission christened in 1989 by the president of the French region of Pays de la Loire, Olivier Guichard, also enabled Xunta de Galicia to represent Galician fishing industry interests to the European institutions by appearing to be the mouthpiece for a transnational territorial body.[37] For the political leaders involved in this type of interregional mobilisation, increasing their respective territories' capacity for direct dialogue with European institutions often counts more than achieving functional cooperation with other territories. From this standpoint, it is once again not by chance that the Galician government chose to handle the coordination of a working group on fishery within the Atlantic Arc Commission, an organisation presided over, moreover, by Manuel Fraga Iribarne. Regular meetings with European Commission representatives, the Atlantic intergroup of the European Parliament and the members of the Regions Committee present many opportunities for Galician professionals to assert their priorities with respect to the CFP without necessarily going through Madrid.

The autonomy of Community institutions

The 1980s hailed political science's rediscovery of institutions under the overall banner of neo-institutionalism. Among American specialists on European integration, this 'return' rekindled the theoretical investigations of the 1960s as to whether Community institutions had their own capacity to shape Community policies or if, on the contrary, only states influenced decisions. Among the theories circulating, that of Andrew Moravcsik is often cited. He considers Community institutions as mere agents aimed at facilitating bargaining among states. On the other end of the spectrum are authors such as Wayne Sandholtz and Alec Stone, for whom the creation of supranational institutions go hand in hand with an increasing autonomy of influence.[38]

In that they are formulated in overreaching terms, the scope of these approaches should be put in perspective. They always involve the same political scientists who share the conviction that there can be no political sociology of European integration without abstract theorising. The autonomy or dependence of Community institutions with respect to states varies by sector and, therefore, their inner workings can only be carefully observed through empirical study of Community policies.[39] Studying fisheries thus provides a means of analysing, without excessive speculation, the European Commission, the European Parliament, the Court of Justice

and the Court of Auditors, which are in fact capable of generating interests and ideas that influence the formulation of the CFP over and above
governments and national administrations. But observing this independence cannot be generalised and is in no way contradictory with another
observation: that government and national administrations continue to
make the final decisions on essential matters with the EU Council of
Ministers.

In addition to national fisheries administrations, the European
Commission is the Community institution best able to unite the most
thorough expertise on all the issues having to do with European fisheries.
Created in 1977 under the administration of Irish diplomat Eamonn
Gallagher, out of the fisheries department that was previously part of the
Directorate General for Agriculture, the Directorate General for Fisheries
(formerly DG XIV) constitutes the locus of expertise. By presenting itself
as the guardians of expert rationality in the face of governments subject
to clientelistic pressures from the fishermen, DG Fish officials occupy a
special place in the formulation of the CFP. Some of them come from the
'biologist' community of fisheries made up by national oceanographic
institutes and federated into a transnational body by the International
Council for the Exploraton of the Sea (ICES). The officials in charge of
conservation and monitoring policy share with their colleagues back in
the capitals the same vision of what motivates a 'good' fisheries policy.
First, any system of common property seems to them naturally to encourage fishermen to increase their catches. And the mission of scientists seems
to them primarily utilitarian: it aims to encourage politico-administrative
officials to offset the recurrent tendency toward overfishing by imposing
regulatory measures.[40] Finally, scientists must be in a position to prove
these risks of overexploitation by having statistical stock assessment
models at their disposal.[41]

The defence and perpetuation of the statistical approach that constitutes 'normal science' has found additional support within the European
Commission's Scientific, Technical and Economic Committee for Fisheries
(STECF) created in 1979 to allow fisheries biologists to issue opinions on
TAC proposals made on the basis of ICES's recommendations. Unlike the
latter organisation, which does not explore the issue from a social science
perspective, the Commission brought economists into the STECF in 1993,
ostensibly to contribute social science expertise to the formulation of the
CFP by examining problems such as fishing company overinvestments,
competition for fishing grounds, etc. This institutional evolution corresponds to the emergence of fisheries economists as an expert community
recognised by several national research institutes, including IFREMER in
France and the Dutch Agronomic Research Institute (LEI-DLO). In
August 1988, they even created a professional association, the European
Association of Fisheries Economists (EAFE), with the aim of reinforcing

their institutional presence in the Commission. Within the STECF, however, fisheries economists have never managed to assert themselves over biologists who have continued to contribute, in the words of a founding member of the EAFE, 'their biological interpretation of social questions'.[42] Whereas fisheries economists originally wanted to mark their distance from the utilitarian science defended by biologists, many of them nevertheless yielded to this temptation by doing nothing more than regularly executing research contracts offered by the Commission.

The DG Fish is placed under the responsibility of a member of the Commission who generally has other attributions to his or her portfolio. Emma Bonino, Italian member of the Santer Commission from 1995 to 1999, held this position along with humanitarian aid and consumer protection. Her successor in the Prodi Commission, Franz Fischler, is responsible for agriculture and fisheries. Rare are those generalist politicians appointed to the Commission who have had prior experience in fisheries problems before taking on their European function. Former Spanish State Secretary for European Affairs, Manuel Marin, in charge of fisheries in the Delors Commission, was, however, highly familiar with fisheries issues for having negotiated his country's membership in the EC. For Commission members, it is typically difficult to capitalise on fisheries problems in terms of image and national career, since most actors they address view Community intervention from a critical perspective. This explains why Fisheries Members of the Commission have rarely sought to represent the EU extensively in the territories by visiting ports and keeping up a direct dialogue with the fishermen, even in their own country. Beginning with Manuel Marin's term in office, the successive Fisheries Members of the Commission (Yannis Paleokrassas, Emma Bonino, Franz Fischler) sought more systematically to invoke the rationality of scientists and environmental NGOs to legitimate the soundness of restrictive measures in matters of resource conservation and fleet reduction, leaving their office and the DG Fish a comparatively large degree of autonomy in the development of the CFP.[43]

The treaties, in particular Article 37 EC, provide for associating the European Parliament with the process of CFP formulation in the form of a simple consultative role. The Assembly in Strasbourg is, however, not at all held at a distance from the CFP. It is in fact the only EU institution that can claim to contribute counter-expertise to the work of the DG Fish. Treated first by a working group, then beginning in 1984 by a subcommittee of the agriculture committee, fisheries was given an independent committee in 1994, with Miguel Arias Cañete, the Spanish PPE – the European People's Party (EPP) – deputy as its first president. Spanish deputies have been intensely involved in presiding over this committee ever since. The predominant style of exchanges in the European Parliament Committee on Fisheries is quite different from that which characterises national parliaments on the same theme. It often gives rise to debates among experts on specialised topics, such as reference laboratories for monitoring marine biotoxins and bacteriological and viral contamination, discussed during a meeting on 30 March 1999.[44] The rhetoric about the plight of the fishermen, which is part of the verbal sparring among national deputies, receives little audience in the European Parliament Committee on Fisheries in that it produces no effect in a transnational assembly that has no reference to a common history.[45]

Over and above technical debates, members of the European Parliament Committee on Fisheries are mainly politicians who act as intermediaries for the fishing industry's territorialised interests in the Community sphere. As Olivier Costa has pointed out, the political activity of MEPs is

> related to the identity and social practices specific to a territory, a territory that is infra-state to most MEPs, since they are neither leading political officials nor a lasting European elite expatriated to Strasbourg and Brussels. Even the MPs on set national lists, who are a little too hastily tagged as pure products of their party, have a political past and future that is directly linked to their establishment in a given electoral stronghold.[46]

The territorialisation of MEPs partly explains why the Committee of the Regions has never managed to play a leading role in the EU. As stated earlier, the Fraga report on the CFP after 2002 very faithfully reflected the positions of Galician high-sea fleet-owners. The report drafted by Irish European MEP Pat 'the Cope' Gallagher in 1999 in favour of extending the coastal waters reserved for the exclusive sovereignty of states to 24 miles and decentralising fisheries management into regional units, also expresses the position defended by the Irish Fishermen's Organisation. The members of the Committee on Fisheries sometimes include voices of professions other than fishermen. A Christian-Democrat elected official from Cuxhaven, in the German *Land* of Lower Saxony, Brigitte Langenhagen, often appears as the spokesperson for the fish-processing industries, which constitute a major source of employment in her region.

The European Parliament is also a Community institution within which environmental non-governmental organisations (ENGOs) such as Greenpeace, the World Wide Fund for Nature (WWF), the Eurogroup for Animal Welfare, which have all had offices in Brussels since the late 1980s, can convey their ideas rather effectively. Various reasons explain the European Parliament's receptivity to ENGOs. First there is the support of green MEPs, whose representation has increased since 1984 and who are now organised into a political group. There is also the strong demand for expertise expressed by MEPs with regard to environmental policy, as they participate in its formulation more directly since the Maastricht Treaty, particularly via the codecision procedure. Lastly, the

European Parliament is highly tolerant of special interests' groups intruding into parliamentary life. Intergroups, created on the pre-existing model of the British Parliament, are the best illustration of this tolerance. These informal debate structures enable MEPs to defend an idea or an interest on the fringe of official legislative work in areas as diverse as federalism, minority protection, consumers, the environment or animal welfare. In the field of maritime affairs, several intergroups exist: fisheries, maritime affairs, the Atlantic Arc. Some have a secretariat handled by an NGO or an interest group.[47] The director of the Eurogroup for Animal Welfare, a British veterinary, handles the secretariat for the Intergroup for Animal Welfare. In 1999, he organised monthly meetings, which no fewer than twenty-five MEPs, most of them British, attended. Their aims are indeed those of an interest group: to increase awareness among all MEPs to respect for animal life by offering a tribune to outside experts, encouraging the committees to draft reports, and giving voting instructions when legislation is passed.[48] In 1998, the Eurogroup for Animal Welfare, just like the intergroup that represents them in the European Parliament, called on the MEPs to vote in favour of the resolution against driftnets, then persuaded the fisheries ministers to agree a total ban of them in the EU Council (see Chapter 6).[49]

Although some intergroups may seem to be clones of the permanent committees, their power of intervention in the formal legislative process nevertheless makes them the preferred contacts for ENGOs. After long having the environment committee as sole liaison, ENGOs have increased their interactions with all the committees, even in areas – such as fisheries – where the European Parliament is merely consulted. Contacts with the Fisheries Committee began to develop in 1994 in the form of hearings, sometimes even seminars, devoted to the various aspects of the CFP: stock management, impact of fishing techniques on marine flora and fauna (dolphins, turtles, etc.). Since NGOs are wells of information that draw on considerable resources of expertise, as does the WWF, their potential to act as a counterweight to Commission proposals is of interest to the Fisheries Committee. In return, the European Parliament serves as a channel to disseminate the NGOs' ideas at a Community level as well as at national and local levels, given the strong territorial base that most MEPs enjoy.

The CJEC and the CFI, as well as the EU Court of Auditors (ECA), have also played sometimes less visible but far from insignificant roles in the development of the CFP. Whether it is following direct appeals by the Community institutions, governments or individuals, or references for preliminary rulings addressed by national courts, the CJEC has been led to issue an opinion on fisheries matters concerning quotas, the free circulation of capital and the EC's authority regarding relations with third countries. Several major decisions have affected Community jurispru-

dence, such as the *Kramer* judgment establishing the principle of an align-
ment of EC external authority with its internal authority,[50] or the
Factortame judgments calling for the elimination of all national provisions contrary to Community law,[51] are the result of litigation relating to
the CFP. These judgments are an indication of the increasing litigiousness
of relations between the various protagonists in fisheries issues due to the
Europeanisation of their activity. As for the actions for failure to fulfil
obligations brought before the CJEC by the Commission, they have often
been aimed at sanctioning monitoring deficiencies of national administrations. Unlike environmental policy, few judgments relating to fisheries
have, however, remained unenforced, which demonstrates a certain legalism on the part of national fisheries administrations once a European
procedure of conflict resolution has been initiated. On 31 December
1998, a single judgment relating to the CFP had not been enforced by a
national administration at the close of a one-year period: the Greek
government did not comply with a November 1997 judgment on the
conditions of granting licences and/or flags.[52]

The ECA, whose legitimacy has increased since the 1980s, as the
budget has become a pre-eminent political subject,[53] has also contributed,
through its annual and special reports, to reforming the CFP, in particular by requiring other institutional actors to justify certain behaviours.
The October 1998 ECA report on the creation of joint companies in third
countries is, for instance, very severe. Criticisms are not directly only at
the procedures for disbursing aid to Community fleet-owners (mainly
Spanish) involved in joint companies, but the very basis of the policy. The
generosity of Community *primes* with respect to other fleet reduction
incentive measures – in particular demolition – was examined in detail,[54]
to such an extent that in its response the Commission pledged to take into
account the ECA audit when the new Community regulations on structural funds were developed, which it in fact did in 1999.

All Community institutions have an obvious capacity to influence
formulation of the CFP with resources (in terms of budget, expertise,
formal legislative authority, etc.), which indicates their autonomy from
national institutions. However, a supranational entrepreneurship model
cannot be opposed to a view of the EU that would be purely intergovernmental. Supranational and intergovernmental dynamics are intricately
interwoven and constitute the very originality of EU policy-making.

In the case of the CFP, evidence of intergovernmentalism can be found
in the Council of Fisheries Ministers where discussion, opposition and
final approval of essential decisions occur. Generally meeting three times
yearly in Brussels or Luxembourg, the Fisheries Council has legislative
powers, which, unlike other Community policies, implies less sharing with
the European Parliament. From this standpoint, the Community treaties
preserve the state's theoretical sovereignty in the field of fisheries more

than in other areas (domestic market or the environment), although the systematic recourse to a qualified majority as well as the rules directly applicable by national administrations, pose certain difficulties to fisheries ministers who must explain the effects to fishermen, themselves seldom prone to compromise on the state's defence of their interests. In June 1998, the French and Irish ministers were for instance forced to yield to a majority that backed the British presidency's proposal to ban the use of driftnets in the Atlantic Ocean and the Mediterranean Sea (see Chapter 6). Prepared jointly by working groups which brought together officials from various national fisheries administrations and permanent representations, and by COREPER – Permanent Representative Committee – 1, Fisheries Councils are the visible outcome of a negotiation process that took place previously in a variety of much more opaque Community and national bodies. In this respect, the Fisheries Councils also help to legitimate the EU among national fishing industries who are aware of deadlines, adhere to the agendas and make use of the decisions to debate the CFP in the respective territories. To a certain degree, the Council of Ministers helps to get the CFP into a public arena of debate in a way that no other Community institution – including the European Parliament – has yet to achieve.

Interest representation

It is at the local level – in ports or maritime areas – that EU fishermen and fleet owners began to organise the representation of their interests, and this as early as the Middle Ages in Spain. During the twentieth century, increasing state intervention in the regulation of fishing activities led fishermen and shipowners to envisage different forms of organisation of their interests in a national context. The corporatist tie between states and fishermen varies in nature from one national context to another. It depends not only on the economic specificities of the sector in each country, but also the global model of political exchange that governs relations between the state and social actors.[55] Though European fishermen may have a supranational interest group, Europêche, that is in charge of representing them in European institutions, the segmentation of professional organisations and the legitimacy of corporatist practices at the national level have not really allowed them to break free of state ties to defend their interests in the Community arena.

Segmentation and corporatism at the national level
As we underlined in the preceding chapter, the fishing industry in the thirteen coastal states is an EU economic activity characterised by a variety of professional techniques and revenues. The socio-economic and territorial difference in turn induces segmentation in the organisation of interests at

the national level, which are well evidenced in the examples of France, Spain and the United Kingdom.

The maritime sections of the major national trade unions such as the Confédération Générale du Travail (CGT) and the Confédération Française Democratique de Travail (CFDT) in France and the Union General de Trabadores (UGT) in Spain, recruited members after the Second World War both among owner-skippers and wage-earning sailors, often disregarding the usual distinction between capital and labour. As regards the specific interests of fleet-owners, the cleavage that marked the Spanish and French institutional landscape is rather one distinguishing between industrial fishing and small-scale fishing. In Spain, the Federación nacional de cofradías de pescadores brings together 225 local brotherhoods of owners and small-scale fishermen (the *cofradías*), a throwback to medieval guilds, the oldest of which were formed in the ports along the coast of Cantabria in the eleventh century. On the other hand, the Federación española de organizaciones pesqueras and the Federación española de armadores de buques de pesca were created to defend the interests of the semi-industrial high-seas fleets, particularly in Galicia. In France, the Coopération maritime[56] is also the descendant of a cooperative started by French fishermen at the end of the nineteenth century to do away with the monopoly of the fish wholesalers. On the other hand, the Union des armateurs à la pêche de France (UAPF) was created to represent the interests of the large fishing industries in Brittany and Boulogne to the state. In both countries, small-scale fishing organisations and industrial and semi-industrial organisations traditionally share the roles at the local level with a sort of tacit compromise.[57] In south Finistère, marketing of catches was, for instance, divided between the Coopération maritime, which controlled the Organisation des producteurs de l'Ouest-Bretagne (OPOB), and the FROM-Bretagne (Fonds régional d'organisation des marchés), whose activity was based on industrial and semi-industrial companies. But the split between small-scale and semi-industrial fishermen began to blur in the 1980s, not without causing tension between organisations.[58] The decision of a number of small-scale fishermen from the port of Lesconil in the Pont-l'Abbé region to join FROM-Bretagne in 1992 was thus perceived by the OPOB as a move to steal its traditional clientele. Similarly, in 1995 the FROM-Bretagne frowned on the decision of Lorient industrial fleet-owner Jégo-Quéré, in which the Spanish firm Pescanova is a major shareholder, to join the Morbihan-Loire-Atlantique producers' association (PROMA) associated with the Coopération maritime. In both cases, the compromise did not hold up to rationales of alliances between fleet-owners and producer organisation representatives at the local level, such that interests win out over historical heritage.

It still holds true that small-scale fishermen defend a cooperative model

of administration, whereas industrials call for more entrepreneurial indi-
vidualism. In southern Brittany, the management groups created by the
Coopération maritime to stand in for owner-skippers in management
matters (accounting, day-to-day administration, supplier relations, etc.)
are often perceived by semi-industrial fleet-owners as a hindrance to
company independence. The latter also criticise the Coopération maritime
for having too long granted loans, in addition to the public subsidies they
receive, to small-scale fishermen through the Crédit Maritime bank to buy
fishing vessels without sufficiently assessing the financial risks run by the
borrowers. Lastly, differing positions on the CFP can sometimes put
small-scale and industrial fishermen at odds. The EU contractual policy
aiming to foster the development of joint companies in third countries in
the course of the 1990s for instance led to a split within the cooperative
of fishing shipowners in Vigo (ARVI), Galicia. In reaction to resistance
from the Vigo high-sea owner-skippers to the idea of creating joint
companies that would make them 'give up the Spanish flag',[59] the port's
major industrial fishing and wholesale fish companies such as Pescanova,
attracted by the relocation of their activities to third countries with abun-
dant stocks and cheap labour, broke away and created their own
association of Spanish fishing companies.

The differences between small-scale and industrial fleet-owners in
Spain and France do not always boil down to a mere divergence of interests. They also have to do with the legitimate image of the fishing trade
that both systems mean to convey to the state and society. In Spain, as in
France, the image of the skipper on board (who may own the ship) defying
the hostile sea and bureaucrats (once national, now European) to ensure
society's food security is still an aspect of the legitimating rhetoric used by
small-scale fishermen with the state, in particular to negotiate public aid.
At the outset of the twenty-first century, the romantic figure of the sailor
as incarnated by Yann, Pierre Loti's character for Paimpol in *Pêcheur
d'Islande*,[60] remains a rhetorical reference. On the other hand, industrial
representatives who are trying to portray more the image of company
executive sometimes find it legitimate to combine other trades with that
of shipowner, such as wholesaler or processor. A French example illustrates this conflict of images. In 1999, the Coopération maritime
unsuccessfully opposed Alain Furic's bid for election to the new state-
created OFIMER. This semi-industrial ship owner who was especially the
largest fish wholesaler in the port of Le Guilvinec, was running for the
presidency of an organization aiming to strengthen collaboration between
producers and fish processors.[61] The position of the Coopération
maritime officials showed the French fishing industry's refusal to be represented by a polyvalent businessman, while the owner-skippers continued
to embody the legitimate representation of the trade in the eyes of the
'cooperatives'.

In Great Britain, the organisation of professional interests meets a territorial criterion. As soon as the UK joined the EC in 1973, Scottish
fishermen, who already accounted for 40 per cent of the British fish catch,
created the Scottish Fishermen's Federation (SFF) to negotiate their integration into the CFP with the government in London and the European
Commission. Given the growing influence of this well-organised Scottish
lobby[62] represented in Westminster as well as in Brussels by Scottish
Office employees, fishermen out of Northern ports such as Grimsby and
Fleetwood, the declining flagships of the large-scale fishing industry,
decided in 1977 to join together as the National Federation of Fishermen's
Organisations (NFFO). Advocating a reactive attitude towards any
expansion of the CFP, the NFFO has emerged as the federating voice of
local fishermen's associations – particularly small-scale fishermen – in
England, Wales and Northern Ireland. Relations between the NFFO and
the SFF have never been very cooperative. Unlike its English counterpart,
in fact, the Scottish organisation never overtly campaigned for the United
Kingdom's withdrawal from the CFP. This is due to the dominant influence of the Scottish high-sea fishermen within the SFF, who see possible
advantages in the CFP for a negotiated regulation of the resource with
respect to both fishermen from other member states and Norwegian fishermen, their main competitors in the North Sea.

The relative segmentation of professional organisations this comparison of the British, Spanish and French situations reveals should be
examined in light of the institutionalisation of the political exchange
between the industry and the state that exists in many European countries.
Such institutionalisation is doubtless the reflection of not only fishery
sector specificities, but also the practices passed down through the history
of corporatist relations between the state and social actors. Despite the
differences between small-scale and industrial fishermen, France has a
Comité national des pêches maritimes et des élevages marins (CNPMEM,
National Committee of Maritime Fisheries and Mariculture) which heads
up thirty-nine local fishery committees and thirteen regional fishery
committees endowed with a legal personality and financial independence.
A legacy of a 1945 ruling that replaced a Vichy law which had established
a Corporation des pêches maritimes,[63] all trades in the fisheries sector –
production, wholesaling, processing – are legally obliged to join the
CNPMEM.[64] Similarly, national committee and regional committee
consultative deliberations are mandatory before implementation of international, Community or national provisions relative to resource
conservation can take place. States have the authority to sanction any lack
of compliance with these deliberations by levying administrative fines or
revoking fishing licences.

The French state's policy that seeks to create a single institutional interlocutor among all of the fishery professionals is similar to the French

model of sector corporatism shown and analysed in other areas.[65] The CNPMEM, made up of representatives who are either elected from trade union lists or nominated by the Coopération maritime, is the place where the various fishing trades – the French speak of the *interprofession* – and the various territories negotiate with the state on a daily basis. The role of the CNPMEM has not been diminished by the creation of the Conseil supérieur d'orientation des politiques halieutique, aquacole et halioali-mentaire (CSO) in 1998, which is made up of fishing industry representatives nominated by the Agriculture Minister to deal with the major issues affecting the sector.[66] Channelling the profession through a corporatist body is advantageous mainly to the French fisheries administration and even more so to the corps of Affaires maritimes administrators, who have little propensity for dealing with social conflict. Entrusting national committee or regional committee industry representatives with official positions, thereby enhancing their status in the sector, is an integral part of mediation as conceived by the French Government.

The CFP has not diminished the CNPMEM's mediational role. On the contrary, shifting the negotiation process – and hence the social compromise – from the state to the EU heightened the French fisheries administration's call for a structure in which professionals can debate issues often perceived as remote, opaque and conflictual. The CNPMEM president (currently Alain Parrès, former general UAPF delegate), director-general (from the corps of Affaires maritimes administrators), and officials assigned to work with them closely follow the debates sparked by the CFP within Community institutions and other EU countries. A position expressed by the president of a Basque *cofradía* in a regional newspaper against the French pelagic trawlers operating in the Bay of Biscay, or a declaration by the NFFO calling for the regionalisation of the CFP will not escape the CNPMEM's attention. It will assess the implications of a given issue both with the professionals concerned and with the fisheries administration.

The main consequence of this institutionalised exchange is that French fishery professionals are seldom invited to consider representing their interests outside of the state framework. The conflict management mechanisms used between French fishermen and certain European fishermen well demonstrates the dominant mediational role that the government continues to play in France via the CNPMEM. Regular CNPMEM-organised meetings with Spanish and Irish professional organisations are designed to accompany diplomatic manoeuvres undertaken in parallel by the French Fisheries Administration with its counterparts in the countries involved. Bilateral structures of crisis prevention, such as the Franco-Spanish Maritime Fishery Committee or the Franco-Irish Committee bring together fishermen's representatives *and* national administrations. Any attempts by French fishermen to escape the filter of the CNPMEM by developing a transnational relationship with professions in other countries will be perceived by the French fisheries administration as an attempt to undermine the system's coherence. This can be seen in the fisheries administration's apprehensive reaction to the Yeu Island fishermen's initiative intending to coordinate their opposition to the EU ban on driftnets with their Italian counterparts in 1997. CNPMEM's mission in this matter was to channel the Vendée fishermen's movement toward transnationalisation so that 'the French position would maintain a certain coherence'[67] within the EU Council, in other words, so as to avert any threat to the state's power to mediate French professional interests in the European arena.

In other EU countries also characterised by the corporatist model, such as the Netherlands and Denmark, public structures institutionalising the dialogue between the state and the fishing industry also help to channel professional representation. In the Netherlands, in the aftermath of the 1929 economic crisis, the state created the Produktschap Vis. This public law company provides for mandatory consultation of fishermen as well as wholesalers, processors and merchants before any major decision is taken in fishery matters. Dutch professionals thus consider the Produktschap Vis as a spokesperson and mediator. Whether it is a question of non-compliance with licences opposing Dutch Inner Sea shrimp fishermen or protectionist legislation imposed by the Belgian Government on Dutch fleet-owners operating trawlers in Flanders, Dutch fishermen will petition the Produktschap Vis to bring their case before the Dutch fisheries administration or even the European Commission if necessary. The Produktschap Vis director epitomises the transnational lobbyist: a polyglot who is up to date on the operational modes of interest representation in Brussels. This special expertise has enabled the Produktschap Vis to be more directly involved in Community negotiation than the CNPMEM, which remains more dependent on the French fisheries administration. The two-tier negotiation – at the national and Community levels – practised by the Produktschap Vis promotes effective representation of Dutch fishery professionals' interests both to the state and the Commission.[68]

In Denmark, representation of fishermen should also be understood in light of consultative government practices, a legacy of neo-corporatism. Any change in legislation having to do with regulation of the fishing effort or structural aids requires the Danish Fishery Administration to call a meeting of a Consultative Committee on Regulations made up of fisheries officials and representatives of the Danish Fishermen's Federation (Danmarks Fiskeriforening), as well as producer, processor and other organisations.[69] As in France and the Netherlands, this institutionalised system of representation forces the social actors to seek solutions through negotiation and compromise with one another and with the state. Denmark is, moreover, the only EU state in which fishery professionals are systematically consulted before any meeting of the Fisheries Council in Brussels.[70] Consultation has the particularity of being conducted not at the government's initiative, but at that of the national parliament, the Folketing. This originality is related to the very strict monitoring procedures to which its parliament has subjected the Danish government since 1973, before any negotiation can take place with Brussels. Indeed, ministers and civil servants cannot take part in a negotiation within a Council or the COREPER unless the Folketing parliamentary committee for Europe has previously expressed its agreement, thereby mandating it. The powerful and respected parliamentary committee has its own channels of expertise in which consultation with the professions takes place.

These various institutionalised consultative practices that have developed in France, the Netherlands and Denmark in order to preserve the states' ability to act with regard to professional interests do not necessarily have an equivalent in other EU countries. In Spain, it was not until March 1999 that the secretariat-general of maritime fisheries decided on a constitutive meeting of a Consultative Fishery Committee to bring together the sector's various representative organisations in preparing decisions affecting the marketing of fishery products, marine research and aquaculture.[71] Until this committee was created, political exchanges between the administration and professionals were governed by ad hoc informal practices. They sometimes drew support from regional or territorial ties of solidarity. For Galician fishing professionals, Galician officials working at the secretariat-general of maritime fisheries in Madrid have thus often played the role of spokesperson to the Spanish Government.

In Great Britain, the state has not historically sought to channel the representation of fishermen through formal consultative institutions. In 1996, John Major's Conservative Government nevertheless created the Fisheries Conservation Group (FCG) bringing together administrators, professionals and scientists with an aim to formulate opinions on the Commission's proposals. Since MAFF has gone along with few of its recommendations, the FCG has sometimes been analysed as a response by the Conservative Government to pressure from its own Eurosceptics in favour of a United Kingdom withdrawal from the CFP.[72] On the contrary, the relative weakness of the corporatist link between the state and British fishermen explains why the latter had been led to invest the national electoral arena more directly, as can be seen in the activity of Save Britain's Fish (SBF). Founded in 1990 in the English port of Grimsby, SBF is a sectional political movement that brings together representatives of the fishing trade, Labour and Conservative party elected officials and trade unionists, all convinced that the drop in activity of English fishing is largely related to poor fisheries regulation by the EU.[73] Popular among small-scale Cornwall fishermen who regularly criticise the CFP for not allocating large enough quotas to them, and who in the 1980s felt very threatened by the phenomenon of quota-hopping, SBF organised press campaigns, meetings and public demonstrations calling for English fishing to revert to national control without it ever having recourse to violence. Since November 1994 the movement has enjoyed the official support of the NFFO (English and Welsh fishermen's federation), and is represented in the House of Commons by the Labour Party and Conservative Party Eurosceptics. Some House of Lords members who are committed to defending small-scale fishing, also support the SBF. In fact, SBF is a political resource that allows certain English professionals to bring their opposition to the CFP into the electoral arena, whereas the British Government has always made sure, more than in other EU countries, to hold them at a distance from public decisions.

A Commission-backed European representation

The close relationship between states and fishermen – although certainly variable from one country to another – helps to explain the relative lack of institutional representation of fishing professionals at the European level. Created in the 1970s, Europêche is a European federation of fifteen national associations of fleet-owners and fishermen modelled on the Eurogroup.[74] The Europêche budget of about €150,000 in 1999, provided solely by national association dues, is modest compared to other Eurogroups such as the COPA/COGECA (agriculture) or the UNICE (business). It allows for the maintenance of an administrative structure in Brussels composed of a half-time secretary-general and an assistant. Certain national fishermen's organisations – for instance Norwegians and Portuguese – are not members because they cannot afford the dues. Other national organisations, Greek in particular, have been excluded because they have been delinquent with their contribution.[75]

In view of the Europêche example, research that systematically likens interest representation in the Community arena to lobbying must be regarded with a critical eye.[76] This Eurogroup's capacity to define common positions so as to put pressure on the Commission is in fact very weak. Faced with the ban on driftnets decided in June 1998 by the EU Council, Europêche could do no more, for instance, than condemn the general principle of prohibiting a fishing technique. Already rather soft, this position was accompanied by an explicit reservation expressed by the Spanish federation of *cofradías*, the Basque members of which spearheaded opposition to driftnets (see Chapter 6). Nor is there any evidence to show that Europêche is exploited by certain national fishermen's associations in order to increase representation of their interests among Community institutions. Lobbying thus seems structurally absent from the activities of Eurogroup.

If another theoretical function of Eurogroups is to inform national members of the regular progress of the European legislative agenda, the added value of Europêche in this area is also limited. Thus, Europêche's *raison d'être* should be sought elsewhere. It is, in fact, to provide a forum or a political arena for national organisation leaders whose legitimacy among their national members also depends on their presence in Brussels. Their participation in Europêche is not so much necessary in order to help build a common fishing policy with other European fishermen, but to show their grassroots members that they are keeping on eye on the government in Community negotiations. The Europêche secretary-general sums up this situation when he declares, 'What matters to my members is bringing home a photograph proving they were in Brussels'.[77]

In 1971, the European Commission instituted a Consultative Committee on Fisheries (CCF) modelled on the Agricultural Committees created some years before by Dutch Commissioner Sicco Mansholt to manage the CAP. By encouraging various representatives of an economic sector to associate (producers, processors, consumers), these committees are reminiscent of the political project of a Commission that, still seeing itself as the future government of Europe, dreamed of establishing the bases of a supranational corporatist system.

Originally, the CCF was made up of forty-five members appointed by the Commission for three years, nominated by the most representative Eurogroups in the sector. This of course involved Europêche for the fishermen, but other organisations as well, such as the European Association of Producers' Organisations (EAPO), which federates producer organisations; the Association of Fish Industries of the EEC (AIPCEE/CEP), which brings together members of the processing industry; and the Federation of European Aquaculture Producers (FEAP). The CCF has never been in a position to really amend the proposals formulated by the DG-Fisheries, which has gradually slipped into the habit of informing about CFP developments rather than consulting on them. The low-reaction capacity of the CCF can be explained by the overwhelming presence of producers within it – twenty-one seats out of forty-five – tethered to very national approaches to the CFP and unable – unlike the farmers – to assert their own expertise in the Commission. Thus, for thirty years, the main *raison d'être* for the CCF boiled down to an exercise in intersecting legitimacies. For the national fishermen's associations, that enabled them to 'increase the number of photo opportunities' in Brussels with Commission heads. For the latter administration suffering from a recurrent legitimacy crisis, this allowed it to protect itself against accusations of regulatory callousness by showcasing true contact with the social actors.

The legitimating value of the CCF did not prevent criticism from developing within the DG-Fisheries starting in the 1990s, in the context of the overall project of an internal reform of the Commission.[78] Criticism regarding the management of the CCF was all the fiercer as travel and

translation expenses incurred by meetings grew considerably with successive enlargements, given that fisheries professionals seldom master foreign
languages and certain organisations cannot afford to cover transportation
to Brussels. The procedure initiated by the DG Fish followed a course
typical of reform methods generally employed in the Commission: an
independent audit was commissioned in 1997, a group was formed to
analyse the proposals associating the social actors involved, and in July
1999, the decision was made to establish a new Consultative Committee
on Fisheries and Aquaculture (CCFA).[79] The reform reduced to twenty
the number of seats in the new CCFA while bringing in actors that previously were not on it, such as environmental and development NGOs. By
diversifying representation and limiting that of fleet- owners and fishermen, the Commission voluntarily undermined the symbolic power of the
profession's major figures, while inviting them to consult each other more
within Eurogroups. The annual €400,000 allocation that the Commission
had announced in 1999 to enable the various fishery sector Eurogroups to
meet more often before the sessions of the new CCFA, attests to the
Commission practice of providing direct support to social actors, a practice that has been noted in other areas such as the environment or
consumer issues.[80] The fisheries sector illustrates a Commission that
backs professional organisations that would have trouble surviving
without its aid, a far cry from the lobbying scenario in which powerfully
organised actors at the European level supposedly put pressure on the
public authorities. This institutionalisation from on high attests to the
Commission's quest for legitimacy among social actors who often
perceive it as a regulatory agency disconnected from the territories, but
also among national administrations that are seeking to make it pay the
political price for regulation that they have nevertheless endorsed within
the Council of Ministers.[81]

The CFP is the product of a system of actors and politico-administrative institutions whose power is established and legitimated at multiple
territorial and spatial levels. Very clearly, governments are not the only
masters in the formulation and implementation of European decisions
with regard to the fisheries sector. They must constantly share the stage
with supranational and infra-national institutions that have resources
allowing them to defend their specific ideas and interests. Hierarchies
among national, supranational and infra-national institutions are fluctu-
ating. They are to a large extent established through the control of
expertise, which is a major stake in the competition.

As for the representation of fishermen's interests, it largely remains
confined to the state framework which perpetuates deep-seated and
powerful corporatist mediational structures. Although forms of
Europeanisation of interests can be observed – particularly through the
formation of Eurogroups such as Europêche – they are backed by the

Commission, which in this way legitimates its own role in the eyes of the state. The obvious gap between EU decisions and interest representation, which still occurs on a very national or infra-national basis, largely explains the legitimacy deficit that fishermen perceive in the implementation of the CFP.

Notes

1 José I. Torreblanca, 'Overlapping Games and Cross-Cutting Coalitions in the European Union', *West European Politics*, 21 (2), April 1998, p. 135.
2 To illustrate this approach of the EU–local collusion that is said to diminish the power of the state, see Gary Marks, Liesbet Hooghe and Kermit Blank, 'European Integration from the 1980s: State-Centric *vs.* Multi-Level Governance', *Journal of Common Market Studies*, 34 (3), 1996, pp. 341–378.
3 Michel Roux, *L'imaginaire marin des Français. Mythe et géographie de la mer*, Paris, L'Harmattan, 1997.
4 Louis Le Pensec, *Ministre à bâbord*, Rennes, Éditions Ouest-France, 1997.
5 Roux, *L'imaginaire marin des Français*, p. 13. In 1995, candidate Jacques Chirac employed the rhetoric of 'France's great seafaring ambition', quoted by Alain Parrès in *Affirmer la place des pêches maritimes françaises face aux défis mondiaux*, Paris, Conseil économique et social, 1997, p. 89.
6 Fernand Braudel, *The Identity of France*, New York, Harper & Row, 1988–90, translated from the French by Siân Reynolds.
7 Law 97–1051 of 17 November 1997, *Journal officiel de la République française (JORF)*, 19 November 1997.
8 Conservative Manifesto, *You Can Only be Sure with the Conservatives*, London, 1997, p. 42.
9 Interview with Colin Breed MP, London, 3 July 1997.
10 I thank Pavel Salz, researcher at LEI-DLO in The Hague, for reminding me of this incident.
11 Now DEFRA: Department for Environment, Food and Rural Affairs.
12 The best history of the French fisheries administration was compiled by Louis Mordrel in 'Les institutions de la pêche maritime française. Essai d'interprétation sociologique', dissertation for a doctorate in law, Université Paris-II, 1972'; see also Michel Morin, 'Les affaires maritimes: une administration au long passé et à l'avenir incertain', *Revue du droit public*, 5, 1999, pp. 1491–1513.
13 These administrators are recruited each year through an internal and external university-level competitive examination.
14 François Dupuis, Jean-Claude Thoenig, *L'administration en miettes*, Paris, Fayard, 1985.
15 Interview with Alain Maucorps, Nantes, 12 March 1997.
16 Interview with John Horwood, Lowestoft, 4 July 1997.
17 Joseph Catanzano and Hélène Rey, 'La recherche halieutique entre science et action: réflexions sur fond de crise', *Natures, sciences, sociétés*, 5 (2), 1997, pp. 18–30.

18   See Patrick Le Galès and Christian Lequesne (eds), *Regions in Europe*, London, Routledge, 1998.

19   Couliou, *La pêche bretonne*.

20   Proutière-Maulion, *La politique communautaire de réduction de l'effort de pêche*.

21   Interview with M. Charton, Ciboure, 16 July 1998.

22   Law of 11 May 1993 reproduced in Juan Carlos Fernandez Lopez, *O sistema xuridico pesqueiro de Galicia*, Santiago de Compostela, Xunta de Galicia, 1995; see also Fernando Criado Alonso, 'Regional Participation in the European Union: the Cases of Galicia, the Basque Country, Scotland and the Fisheries Policy', dissertation for Masters' degree in European Studies, Bruges, Collège d'Europe, 1996.

23   Ramon Maiz and Antonio Losada, 'La Galice et le difficile chemin de l'autonomie', *Hérodote*, 91, 1998, p. 192.

24   Gwenaële Proutière-Maulion, 'L'encadrement juridique des pêches maritimes en Espagne: l'exemple de la Galice', *Annuaire de droit maritime et océanique*, 15, 1997, pp. 262–278.

25   Interviews with Victor Vasquez Seijas and Ana Maria Gallego Castro, Saint-Jacques-de-Compostelle, 28 October 1997.

26   Interview with Edwin J. Derriman, Penzance, 6 July 1998.

27   Michael Keating and Arthur Midwinter, *The Government of Scotland*, Edinburgh, Mainstream, 1983.

28   *Specific Concordat between MAFF and the Scottish Executive on Fisheries* (www.scotland.gov.uk/concordats).

29   Jacques Leruez, *L'Écosse. Vieille nation, jeune État*, Crozon, Éditions Armeline, 2000.

30   At the request of Germany and Belgium, Article 146 EC Treaty – now Article 203 – was modified during the Maastricht Treaty negotiations to allow ministers of sub-national governments to represent officially the state in the EU Council.

31   Caitriona A. Carter, *Third-Level Assemblies and Scrutiny of European Legislation*, Comité de recherche sur l'intégration européenne, IPSA, Brussels, 2–3 December 1999.

32   In the Scottish Parliament, Labour has formed a coalition with the Liberal-Democrats.

33   Laurence Burgogne Larsen, *L'Espagne et la Communauté européenne*, Brussels, Bruylant, 1995.

34   Emmanuel Négrier, 'Intégration européenne et échanges politiques territorialisés', *Pôle Sud*, 3, 1995.

35   Carmen Fraga Estévez, *Rapport sur la politique commune des pêches après l'an 2002*, Luxembourg, European Parliament, 1997; interview with José A. Suarez-Llanos Rodriguez, Vigo, 30 October 1997.

36   Tanja A. Börzel, 'Towards Convergence in Europe? Institutional Adaptation to Europeanization in Germany and Spain', *Journal of Common Market Studies*, 37 (4), December 1999, pp. 573–596.

37   Richard Balme, Sylvain Brouard and, François Burbaud, *Politique de coopérations atlantiques. Mobilisations inter-régionales et intégration régionale*, Bordeaux, CERVL, December 1995.

38   Moravcsik, *Choice for Europe*; Sandholtz and Stone (eds), *European Integration*.
39   Susanne K. Schmidt, 'Sterile Debates and Dubious Generalisations: European Integration Theory Tested by Telecommunications and Electricity', *Journal of Public Policy*, 16 (3), 1997, pp. 233–271.
40   Catanzano and Rey, 'La recherche halieutique'.
41   Regarding the scientific debate over biometric stock assessment models, see Jean-Pierre Revéret, *La pratique des pêches,* Paris, L'Harmattan, coll. 'Environnement', 1991.
42   Interview with Jacques Weber, Nogent-sur-Marne, 20 June 1997.
43   See Emma Bonino's article in *El Anzuelo*, 3, 1999.
44   On this topic, see Olivier Costa, *La délibération au Parlement européen*, Éditions de l'Université de Bruxelles, forthcoming.
45   Marc Abélès, *La vie quotidienne au Parlement européen*, Paris, Hachette, 1992.
46   Olivier Costa, 'L'Europe par les régions au Parlement européen', *Critique internationale*, 5, autumn 1999, p. 17.
47   Costa, 'L'Europe par les régions au Parlement européen'.
48   Interview with David Wilkins, Brussels, 31 March 1999.
49   Eurogroup for Animal Welfare and RSPCA, *Memorandum on Animal Welfare to the United Kingdom Presidency of the Council of the European Union*, brochure, Brussels and London, November 1999.
50   Joined cases C-3/76, C-4/76 and C-6/76.
51   Cases C-213/89, C-221/89, C-46/93 and C-46/93; see Chapter 5.
52   Seizième rapport annuel de la Commission sur le contrôle de l'application du droit communautaire, *OJEC*, C 354, 7 December 1999.
53   Brigid Lafan, 'Becoming a "Living Institution": The Evolution of the European Court of Auditors', *Journal of Common Market Studies*, 27 (2), June 1999, pp. 251–268.
54   Court of Auditors, Special Report 18/98, *OJEC*, C 393, 16 December 1999.
55   Shackleton, *Politics of Fishing*, p. 9.
56   The precise name of the organisation is the Confédération de la coopération, de la mutualité et du crédit maritimes.
57   Couliou, *La pêche bretonne*, p. 100.
58   It is interesting to note that French fishermen tend to use the term 'family' to refer to their membership in one organisation or another. In their speech they often refer to the 'Coopération maritime family' or the 'UAPF family'.
59   Interview with Alberto Gonzalez-Garces Santiso, Vigo, 29 October 1997.
60   Pierre Loti, *Pêcheur d'Islande*, Paris, Gallimard/Folio, 1988. Regarding novelists' image of the sea, Roux, *L'imaginaire marin des Français* is worthwhile reading.
61   *Le Marin*, 19 February 1999.
62   Mireille Thom, 'A Comparison of British and French Fishing Policies', in Gray, *Politics of Fishing*, p. 131.
63   The best analysis of the history of the CNPMEM is to be found in Louis Mordrel, *Les institutions de la pêche*.
64   Law no. 91–411 of 2 May 1991, in the *Journal Officiel de la République*

Française (lois et décrets), 7 May 1991.

65 Bruno Jobert and Pierre Muller, *L'État en action*, Paris, PUF, 1987.

66 Law no. 98–1060 of 24 September 1998, *Journal Officiel de la République Française* (lois et décrets), 273, 25 November 1998.

67 Interview with Alain Parrès, Paris, 9 February 1998.

68 Interview with Dirk Langstraat, The Hague, 2 April 1998.

69 Interviews with Ole Poulsen and Mogens Schou, Copenhagen, 12 April 1999.

70 David Symes (ed.), *Devolved and Regional Management Systems in Fisheries*, final report, Hull, School of Geography, January 1996.

71 Secretariat General de Pesca Maritima, *Noticia de Fecha*, Madrid, 3 March 1999 (www.from.mag.es/lec.asp).

72 Mark Gray, 'Recent Industry Participation in UK Fisheries Policy: Decentralization of Political Expediency?', in Tim S. Gray (ed.), *The Politics of Fishing*, Basingstoke, Macmillan.

73 *Save Britain's Fish's* website is available (www.savebritfish.demon.co. uk/hedfsh.htm).

74 Justin Greenwood and Mark Aspinwall (eds), *Collective Action in the European Union*, London, Sage, 1998.

75 Interview with Guy Vernaeve, Brussels, 31 March 1999.

76 Like Sonia Mazey and Jeremy Richardson (eds), *Lobbying in the European Community*, Oxford, Oxford University Press, 1993. For a critical perspective, see Andy Smith, 'Au-delà d'une Europe du lobbying – l'exemple des rapports entre régions et Commission', in Paul-Henri Claeys *et al.* (ed.), *Lobbyisme, pluralisme et intégration européenne*, Brussels, Presses interuniversitaires européennes, 1998, pp. 58–82.

77 Interview with Guy Vernaeve, Brussels, 31 March 1999.

78 Christian Lequesne, 'The European Commission: A Balancing Act between Autonomy and Dependence', in Karlheinz Neunreither and Antje Wiener (eds), *European Integration after Amsterdam. Institutional Dynamics and Prospects for Democracy*, Oxford, Oxford University Press, 1999, pp. 36–51.

79 *OJEC*, 20 July 1999.

80 Simon Hix, *The Political System of the European Union*, London, Macmillan, 1999; Ruth Webster, 'Environmental Collective Action', in Justin Greenwood and Mark Aspinwall (eds), *Collective Action in the European Union*, p. 176–195.

81 Giandomenico Majone, *La Communauté européenne: un État régulateur*, Paris, Montchrestien, coll. 'Clefs', 1996.

3

Conserving the resource: from supply of to demand for European regulation

Established in the seventeenth century as a principle of international law, freedom to sail to other nations entails by the same token the freedom to fish. In his *Mare Liberum* published in 1609, Grotius discussed 'the capture of fish in rivers, which cannot be free for it would soon exhaust the river of fish, but fishing in the sea is free, for it is impossible to exhaust its wealth'.[1] Opposite to this reasoning, some contemporary legal experts underscored the need to preserve living maritime resources. In 1653, Scottish law professor William Welwood refuted Grotius's arguments, noting that freedom to fish led to an overexploitation of stocks off the coast of Scotland. By revolutionising fishing with the arrival of steam-powered vessels,[2] the industrial era of the late nineteenth century brought the debate on conservation of the resource around to seeking institutional solutions at the international level. In the scientific field, the pursuit of this aim led to the creation of the International Council for the Exploration of the Sea (ICES) in 1902, then, in the intergovernmental field, to setting up a network of regional fishery bodies (RFB) in 1911 that were to allow states to better monitor the activity of their fishermen.

Intended to restrict the volume of catches, resource conservation measures initiated by the EC in the 1980s – not without a certain reluctance on behalf of some governments – were not fundamentally innovative with respect to those advocated previously by the regional fishery bodies (RFBs). These measures nevertheless evolved into other forms of regulation that were meant to frame more than just catches and now included the fishing effort (limiting fleet engine power, granting of licences, etc.). Moreover, Community measures fit into an original institutional context within which a supranational institution, the European Commission, acting as a regulatory agency, and a set of supranational legal norms, were to hold sway over member states.

In the vein of research by scholars such as Giandomenico Majone, Community policy on the conservation of fishery resources raises the question of the means of production and legitimation of a European political action that is not exclusively but to a large extent regulatory in nature, in other words that consists of 'a sustained and focused control exercised by a public agency, on the basis of a legislative mandate, over activities that are generally regarded as desirable to society'.[3] This chapter begins by examining the various regulatory measures that have characterised the European fishery resources conservation policy since its inception, and which have emerged on the EU political agenda largely as a result of European Commission input. It then shows the difficulties involved in implementing European regulations and monitoring them on the national level. Via the question of Community monitoring of resource conservation measures, this chapter ends by examining the conditions under which European regulation, first initiated by the Commission, has become regulation that meets the demands of social actors.

From catch limitation to reduction of the fishing effort: supply-sided regulation

Modern political–economic theories distinguish several forms of state intervention in the economy, such as income redistribution, macroeconomic stabilisation and regulation. For Giandomenico Majone, regulation 'attempts to correct various forms of market deficiencies, such as the power of monopolies, negative externalities, information deficits or a lack of supply of collective goods'.[4] This liberal theorem, according to which the lack of trade barriers results in the efficient allocation of collective goods, is impossible to apply to natural resources. Indeed, a natural resource is by nature exhaustible and hence, as all the studies on 'the governance of the commons' have reiterated, freedom of access and exploitation results in more and more actors seeking to draw maximum benefits. This eventually leads to overexploitation and depletion of collective goods, which Garrett Harding called 'the tragedy of the commons'.[5] In the field of maritime fishing specifically, the problem of regulation is therefore posed in terms of framing the free access of vessels via restrictive measures governing exploitation of the resource.

Free access of European member states to Community waters was decided in 1970, in compliance with the general principle of equal treatment of economic actors set out by the Treaty of Rome and regularly reaffirmed by the Court in Luxembourg in its case law. The principle of free access also governed the establishment of the EU 200-mile fishing zone, which was accompanied by resource regulation measures. The first of these measures was the setting of Total Allowable Catches (TACs) applicable to certain species and certain fishing areas. It was followed by the establishment of technical regulations and finally, by a policy of limiting the fishing effort. All these measures have the specificity of being on the supply side of regulation, in other words, they have more or less been concocted by European Commission experts and civil servants. As is the case in any bureaucratic organisation, Commission officials have been tempted by this useful function to extend their power over the fishing sector by circumventing the constraints of a Community budget whose modest allowances set limits on other forms of intervention. In this regard, the regulatory action of the European Commission over the conservation of fishery resources disproves traditional theories of public decision-making, which hold that budget maximisation is the sole source of power for administrations.

The TAC and quotas system
The TAC and quotas system, passed by the EC in 1983, drew its inspiration from what the regional fishery bodies, particularly the North-East Atlantic Fisheries Commission (NEAFC). The instrument was recognised by the 1982 Montego Bay International Convention for the Law of the Sea, which authorised any coastal state wanting to preserve and exploit its biological resources 'to determine the allowable catch of the living resources in its exclusive economic zone'.[6] Some 120 fish and shellfish stocks in the Atlantic, the English Channel, the North Sea and the Baltic Sea thus come under the EU's TAC and quotas system.[7] Given that in 1977 the Mediterranean was not subject to the EEZ system, in 1983 the EC fisheries ministers felt that it was exempt from the TAC regulations. Following a recommendation issued by the International Commission for the Conservation of Atlantic Tunas (ICCAT) reporting a threat to the stock of bluefin tuna, in December 1998 the EU Council nevertheless decided to establish a TAC on this species, applicable not only to catches in the Atlantic Ocean but in the Mediterranean as well.

The yearly setting of TACs and quotas by European fisheries ministers that frames the activity of fishermen throughout the following year is a ritual exercise during which the rationality of expertise confronts political rationality. It begins with an assessment that is primarily in the realm of scientific expertise. In October or November at the earliest, an annual report compiled by fishery biologists on the ICES's Advisory Committee on Fisheries Management (ACFM) is filed with the Commission's DG-Fisheries. The opinions therein, which set the main TACs by species and geographical zone, apply strictly to Community stocks and those shared with certain neighbouring countries such as Norway, the Faroe Islands or the Baltic countries. They usually distinguish analytical TACs, established on the basis of assessments the scientists consider to be verified, from precautionary TACs intended to protect an endangered species, although precise data does not allow the risk to be entirely proven.

The European Commission's Scientific, Technical and Economic Committee for Fisheries (STECF), many experts of which also sit on the ACFM, generally ratify scientific opinion without modification. This then constitutes the basis on which the DG Fish Conservation and Control Directorate bases its proposal to distribute the TACs into national quotas. Feeling invested with a mission of 'guardian of the stocks', DG Fish officials often validate the opinion of scientific committees knowing full well that national ministers and officials will then seek to review their proposals to make them more favourable to their respective fishermen. When the Commission has put its proposal to the national administrations in November, the rationale of the negotiation actually switches from the problem of protecting fish stocks to that of protecting territories, or from resource management to keeping the social peace.

The importance of the political aspect disproves Giandomenico Majone's thesis according to which European regulation is primarily a matter of administrative authorities acting on the basis of 'research reports',[8] just as it invalidates the widespread idea among certain social scientists working on the CFP that the latter is overly focused on the DG-Fisheries's biological and economic goals and neglects to take the fishermen into account.[9] On the contrary, as Jean Boncœur and Benoît Mesnil have pointed out, themselves drawing on research conducted by Anthony T. Charles, the social/Community paradigm' that prefers to 'minimize the risks of conflict between fishermen and with fishermen in the short term' dominates the process of developing the CFP.[10] Another manifestation of the supremacy of politics over biology and economics – in the sense of maximising the income from fishing – can be seen in the founding principle of relative stability, which acknowledges for each state a set proportion of the TACs established for each stock on the mere basis of previous catches by the nation's fleet. The principle of relative stability, as well as the division of TACs into national quotas, illustrates the difficulty of sometimes drawing a precise line between what would come under regulatory policies and distributive policies respectively, as certain public policy typologies tend to do.[11] The division of TACs into quotas shows, on the contrary, how a form of control exercised by a public authority over an activity having a social value for all (regulation) is intricately bound up with a differentiated transfer of resources to social groups (redistribution).

The annual fixing of TACs also illustrates the limits of analyses that boil European regulation down to a negotiation between experts trying to produce 'rational decisions' in sectors characterised by a strong technical complexity, even if government officials later must overstep them in the implementation phase.[12] It in fact brings into play not only Commission officials and expert committees whose expectations are to a large degree disconnected from election cycles, but also political actors whose decision-making rationale is dictated by the preservation of social peace in the national territories, even when this is likely to be threatened by a very limited social group such as fishermen. It can even be asserted in this regard that the concerns of the latter tend to prevail over those of the former, keeping the social peace taking precedence over the future of fish stocks.

Table 3.1 Division of TACs in area IIa, North Sea (2000)

Country	TACs *(in tonnes)*
Belgium	2,530
Denmark	200,200
Germany	2,530
France	2,530
The Netherlands	2,530
Sweden	1,330
UK	8,350
EC total	220,000
Norway	5,000
Faroe Islands	2,000
Total TAC	225,000

Source: Official Journal of the European Communities, L 341, 31 December 1999, p. 25

Technical regulations

The CFP also exemplifies the preponderant weight occupied by regulations as a specific way of managing fisheries. Since 1983, European fisheries resource conservation policy has in effect been based on a plethora of technical regulations aiming to frame fishing by setting standards for net mesh sizes, conditions for storing special nets aboard vessels, minimum landing sizes for species, imposing fishing bans or restrictions on certain types of vessel or in certain areas. Even more so than the TACs, these rules are on the supply side of regulation, for they are often initiated by DG-Fisheries officials on the basis of expert research. There is without doubt a community of ideas among experts and Commission officials which can be likened to what Peter Haas has termed an 'epistemic community',[13] as to the fact that TACs are no longer sufficient to ensure lasting fish stocks in Community waters, and that other forms of management must be found.

Unlike the TACs, technical regulations are a matter regarding which national political–administrative heads and the fishermen – via their representational bodies – have more trouble influencing Commission proposals, since they are unable to bring in alternative expertise to that of the DG Fish. The projected overhaul of technical regulations submitted to the Council in late 1995 by the Commission, aiming to create a single body of texts (protection of young species, minimal net mesh sizes, etc.), has thus encountered many reservations on the part of several national governments that must deal with the reluctance of their professionals. It was nevertheless adopted without the Commission's original proposals being significantly amended by the states.[14]

Limiting the fishing effort

Beginning in the 1990s, it was recurrently acknowledged that TACs and quotas were not enough to curb overfishing because the European decision-making processes were too dependent on keeping the social peace. Commission officials therefore began to explore another dimension of conservation policy. This involved limiting the fishing effort by instituting licences, limiting the time at sea and most of all restructuring fleets. The mobilisation of experts (biologists as well as economists) in charge of drafting the reports points up the experimental nature of the process of concocting regulations at the European level.[15] The experimental aspect explains why the Commission constantly suggests new measures to limit overfishing that supplement, but never replace existing measures. Alain Parrès, the French president of the CNPMEM, described this phenomenon as the 'layer-cake method'.[16] Each layer of regulation in fact corresponds to the pursuit of a better solution than the preceding one, the latter which, however, must not be totally eliminated since it has not proven entirely ineffectual. The resulting impression among social actors at the national level is naturally that European measures lack effectiveness.

The introduction of fishing licences to reduce the fishing effort is not a novel measure with regard to common practice in most member states. In Spain, a licensing scheme was established in 1980 that included specific lists for each occupation performed. In the Netherlands, a fishing permit system was introduced for cod in 1981 and was extended to other species in 1987. Although French fishermen have often criticised licensing as hindering young fishermen from getting started in the profession, they have often been used to manage local fisheries, such as scallops in the bay of Saint Brieuc, shrimp in Guiana and elver (small eel) in the Loire-Atlantique department.[17] While fisheries experts, particularly in Organisation for Economic Cooperation and Development (OECD) reports, have often demonstrated that limiting factors of production in a fishery through licensing does not solve overfishing, the Commission nevertheless wanted to promote this instrument at the Community level.[18] Following the December 1992 framework regulation instituting the Community system for fisheries and aquaculture, the DG Fish made proposals to national administrations to establish a Community licensing scheme intended to frame certain activities in the Community fishing zone, in third-country waters and on the high seas. In view of opposition from several national professional organisations to a proposal that would limit their members' access to certain fisheries, on 20 December 1993 the EU fisheries ministers adopted a compromise that fell well short of the DG-Fisheries' expectations. Regulation 3690/93[19] stipulating that member states shall issue fishing licences for all vessels, and that the information contained in such a document should match that contained in Community records of fishing fleets set up by the Commission in 1989. The added value of this Community regulation on licences resides to some extent in better harmonisation of the information contained in national documents. This text would have gone fairly unnoticed had not Commission officials, entrepreneurs in the habit of pestering national administrations,[20] managed to get another regulation (1627/94) passed by the Fisheries Council in June 1994, which established the framework for issuing special fishing permits (SFPs). This measure to limit the fishing effort allowed member states to grant fishing licences validated by the Commission to individual boats exploiting certain fishing areas during given periods. In force as of 1 January 1996, these Community SFPs were only used to regulate fishing of rare species such as scallops, shellfish and certain deep-sea stocks. They nevertheless obliged national administrations to conduct a regular review of their fishing effort of these species and draw up a register of vessels involved in these types of fisheries. Unlike the TACs, the institution of a licensing scheme was not especially perceived by the fishermen as an instrument of top-down centralisation symbolising the Commission's interventionism in the regulation of their activity. But nor have licences, which experts endlessly proclaim are an inadequate means of limiting the fishing effort, ever constituted the primary instrument on which the Commission has sought to found a Community policy for resource conservation.

The situation is different with the two other methods offered by the Commission: limiting the time spent at sea and, to a greater extent, the restructuring of national fleets through MAGPs. The first measure figured among the incentives of the 1992 framework regulation aiming to ensure a 'rational and responsible exploitation of resources on a sustainable basis'. Limiting the time spent by fishermen at sea is another form of regulation that Commission officials and experts modelled on experiments conducted in certain third countries, knowing from the start that there, too, these were not a cure-all solution. Restrictions on the duration of trips out to sea to fish Pacific halibut introduced in 1979 in Canada were not, for instance, effective in limiting the increase of the fishing effort. Similarly, the limitations on the frequency of fishing trips introduced in 1981 in certain United States fishing zones did not result in a real reconstitution of stocks.[21] As usual, DG Fish officials were mainly concerned with encouraging national administrations and fishermen to test new regulatory methods through innovation. In the context of the 1990s where the subsidiarity principle tended to hold sway as a new legitimate means of public action within the EU, national governments were encouraged rather than obliged to introduce the time spent at sea as a complementary method to the TACs and quotas. The instrument was only actually put into practice by certain national administrations – for instance in Denmark, Great Britain and the Netherlands – with a view to regulating certain specific fisheries. In Great Britain, the *Days at Sea* plan set up by MAFF was basically targeted at pelagic vessels and beam trawlers. The Community measure was to a great extent exploited by British MAFF officials to impose on professionals a new effort deemed necessary to regulate the resource, to such an extent that the NFFO quickly disputed the rationality of a measure that, being basically designed to limit the yield of Scottish vessels, could be extended to other segments of the fleet, and therefore more directly concern English and Welsh fishermen.[22] What is interesting to note in the NFFO position with regard to the *Days at Sea* plan is an opposition to a Community regulatory measure of which the enforcement was intended to be optional, not obligatory. To a certain extent, the fishermen, constantly advocating increased decentralisation of the CFP in their rhetoric, in this case were paradoxically led to dispute the legitimacy of an EU-proposed regulation because it was not imposed uniformly over all European actors in the sector.

From the start, limitation of the fishing effort set up by the MAGPs was situated by the Commission at the crossroads of resource conservation policy and structural aid policy. Designed as an incentive to curb the chronic overcapacity of the Community fleet, the MAGP has gradually become a restrictive programme of multiannual reduction of national fleets, negotiated by the Commission with each state with an aim to achieve, segment by segment, a more balanced equation between the fishing effort and available stocks. With the third MAGP (1992–96), the instrument – which is expressed in terms of tonnage and vessel power – has, in the eyes of European fishermen regardless of their occupation or their economic situation, embodied a regulation policy centralised in Brussels aiming to bring their activity under its supervision. It is true that MAGP incentives to break up vessels constitute a particularly powerful symbolic measure since they encourage destroying the tool of the trade. The MAGP is a perfect illustration of the way in which a regulatory policy is structured at the European level, the issues and the conflicts that it raises and the central position that the Commission occupies in it. The first two MAGPs (1983–86 and 1987–91) in no way helped to reduce the overcapacity of Community fleets. On the contrary, the latter even tended to increase it through the financial aid granted at the same time by the EU, the states and the regions. From 1986 to 1988, the capacity of the French fishing fleet rose for example by 7 per cent whereas is should have decreased by 2.7 per cent at the end of MAGP 2.[23] Though the ineffectiveness of MAGPs 1 and 2 has often been explained by their non-binding nature, it was primarily due to the national administrations' lack of reliable methods for calculating vessel capacity and classifying them into set categories.[24] The Commission's DG Fish learned from this that to ensure effective regulation of the resource through MAGPs, better data on vessel capacity had to be collected, which required improved monitoring of national records on fleets. It was in the aim of legitimating increased monitoring of data held by national administrations that the Commission proposed, for the first time with MAGP 3 (1992–96), a more sophisticated method of calculating fleet reduction since it was divided by segment (a given per centage of reduction for the pelagic fleet, another for the demersal fleet, etc.). Finding justification once again in reports outside the Commission,[25] this proposal has to do with the very definition of the regulatory supply offered by a public authority, that is, to gain legitimacy by advocating control of all social actors.[26] The demand for increased monitoring of national fleet records came along with specific Commission practices to foster implementation of Community policies at the national level. As does the legal department in matters of non-compliance with Community law or by the Competition DG in matters of state aid, beginning with the MAGP 3, the DG Fish indeed began to publicise the annual results of programme implementation within each state and each segment of fleet. The ranking of states and occupations as 'good' or 'bad' pupils of the CFP is clearly intended as a political means to invite national administrations to demand additional efforts from fleet-owners and fishermen. In May 1999, a Commission report showed that the French and Dutch fleets did not always comply with the goals of MAGP 3 (1992–96), whereas other fleets (Portuguese, Spanish and Danish) had already anticipated the goals of the MAGP 4 for the 1997–2001 period.[27] This political measure of competitive publicity was supplemented by another that involved linking the goals of one Community policy to those of another. Thus the grant of aids to building and modernising vessels was conditional upon compliance with the MAGP. In late 1998, the French administration thus had to oversee the elimination of 20,000 kW of power required by the MAGP 3 (1992–96) to be able to authorise certain professionals to build new boats. The Commission has even managed to get the fisheries ministers to strengthen this conditionality by way of a reform of structural funds. The December 1999 regulation defining new guidelines for aid to the fishing sector in fact stipulates, for segments of fleets that are not in compliance with the goal set by the MAGP, that shipowners who wish to benefit from a Community grant to build new boats must offer in exchange to withdraw an additional 30 per cent of their capacity (see Chapter 4). The example of the MAGP is a good illustration of supply-sided regulation of public action as it functions at the European level. But EU member states differ as to the conditions in which they implement and monitor this European regulation.

Diversity of implementation and monitoring at the national level

Implementation and monitoring of fishery resources regulation continues to take place within member states that have differing historical and institutional itineraries as well as configurations of actors. As a result, there are discrepancies both in the conditions of implementation and monitoring and in the capacity of social actors to comply with them.

Territory-based implementation

Implementation of European resource conservation management mainly involves regulations that are directly applicable in national legislation. Unlike directives, regulations do not need to be formally transposed by national institutions, their content usually being subsumed by national ministers in administrative measures that do not require the involvement of national Parliaments.[28] Resorting to regulations rather than directives illustrates the original plan of Commission officials to establish a unified European administration of the CFP in the territories, drawing inspiration directly from CAP methods. Although Community resource conservation regulations have multiplied since the 1980s, the implementation of them should not be seen as merely a process of legally transcribing the European norm with which fishermen would then simply comply. Implementation at the national level on the contrary involves a process of translation and reinterpretation of European regulations that varies depending on institutional factors specific to each national context. By comparing France, Great Britain and the Netherlands, it is possible to show the influence these respective factors have on different forms of implementation of the TACs and quotas, as well as the MAGPs.

Different institutions are mobilised in each of the three countries to implement the TACs. In France, the state distributes the TACs each year by allocating sub-quotas to producer organisations (POs), or even more marginally to the fishing companies for certain specific species. In France, most POs do not assign sub-quotas individually by vessel, so members of the PO fish until the national administration declares that the quota has been reached. Regional market organisations FROM-Bretagne and FROM-Nord nevertheless monitor ship logs, enabling them to inform their members when a sub-quota has been reached. FROM-Nord even makes some allocations to individual ships. Non-individual allocations in a majority of POs underscore the refusal of French fishermen (especially small-scale fishermen) to accept any move toward some form of allocating fishery resources to individuals. It is not by chance that the 18 November 1997 framework law on maritime fishing and mariculture set the goals of 'allowing the sustainable exploitation and enhancement of the collective wealth constituted by the fisheries resources to which France has access'.

In Great Britain, 95 per cent of the TACs are managed by nineteen POs that are responsible for catches made by their members. Most of the British POs allocate sub-quotas to member vessels on a monthly or annual basis. This boils down to a de facto distribution of property rights in the form of individual quotas.[29] Although the English, Scottish and North Irish fisheries administrations continue to directly manage 5 per cent of the quotas not assigned to the POs, authority is largely delegated to the British fishing industry, which manages the TACs with a higher degree of responsibility than the French POs. We shall return to the bases for this delegation of authority in Great Britain, which illustrates a very different relationship between the state and social actors in the management the public goods from that which exists in France.[30]

In the Netherlands, even before Community TACs were established, the fisheries administration decided to introduce a system of individual transferable quotas (ITQ) per vessel to manage flatfish catches – plaice and sole – in the North Sea, based on previous catches. Unlike most EU countries, the idea of individualising fishery resources has never been taboo to Dutch high-sea fleet owners who, having a long tradition of free enterprise, perceived the possibility of grouping boats together to have a greater ITQ as an advantage. However, the increase in the fishing effort due to higher ITQs encouraged Dutch fishermen to overfish, even step up fraud and illegal unloading. This situation, which led the Dutch agriculture minister to resign in September 1990, prompted the Dutch fisheries administration to suggest a codetermination of quotas by the state and the profession which, in this case, clearly harks back to the neo-corporatist heritage. Quota management groups, known as *Biesheuvel* groups, which have no other equivalent in any other EU country, were created in 1993. Always presided over by a figure from outside the fishing industry, these groups – seven of which were in existence in 1998 – bring together fishermen belonging to a single producers organisation, who delegate the right to manage their ITQs to a board of directors. They must regularly declare their catches and obey the rule of time spent at sea managed by this same board of directors which, moreover, can levy fines, while remaining collectively responsible to the administration for exceeding quotas. Of Dutch beam trawler owners fishing flatfishes 97 per cent were members of a *Biesheuvel* group in 1998, and it has been estimated that no quotas have been exceeded since 1994, thanks to management by these delegated structures.[31]

Comparative analysis of the institutions in charge of implementing the TACs in Great Britain, France and the Netherlands shows European regulation translates differently from one country to another. A number of institutional factors contributing to the differentiated implementation of TACs and quotas can be highlighted, as well as certain technical measures.

In the first place, the extensive involvement of the fisheries administration in France indicates a refusal on the part of most French fishermen – particularly in the small-scale sector – to consider a shift toward a privatised or delegated management of the resource base. This is a notable difference with respect to the Netherlands, and even Great Britain, where acceptance of a form of individual ownership of the resource goes together with a greater capacity among professionals to take responsibility for determining quotas. The state/industry co-management much touted in the literature on the governance of the commons,[32] does not always lead to more effective implementation. In Great Britain, the rigour that the POs demonstrate in allocating and managing quotas is a factor that encourages fraudulent practices. Illegal unloadings are so widespread that the Anglo-Welsh and Scottish fisheries administrations have obliged vessels over 20 metres long to unload their catches exclusively in designated ports at fixed times. The national models are not, moreover, necessarily duplicable from one territory to another. Most French or Spanish fishermen would consider the Dutch model of *Biesheuvel* groups illegitimate. The head of one Breton PO described it in the highly revealing terms as being a system that encourages fishermen to be 'collaborationists'.[33]

Secondly, the relationship that has developed historically between each state and its fishermen's organisations has an impact on the implementation of European regulation. In France, the relationship between the state and the fishermen has been forged partly by a compromise that can be expressed as social peace in exchange for tolerance of non-compliance with the law. Although opinion must be qualified according to the different local situations, the fisheries administration in France tends to be rather lenient in its enforcement of European regulations when social peace is threatened. In the aftermath of the social movement that struck southern Brittany in 1993–1994, the fisheries administration proved itself to be particularly tolerant toward high-sea fishermen that did not log their catches as stipulated in a Community regulation, because the order from the French fisheries administration was to indulge the profession.[34] The British situation differs from France in this respect. Both MAFF and the Scottish Executive Rural Affairs Department as well as the sea fisheries authorities at the local level, have a more legalistic approach to implementing European regulation, because they are less subject to pressure from fishermen's organisations likely to breach the social peace.

Thirdly, the structure of national fleets is an institutional factor that influences implementation of European regulation. Coastal fishermen feel less bound by the European regulation of the resource base and technical measures than do high-sea fishermen because they are less constrained by formal obligations such as keeping a logbook or notifying changes in fishing areas. Implementation of European regulation also varies in all countries according to the size of the fishing company. Industrial and semi-industrial fleet-owners and fishing captains operating in Community fishing areas have a tendency to comply with regulations for economic reasons. They are in fact more inclined to perceive the impounding of a vessel by the supervisory authorities as an economic difficulty. A manager of the Pétrel-Scarfel fleet, whose trawlers in 2000 brought in one-third of the stock sold at the Lorient fishery product auction emphasised his obligation to comply with Community legislation on the TACs and technical measures, because his company management, associated with the large retail chain Intermarché, could not afford repeated detentions of their vessels for being suspected by the supervisory authorities of infringing the law.[35]

The obvious discrepancies in the implementation of TACs and quotas and technical measures also hold true for MAGPs. This is often what leads fishermen to dispute the legitimacy of regulating the fishing effort through MAGPs. British fishermen for example feel discriminated against due to the fact that the United Kingdom Treasury, for reasons of budgetary rigour, has always been opposed to the allocation of a national or regional complement to the Community premium for final cessation of activity provided by the MAGP, as is current practice in Spain or in France. The variety of implementation processes feeds the sentiment among all fishermen that they are not subjected to fair rules. This constitutes a fundamental limit to the legitimation of the CFP in particular and to the EU in general.

Control: still a national prerogative

In a top-down approach, effective implementation of European regulation at the national level should be the result of a 'self-conscious oversight, on the basis of authority, by defined individuals or offices endowed with formal rights or duties to inquire, call for changes in behaviour and (in come cases) to punish'.[36] Theoretically, the European Commission could exercise this control over implementation on the model of a federal regulatory agency such as those that exist in the United States. As concerns competition and aid allocation, this is partly how it functions. The situation is different with regard to fisheries policy, because national governments have preferred, for reasons we shall analyse further on, to exercise control of implementation of European regulation themselves rather than delegate it to the Commission. This political choice of EU member states leads us to ponder their capacity to exercise national control, a problem that in turn raises the question of how states assert their authority over the fishermen.

Control is handled through national institutions whose resources and effectiveness also vary considerably from one territory to another. Despite national differences, we can nevertheless underline a number of common traits. First, control of fishermen's activity requires national administrations to deploy considerable means for sea and port surveillance (inspection staff, surveillance vessels and planes). This effort involves considerable state budget expenditures the legitimacy of which is often disputed by national fiscal administrations, given the low contribution of fisheries to the national GDP. In England and Wales, the cost of inspections at sea conducted by the Royal Navy for MAFF was estimated in 1998 to be approximately £20,000 per day, an amount deemed too costly by the British Treasury.[37] Lastly, control is rarely exercised by a single national authority but instead relies on the intervention of several civil and military and/or central and regional administrations. These exchanges tend to be characterised by bureaucratic competition. In member states such as France, Great Britain and Belgium where the national navies are used to ensuring control of fishing vessels, there is even a conservative reflex on the part of the latter, not wishing to give up an aspect of their activity long considered not to be the most 'noble' part of their trade. Policing fisheries in fact compensates for the decreased utility of national navies in military operations that have become rare. One must be cautious, certainly, in attempting to draw up national models of CFP control. Like the policy styles developed twenty years ago by Richardson *et al.*, the notion of national model of control tends in fact to be overly general and neglect the internal diversity of a national territory.[38] Variants ascribable to national factors can nevertheless be observed in the control of fishing activities. Among these are the nature of public debate on fishery resources, the state's institutional structure, the nature of the relationship between the state and the fishermen, and the legal regime sanctioning fraud.

To take the case of Spain, up until 1986, control of the fishing industry by the state was very poorly organised, both at sea and on land. Accession to the EC forced the state to set up a control of the fishing effort, because the Act of Accession provided for strict reductions in fleet power. At the same time, the state and the autonomous communities established technical regulations and control measures for catches, although these were relatively unenforced compared to the size of the catches landed. With respect to the four institutional factors mentioned above, the situation in Spain is perfectly explicable. First of all, the continental shelf in the Atlantic portion of Spain's EEZ is so narrow that most fishing activity is done outside national waters. There is hence no real public debate in Spain regarding the protection of national fishery resources as there is in Great Britain or Ireland. Spanish fishermen tend, in fact, to use up the quotas attributed by the EU and feel that they were underevaluated with respect to market capacities when Spain joined. As a result of this perceived discrimination, Spanish high-sea fishermen have trouble accepting the legitimacy of Community regulation of the resource, echoing analyses that, since Max Weber, have established a link between a sense of fairness and compliance with the law.[39] Consequently, the central and autonomous administrations in Spain demonstrate a certain tolerance of fraud, considered to be the inevitable effect of a lack of quotas. Second, the effect of regionalisation of the state in Spain is a vertical distribution of control that fosters bureaucratic competition. Inspectors answering to the central government share surveillance of fisheries and related activity with inspectors from the autonomous communities on the basis of a perfectly random criterion: the origin of the catches to be unloaded. Fish caught beyond the base lines recognised by the international law of the sea come under the authority of inspectors from Madrid, whereas catches made inside these lines come under the responsibility of their colleagues in the autonomous communities. Control of the first sale of fish on the market also falls to the Madrid inspectors, whatever the origin of the catches, whereas that of subsequent sales comes under the authority of regional inspectors. Such a fragmented administrative system reduces the effectiveness of controls not necessarily because of its two-tier organization, but because it is poorly accepted by certain regional authorities which do not cooperate with the inspectors in Madrid. Third, if the relationship between Spanish fishermen and the central government is less corporatist in Spain than in France, their interactions with the autonomous governments are sometimes much more so, which tends to limit the effectiveness of controls. Fleet owners, fishermen and wholesale traders in Galicia form a clientelistic backing of the Partido popular, one reward of which is leniency on behalf of the autonomous administration in the local enforcement of European regulation of the resource. Finally, the legal sanctions decreed by the Spanish courts are generally not very dissuasive. The maximum fine provided for in Spanish law for quota infringement or fishing with non-regulation vessels is two times lower than in Germany and Great Britain and four times lower than in Ireland. The contrast with Irish legislation is such that the fines levied by the courts there against Spanish fishermen have once again been perceived as discriminatory by shipowners who are unaccustomed to such sanctions at home.[40]

Unlike Spain, the waters in the French EEZ constitute an important reservoir of marketable species such as sole, anglerfish and anchovy. A debate on national protection of the resource base exists in France and has repercussions on administrative practices. However, since most of the TACs attributed to French fishermen rarely exceed the capacity of the fleets (which does not preclude frequent exhaustion of certain quotas), the French administration is not inclined to control strictly the use of quotas by French vessels. It is more vigilant over the use of quotas in the French EEZ by boats of other member states, in particular Spanish vessels operating in the Bay of Biscay. Second, control at sea in the middle-water fishing area, in other words between the 12- and 200-mile line, is divided in France among four state administrations, each of them interested in preserving its prerogatives. Although the fisheries administration coordinates the operational means to control overfishing from their *centres régionaux opérationnels de surveillance et de sauvetage* (CROSS), inspections are conducted by the fisheries administration themselves, the French navy, the maritime *gendarmerie* and lastly by the customs office. Controls on land and in the coastal area are subject to a less marked administrative sectorisation following a reform in 1995 creating fourteen French Fisheries Administration Coastal Units (*unités littorales des Affaires maritimes*, ULAM). Third, in France, any technical improvement in control runs up against the political relationship established historically between the state and the fishermen. In response to the threat of disrupting the social peace brandished by the fishermen, tolerance of fraud is a fact. This situation is reinforced by the ambiguous dual role of lawkeeper and social worker that the French fisheries administrators fulfil in the ports. As one of them remarked, 'it is hard to report an infringement of a fisherman you'll have in your office the next morning to discuss how to finance his retirement.'[41] The leeway that the French fisheries administration has varies, however, from one port to another depending on the capacity of the profession to organise as an interest group. In southern Brittany, there is a port where the administration's control over the fishing of undersized hake by certain well-organised professionals with considerable influence among local elected officials boils down to the order 'make no waves'.[42] The situation is different in neighbouring ports where the fisheries administration has less difficulty controlling and reporting offending fishermen and wholesale traders. Lastly, sanctions in France, like in Spain, are not very dissuasive, in that fraudulent fishermen are not always subject to prosecution. Numerous infractions are simply punished by administrative fines that are low with respect to the profits the fisherman can hope to make. French law, moreover, allows the fisheries administration official to bargain with the offender. This is a halfway procedure between calling off the offence and prosecuting it, which allows offending fishermen to avoid legal action in exchange for the payment of an indemnity to the administration.[43] This procedure illustrates the corporatist nature of the relationship that has been established between the state and the fishermen in France. This does not, of course, mean that fisheries administration officials will not sometimes have recourse to the law for the most serious offences. But French judges are often indulgent with regard to offences they consider more as a matter of risk-taking than ordinary delinquency, which in turn contributes to making fraud more prevalent. Since 1997, some French criminal courts have nevertheless been obliged to deliver harsher verdicts – fines of up to €45,700 – for concealing undersized fish on board trawlers. It is true that these fines have often applied to Spanish boats, though it is impossible to affirm whether this is due to a lucrative market for undersized fish that encourages Spanish fishermen to cheat more or if the French administration inspects them with particular fervour.

In Great Britain, protection of the resource base took the form of a national political debate starting in 1973, given the 850,000 square kilometres of waters under its jurisdiction, the great wealth of stocks and the feeling among its fishermen that free access was imposed on them during EU accession negotiations. Some British fishermen's organisations are calling for the renationalisation of the CFP in general and of resource management in particular, a demand with virtually no equivalent in other member states, except for perhaps in Ireland and Portugal. This debate, conveyed to society by the political parties, has led the British administration to justify the effectiveness of national control of fishery activities. Control in Great Britain is administered on a regional basis. In England and Wales, sea fisheries authorities inspectors handle control of technical measures in the 6-mile zone, whereas MAFF inspectors are in charge of overseeing marketing in the wholesale auctions, and the Royal Navy performs most of the controls at sea within the 200-mile zone. In Scotland and Northern Ireland, organizations within the regional agriculture ministries have their own vessels to enforce resource regulation measures, while benefiting from occasional aid from the Royal Navy. The controls performed by the Royal Navy are tightly enforced in a non-discriminatory manner on British and Community fishing vessels alike. This legalism does not solve the problem of perceived unfairness in national control, in that British fleet-owners and fishermen feel discriminated against by a regulatory framework they feel to be much more stringent than in other member states.[44] This situation also explains the widespread phenomenon of illegal unloadings and sales under fake labels in Great Britain, despite an administrative policy that aims to bring all offences systematically before the courts. Fraud is, however, not sanctioned any more than in other member states, because the British courts require material evidence that is not easy to bring together when controls are performed after unloading.[45] Impunity is hence fairly widespread in Great Britain as well.

Implementation and national control of European regulatory measures over fishery resources can thus hardly be boiled down to a problem of adaptation to European norms imposed on the state from outside. They correspond on the contrary to political processes in which national institutions have autonomous capacity to reinterpret and translate the European norm according to factors that are specific to each state and each national society. What is observable in the area of fisheries probably also holds true in other sectors of Community activity. For instance, the institutions of applicant countries to the EU do not only adapt to the Community *acquis*, but also translate regulations nationally in different ways. The voluminous research on the Europeanisation of national institutions and policies, which often highlights national convergences rather than differences, should therefore be put in perspective. European regulation of fishery resources has not totally destabilised the relations that have historically developed between each state, the social actors and national legislation. It has rather incorporated these relationships into a variety of forms and procedures. Like most Community policies, the CFP also contributes to a debate on the convergence or an increased Europeanisation of national practices.

Europeanising control: fishermen in pursuit of fairness

Establishing direct control of fisheries by the EU is a project that Commission civil servants have had since the early 1980s. For lack of favour among the main national fisheries administrations and fishermen, this project has given rise to a form of compromise that in 1983 resulted in the creation of a Community Fisheries Inspectorate in charge of controlling the national controlling authorities. The project, which aimed to strengthen control of the CFP in member state waters, gained a certain topicality in the 1990s, backed by a demand from the fishermen.

Controlling the controllers

Putting a resource conservation policy on the agenda in 1983 logically led DG Fish officials to study the establishment of a centralised control policy at the European level at the same time. As a Commission document underlined, a Community system of control 'would have probably been in a good position to enforce a coherent set of modalities and sanctions in the event of non-compliance. Furthermore, it would have shown greater impartiality in its surveillance and inspection activities, whereas national agencies are vulnerable, given the pressure national industries exert'.[46] The proposal, however, did not hold sway with the majority of governments, who refused to allow the Commission to become a regulatory agency in charge of direct control of fishermen in Community waters. One reason for the refusal had to do with beliefs that most national administrators and fishermen still held in the early 1980s about the relationship between fishing and the exercise of sovereignty. Although Community resource management measures had been effective, fishing remained a sector of activity in which it was not considered legitimate to replace national navies' vessels with those from a supranational institution in order to enforce the law. A second reason was related to an organisational problem. Since each member state possessed, in one form or another, a national system for monitoring fishing activities, the administrations involved were more interested in maintaining and improving them than replacing them. A third reason had to do with the desire not to renounce using the national legal apparatus to sanction fraud, in the absence of

European criminal law.[47] The compromised established in the Fisheries Council could not help, then, but result in reiterating each member state's authority over the control of the CFP in its waters and on its territory, while creating a fisheries inspectorate within the Commission having a limited remit.

When it was created in 1983, the Community Fisheries Inspectorate employed seven inspectors who were recruited on a contractual basis from national civil and military inspectorates. In 2000, twenty-four inspectors performed a task that theoretically remained governed by the same bases as when it was created. The EC having obtained the right to stand in for member states in regional fishery bodies following a legal battle settled by the CJEC in 1976,[48] the governments agreed to let Community inspectors participate directly in the inspection programmes of these organisations. Within the North-West Atlantic Fisheries Organisation (NAFO), the European Commission is responsible for inspections aboard boats it operates or that are made available by a member state in return for a Community budget expenditure. Representation of the EU on the international scene lends the Commission particular power. This search for legitimacy by the Commission through external sources – which can in fact be observed in other sectors besides fisheries – nevertheless has its limits. The main one is the small size of the Community budget, which prevents the Commission from assuming the additional costs of externalisation. But the main mission of Community inspectors is to control the activities of national authorities in the waters of member states, in other words to 'regulate the regulators'.[49] Although Community regulation 2847/93 authorises Community inspectors to intervene without warning in the event that serious fraud is suspected, their autonomy with respect to the national authorities they are supposed to control is fairly narrow. The corporatist nature of relations binding the fisheries administrations and fishermen in certain countries is not conducive to cooperation. It even happens that national administrations, warn 'their' fishermen of the imminent visit of Community inspectors if they have prior information to that effect. In so far as they remain confidential, inspection reports addressed by the Commission to national control authorities carry little weight, except when the Commission decides to investigate an infringement report leading to a referral before the CJEC. In June 1991, a judgment was thus rendered against France by Community judges after Commission inspectors had already noted that the French fisheries administration allowed the continuation of catches of undersized hake, which was in high demand on the Spanish market.[50]

This limited authority has nevertheless enabled the DG Fish to endow control gradually with the status of Community policy. As Andy Smith has pointed out, Commission civil servants enjoy time and stability in the exercise of their functions, unquestionable assets when it comes to influencing the EU agenda.[51] Since the early 1990s, within the DG-Fisheries ideas have emerged aiming to strengthen control. These ideas have a certain resonance with those of actors outside the Commission, such as ENGOs and the Fisheries Committee of the European Parliament. Such a dynamic context has prompted Commission officials to seek to convert these ideas into a supply of European regulation by relying on a range of modus operandi characteristic of their institution. One mode of operation consists in giving a political visibility to a social problem by publishing expert reports. Specifically, this has meant publishing assessment reports on control deficiencies at the national level. The 1992 and 1996 Commission reports well illustrate this method in two stages.[52] Through these 'public policy narratives',[53] the main goal of the DG Fish is to underline the shortfalls of the national means of control available and those undertaken, examine the legal sanction schemes, and conclude as to the need for coordinated institutional responses within the EU. Another standard modus operandi of the Commission is to foster exchange among national actors involved in control by organising regular meetings in Brussels with a common agenda and facilitating bilateral cooperation among operational departments. With regard to national authorities used to thinking of themselves as sovereign administrations and having little inclination to exchange beyond the state's borders, this appeal to transnationalisation has had an obvious impact on their practices. Control missions have developed within central fisheries administrations. Meeting in Brussels, fisheries administration heads have promoted the idea among operational departments that a Europeananisation of control practices has enabled more effective preservation of fishery resources.[54] For instance, a state's control authorities can inform authorities of another state of vessels likely to unload fish illegally, which was unthinkable a few years before.[55] A third modus operandi used by the Commission to legitimate a European policy of control aims to distribute budget aids to national administrations to acquire or modernise their equipment. It is unnecessary to restate the modesty of the Community budget with respect to national budgets. The Community nevertheless has funding available that the Commission can direct to actions in keeping with the political priorities it has defined; this is the case with fisheries control. In 2000, it was thus decided that 50 per cent of the expenditures relating to investment costs, such as purchasing control vessels or equipping fishing boats with satellite radars, would be paid for out of the EU budget.[56] National controllers and fishermen are aware of this financial contribution, which helps the EU to establish progressively the legitimacy of a European control policy. To refer to the various processes of legitimation of the EU inventoried in the literature, we are here faced with a process of legitimation by utilitarian justification of the intervention.[57]

The fishermen's demand for more Europe

Though the Commission indeed relaunched the project for a European policy of control in the 1990s, seeking mainly to associate national administrations, it benefited at the same time from a shift in the debate among fleet owners and fishermen. The fear of resource depletion in the Community fishing area due to insufficient regulation in fact concerned the trade in general and those in the high-sea sector in particular. Although the latter did not abandoned short-term productivist practices, they integrated as a plausible hypothesis a massive resource crisis and engaged in discussion on the theme with national and Community administrations, scientists and ENGOs. Meetings on the reform of the CFP in 2002 held by the DG Fish in 1999 in the thirteen countries involved, revealed this evolution in the debate among fishermen, which has now led them to formulate on their own a demand for European control. Two decades of experience with different national systems of control, moreover, had led many European high-sea fishermen to feel that control ensured by the Commission would remove the main obstacle of discrimination by nationality.[58] This concern of the European fishing trade illustrates the analyses made by international relations specialists who explain the creation of international environmental institutions as a response by social actors to the heterogeneity of national regulations.[59] It also supports what Giandomenico Majone has called the demand-sided production of European regulation. Disconnected from electoral considerations, the Commission appears in the eyes of social actors as a more legitimate regulatory authority because it is less captive of the very interests it is supposed to regulate.[60] The fishermen's demand for increased EU intervention in the operational control of their activities does not run counter to the principle of subsidiarity in that the latter considers a Community regulation acceptable as long as it proves to be more effective than national regulations. It can, however, contradict the idea of an increased decentralisation or regionalisation of the CFP advocated by the Irish and British organisations, who remain more in favour of the idea of national control. For Commission officials, strengthening European control policy no longer means, however, conferring all the powers on European inspectors who would replace national authorities.[61] They instead conceive of regulation as the production of common standards aiming to bring together the national authorities in a harmonised model of public policy. The Communication from the Commission in February 1999 devoted to the control of EU fisheries activities did not call for a substitution of national authorities by the EU, but a networking of national practices of identification and treatment of fraud. It is interesting to note that this search for a role by bringing national practices closer together is at odds with the fishermen's perceptions, which tend to view European intervention in terms of a substitution of authority.

European regulation of fishery resources was born out of the convergent effort of Commission civil servants and experts who share the conviction that preservation of the stocks calls for solutions that are more effective on the European than the national level. This initial observation does not automatically validate the hypothesis that in the EU political system the power of the technocrats is imposed on that of national political leaders and social actors. Analysing the EU political system by opposing expertise and politics is a pointless exercise.[62] The empirical reality hints at the emergence of transnational experts who undertake projects in the spirit of political exchange, that is, characterised by power games between institutions and interest groups. The annual negotiation on determining TACs and quotas even shows that the political rationality that encourages governments primarily to seek compromises in order to keep the social peace in their territories tends to take precedence over the expert rationality of the Commission and scientific forums.

Implementation of European regulations remains subject to marked differences because national administrations maintain room to manoeuvre in translating them. This differentiated implementation provokes a sense of unfairness among the social actors involved, stimulating a desire among fishermen to see European institutions (particularly the Commission) stand in for national authorities to control implementation of regulation. This shift from a supply-sided European regulation expressed solely by the Commission and experts to a demand expressed by the trade itself does not, however, prompt Commission officials to want to replace national administrations. The case of fisheries shows that, on the contrary, the Commission intends instead to favour the networking of national institutions. Legitimate implementation of European regulation in a way poses less a problem of creating new supranational institutions than one of convergence among national institutions and practices.

Notes

1   Cited by Jean-Pierre Beurier, 'Le droit international des pêches maritimes', *Droits maritimes*, vol. III, Lyon, Éditions Juris, 1998, pp. 17–18.
2   *Ibid.*, p. 18.
3   Philip Selznick, 'Focusing Organizational Research on Regulation', in R. G. Noll (ed.), *Regulation Policy and the Social Sciences*, Berkeley and Los Angeles, University of California Press, 1985, quoted in Giandomenico Majone, *Regulating Europe*, London, Routledge, 1996, p. 9.
4   Giandomenico Majone, *La Communauté européenne: un État régulateur*, Paris, Montchrestien, coll. 'Clefs', 1996, p. 13.
5   Garrett Harding, 'The Tragedy of the Commons', *Science*, 162, December 1968, pp. 1243–1248.
6   Quoted by Proutière-Maulion, *La politique commonautaire*, p. 81.

7   A. Karagiannakos, 'Total Allowance Catch (TAC) and Quota Management System in the European Union', *Marine Policy*, 30 (3), 1996, pp. 235–248.

8   Majone, *Regulating Europe*, p. 59.

9   See for instance Kevin Crean, David Symes (eds), *Fisheries Management in Crisis*, Oxford, Fishing News Books, 1996.

10 Jean Boncœur and Benoît Mesnil, 'Quelle politique de la pêche? L'exemple de l'Union européenne', *Problèmes économiques*, 2650, 2 February 2000, pp. 5–9; Anthony T. Charles, 'Fisheries Conflicts: A Unified Framework', *Marine Policy*, 16, pp. 379–393.

11 See Theodore J. Lowi, 'Four Systems of Policy, Politics and Choice', *Public Administration Review*, 32, 1972, pp. 298–310.

12 Fritz Scharpf, *Gouverner l'Europe*, Paris, Presses de Sciences Po, 2000, p. 25.

13 Peter Haas, 'Knowledge, Power and International Policy Coordination', *International Organization*, 46 (1), Winter 1992.

14 Parrès, *Affirmer la place des pêches*, p. 140.

15 See for instance the Gulland and Lassen reports on the measures to restructure national fishing fleets submitted to the Commission in 1990 and 1996 respectively, internal Commission documents.

16 'La méthode du mille feuilles', interview with Alain Parrès, Paris, 9 February 1999.

17 Proutière-Maulion, *La politique communautaire*.

18 Since the 1983 Regulation concerning conservation, the Commission has managed a licensing scheme that applies to German, Belgian, British and French vessels allowed to operate in the Shetland Box area.

19 Regulation 3690/93 CE du 20 December 1993, JOCE, L 341, 31 December 1993.

20 Christian Lequesne, 'La Commission européenne entre autonomie et dépendance', *Revue française de science politique*, 46 (3), 1996, pp. 389–408.

21 Philip Rodgers and Gregory Valatin, *Common Fisheries Policy beyond 2002: Alternative Options to the TACs and Quotas System for the Conservation and Management of Fisheries Resources*, European Parliament working document, Brussels, Directorate General for Research, 1997.

22 'Stop Days at Sea Now. NFFO Warns of More to Come', *Fishing News*, 20 March 1998.

23 Proutière-Maulion, *La politique communautaire*, p. 126.

24 See the 1991 Commission progress report on the CFP.

25 The Gulland report. See note 15.

26 Lawrence M. Friedman, 'On Regulation and Legal Process', in Noll, *Regulation Policy*, p. 111.

27 *Agence Europe*, 6 May 1999.

28 See Heinrich Siedentopf and Jacques Ziller (eds), *Making European Policies Work: The Implementation of Community Legislation in Member States*, vol. 2, London, Sage, 1988.

29 John Goodlad, 'Sectoral Quota Management: Fisheries Management by Fish Producers Organizations', in Gray, *Politics of Fishing*.

30 Thom, 'Comparison of British and French Fishing Policies', in Gray, *Politics of Fishing*.

31   Interview with Dirk Langstraat, The Hague, 2 April 1998.
32   Svein Jentoft, 'Fisheries Management, Delegating Government Responsibility to Fishermen's Organisations', *Marine Policy*, April 1989, pp. 137–154.
33   Interview, 22 July 1998.
34   Interview with Alain Maucorps, Nantes, 12 March 1997.
35   Interview with Vincent Cocozza, Lorient, 4 February 2000.
36   Christopher Hood, 'Concepts of Control over Public Bureaucracies: "Comptrol" and "Interpolable Balance"', in Franz-Xaver Kaufman (ed.), *The Public Sector*, Berlin and New York, De Gruyter, 1991, p. 347.
37   Interview with S. G. Ellson, London, 8 July 1998.
38   Jeremy Richardson, G. Gustafson and G. Joran (eds), *Policy Styles in Western Europe*, London, George Allen & Unwin, 1982.
39   See Tom R. Tyler, *Why People Obey the Law*, New Haven and London, Yale University Press, 1990.
40   Interview with José A. Suarez-Llanos Rodriguez, Vigo, 30 October 1997.
41   Interview, 9 February 2000.
42   In July 1998, the French fisheries administrator of this port allowed me to consult his annual reports on local fishing in his office. He did not, however, wish to answer my questions about exercising control.
43   See law no. 89–554 of 2 August 1989, *JORF* of 10 August 1989, and the circular of 9 January 1990, *JORF* of 3 February 1990.
44   Interview with Elisabeth Stevenson, Newlyn, 6 July 1998.
45   *Monitoring the Common Fisheries Policy*, COM (96) 100 final, Brussels, 18 March 1996, p. 111.
46   European Commission, *Le contrôle des activités de la filière 'pêche'*, Luxembourg, OPOCE, 1996, p. 15 (translated into English by the author).
47   Mireille Delmas-Marty, 'Union européenne et droit pénal', *Cahiers de droit européen*, 5–6, 1997, pp. 607–653.
48   *Kramer* judgment, 1976.
49   Majone, *Regulating Europe*, p. 145.
50   Judgment C-64/88. From the Commission's viewpoint, execution of this judgment proved to be unsatisfactory for a number of years.
51   Andy Smith, *L'Europe politique au miroir du local*, Paris, L'Harmattan, 1996.
52   Final SEC (92) 394 report of 6 March 1992 and final COM (96) report of 18 March 1996.
53   Claudio M. Radaelli, 'Logique de pouvoir et récits dans les politiques publiques de l'Union européenne', *Revue française de science politique*, 50 (2), April 2000, pp. 255–275.
54   I had observed a similar function of disseminating European norms in studying the European cells of French ministries in my book *Paris–Brussels. Comment se fait la politique européenne de la France*, Paris, Presses de Sciences Po, 1993.
55   Interview with Philippe Forin and Yves Auffret, Paris, 9 February 2000.
56   Ireland negotiated Community budget participation rates of over 50 per cent; see the Commission decision of 24 January 2000, *OJEC*, L 33, 8 February 2000.

57 David Beetham and Christopher Lord, *Legitimacy in the EU*, London, Longman, 1998.
58 Interviews, Vigo, 30 October 1997 and Concarneau, 4 February 2000.
59 See Oran Young, 'Gérer les biens communs planétaires. Réflexions sur un changement d'échelle', *Critique internationale*, 9 October 2000.
60 Majone, *La Communauté européenne*, pp. 64–65.
61 After the shipwreck of oil tanker *Erika*, there was an outcry from among the French maritime community calling for the creation of an operational European maritime agency, a sort of prefiguration of a European coast guard (*Le Marin*, 21 January 2000).
62 Claudio M. Radaelli, 'The Public Policy of the European Union: Whither Politics of Expertise?', *Journal of European Public Policy*, 6 (5), 1999, pp. 757–774.

4

Europe's distribution mechanisms

Giandomenico Majone's observation that the EU's predisposition to regulation is a sign of the 'unfeasibility of the European welfare state' due to the modesty of the Community budget, the impossible emergence of a feeling of solidarity in a transnational space and the diversity of reference models, calls for some qualification.[1] Admittedly, the EU budget's distributive and redistributive efforts cannot compare to those of national budgets. In 2000, its €93 billion represented hardly 2.4 per cent of member states' public sector expenditure and was equivalent to 1.13 per cent of the Community GDP (Table 4.1). 'By comparison, national and local governments spend around 50 per cent of the wealth produced in the EU.'[2] The fact remains, however, that a distributive policy in the form of price support to agricultural markets, and a redistributive policy, through regional development, nonetheless absorbed 70 per cent of the EU budget expenditure in 2000 (Table 4.2). The difference between a distributive policy and a redistributive policy sometimes does not hold up to the test of empirical analysis. However, a distributive policy can be said to consist in allocating public resources to groups or activities, whereas a redistributive policy aims at transferring resources from one group of individuals, regions or countries to another group.

Since the CFP's inception, the fishing sector has benefited from EU financial transfers, albeit on a scale in no way comparable to agriculture. This chapter examines the forms of distribution and redistribution exercised by the EU budget in support of the fishing industry, through both structural funding and the Common Organisation of Markets (COM). It aims to highlight the mobilisations that these transfers bring about in territories and examines their contribution to the process of legitimating the EU political system.

Table 4.1 General expenditure of the EU (1970, 1980 and 1990–2000) (including ECSC[a], EAEC[b] and EDF[c])

	1970	1980	1990	1991	1992	1993	1994	1995	1996	1997	1998	1999	2000
Total expenditure (in millions of euros)	3,576	16,454	45,608	55,016	60,844	66,733	61,478	68,408	78,604	81,798	82,798	87,213	91,997
Expenditure per inhabitant (in euros)	19	63	139	159	175	191	176	183	210	217	220	232	244
Expenditure in relation to public expenditure of member states (%)	2	1.7	2	2.1	2.2	2.3	2.1	2.1	2.3	2.3	2.3	2.3	2.4
Expenditure relation to GDP Community (%)	0.74	0.80	0.95	1.05	1.11	1.21	1.06	1.06	1.16	1.14	1.11	1.11	1.13
Annual growth in Community expenditure (%)		11.4	7.9	20.6	10.6	9.7	–7.9	11.3	14.9	3.7	1.6	5.3	5.5

Source: Vade-mecum budgetaire 1999, Luxembourg, Office of EC publications, 1999
[a]European Coal and Steel Community [b]European Atomic Energy Community [c]European Development Fund

Table 4.2   Structure of EU budget expenditure (2000) (in € million)

Sub-section	amount	%
European Agricultural Guidance and Guarantee Fund, Guarantee section	41,493.9	44.5
Structural Actions, structural and cohesion expenditure, financial mechanisms, other agricultural, and regional, transport and fishing actions	32,811.5	35.2
Training, youth, culture, audiovisual, information and other social actions	841.6	0.9
Energy, control of nuclear security of Euratom and environment	211.2	0.2
Consumer protection, internal market, industry, trans-European networks, open space, security and justice	1,210.7	1.3
Technological research and development	3,630.0	3.9
External Actions	8,127.8	8.7
Foreign policy and common security	47.0	0.1
Guarantees, reserves and compensations	203.0	0.2
Administrative Expenses (of all the institutions)	4,703.7	5.0
Total	93,280.4	100.0

Source: European Commission, Directorate General budgets

Structural funds: legitimisation through outputs?

The structural component of the CFP was French inspired, growing out of a projection onto the Community level of the practices of a state used to granting public aid to its fishermen. What main developments has this structural policy undergone over the past thirty years? And what impact has it had on local actors?

The stages of the structural policy

The funding of structural policy in the fishing sector was originally managed by the European Agricultural Guidance and Guarantee Fund (EAGGF). Conceived as complements to national subsidies, Community aid intended to support projects either in the catching aspect of the sector, such as building or converting fishing vessels, or the marketing aspect of the sector, such as improving commercial channels. Although modest in relation to the overall structural funding allocation, the budget agreed for fishing grew appreciably from the 1980s onwards, with funds committed rising from 32 million ecus in 1983 to 330 million ecus in 1993.[3] This evolution was a direct consequence of Spain and Portugal's accession to the EU, their governments having negotiated substantial aid to modernise their fleets in exchange for dispensations imposed on their fishermen's access to Community waters. But at the same time this also led, particularly in Spain, to an increase in fleets' fishing capacity, which ran counter to the Commission's priority to improve the balance between the fishing effort and resource management through MAGPs. Given the weak implementation of the latter in many member states, the DG Fish called for a reduction in Community subsidies for the building of new fishing vessels, starting in 1988. The 1988–93 period, following the first reform of structural funding intended to support the internal market,[4] resulted in a progressive modification of the distribution of Community aid to fishing. Still at the instigation of the DG Fish, spending on adjusting fishing capacities, through temporary or definitive stopping of the activity, was gradually replaced by expenditure on modernising and building fishing vessels.[5] As a result, fishermen's representation of the EU's structural policy has likewise changed. The latter have increasingly assimilated this policy under pressure from MAGPs, i.e. a regulatory policy aimed at reducing their activity.

At the conclusion of the European Council of Edinburgh in December 1992, which outlined the new financial prospects for the period 1994–99, a second reform of structural funding took place. It was within this framework that, at the Commission's suggestion, the Financial Instrument for Fisheries Guidance (FIFG) was created in July 1993.[6] Allocated 2.9 billion ecus (1.9 per cent of the total structural funding allocation), this fund, specifically earmarked for fishing, was intended to help achieve the new objective 5a of the policy of economic and social cohesion, whose aid was aimed at adapting agricultural and fishing structures. The latter continued, moreover, to benefit from other structural funding interventions, notably from the European Regional Development Fund (ERDF) and the European Social Fund (ESF), in regions categorised under objective 1 (lagging behind in development), objective 2 (industrial retraining) and in objective 5b (vulnerable rural zones). A specific Community-initiated programme (PESCA) was also created to aid areas dependent on fishing. From 1994 to 1999, the main beneficiaries of structural aid to fishing were primarily the Spanish fishing industry (40 per cent of scheduled allocations), followed by the Italian, Portuguese and French industries. In addition to adjusting the fishing effort, the Commission's priority objective with regard to MAGPs, actions financed from the Community budget mainly concerned modernising fishing vessels, developing food-processing and marketing of products, and socio-economic measures to encourage the retraining of fishermen. For coastal regions like Galicia, Brittany or Scotland these Community aids, added to national and regional aid and along with private finance, amounted to a significant capital contribution. Between 1994 and 1999, the Community budget allocated 513 million ecus to Galicia alone to finance various structural programmes related to fishing. During the same period Brittany benefited from 72 million ecus and Scotland from 65 million ecus.[7]

Adopted within the framework of the 2000–6 financial perspectives known as Agenda 2000, the structural-funding reform approved by the EU Council in June 1999 aimed at a greater territorial concentration of structural funding assistance with a view to the EU's future enlargement to the East. The global financial allocation decided for actions in the EU's coastal regions was, however, quite similar to that of the previous period. Although the PESCA programme disappeared along with nine other programmes of Community interest, the FIFG was continued and financed actions that were not tied to any particular zoning area. Within the framework of the three new objectives adopted by the Agenda reform, the new objective 2 was additionally intended for fishing-dependent areas in crisis – among others – constituting a kind of 'extra' for the coastal regions concerned.[8] The increased concentration of structural actions provoked protests by fishing professionals over their distribution, in particular in countries like France, which no longer benefited from objective 1 (with the exception of overseas territories). In Brittany, over 1998 and 1999, Finistère professionals made representations to elected officials and the region's prefect relating, for example, to the zoning of the new objective 2, which no longer included all the cantons of the Quimper region that could previously lay claim to assistance from the PESCA programme.[9]

This pressure on the state by social actors did not prevent the Délégation à l'aménagement du territoire et à l'action territoriale (DATAR) planning board from sending to the Commission the zoning project it had initially decided. Moreover, the new conditions for assistance relating to the renewal and modernisation of fishing fleets were the subject of arguments between the scientists and the Commission on one side, and on the other, national administrations and professional organisations. Determined not to give way on resource conservation, in 1998 the DG Fish suggested banning any aid to fishermen who did not respect the MAGP objectives of annual reduction and that public aid be granted only on condition that construction of a vessel corresponded to the scrapping of 30 per cent of surplus capacity (see Chapter 3). Welcomed only by the British and Danish administrations, the Commission's proposal was contested by eight other states (including France, Italy, Spain and the Netherlands) who demanded that a one-to-one parity between the construction and the withdrawal of a fishing vessel should be applied. A compromise was finally reached by the fishery ministers under the Finnish presidency in November 1999. This provided that the 30 per cent of additional withdrawal required for the granting of aid would not be applied until the end of 2001 and also spared small-scale fishing vessels under 12 metres other than trawlers.[10] But, once again, a majority of organisations of ship-owning businesses and European fishermen, including those in a country like Spain whose fleet generally respected the MAGP prescriptions, essentially perceived the measure's dimension as regulatory rather than redistributive.

The impact on local actors

As with any policy of economic and social cohesion, it is difficult to assess the economic and social impact of structural funding on the fishing industry.[11] Although for thirty years the fishing industry participated in the adaptation of activities, by funding expenditure on infrastructure and occupational redeployment measures, its actions attracted a fair amount of criticism. First of all, despite the scheduling imposed by Community rules on states and local operators, the EU's cumulative financial contribution along with that from other levels of government (states, sub-national authorities) did not encourage selectivity of projects. Over the 1990s, several ports in southern Brittany, for example, benefited from Community aid to mobilise other public funding with a view to modernising their auctions (the fish are sold by auction sale), whereas a decrease of contributions would logically have called for a regrouping of fish-processing sites.[12]

Secondly, the flexibility of the funding rules set by the EU sometimes tended to incite competition between territories instead of calming it. In Spain, Basque fishermen have always found it difficult to accept that their Galician colleagues, whom they consider no less prosperous than themselves, enjoyed higher levels of assistance than they did, because Galicia, and not the Basque Country, was classified by the EU as a ' region lagging behind in development' (objective 1 of the economic and social cohesion policy). More fundamentally, the regional redistribution supported by structural funds did not necessarily prove effective as an instrument of social policy to reduce individual inequalities to help the least thriving fishermen.[13] The aid allocated to creating joint enterprises in non-member countries is an example of aid which has sometimes ended up subsidising the most thriving industrial shipowning businesses, notably the Spanish, which could have delocalised their fishing vessels perfectly well without them. These actions even encouraged some of these actors well versed in the workings of Community subsidies to misappropriate funding. In 1998, an inquiry conducted by the Unit for the Coordination of Fraud Prevention (UCLAF), attached to the European Commission, revealed that the French shipowning business Jégo-Quéré, a Pescanova subsidiary, had received 10.5 million fr. to reflag a vessel under Guinean flag which, shortly after the Community subsidy had been banked, was then resold to another Pescanova subsidiary.[14] Finally, despite all the Commission's control mechanisms with respect to application of the MAGPs, Community subsidies have contributed to increasing the fishing capacity of some fleets at the expense of the reduction of the fishing effort needed to prevent deterioration of the fisheries resource.[15]

   The financial windfall that structural funding represented did not, however, prevent some local fishing actors from taking a different position regarding the EU, not only by reacting against a Community regulation considered oppressive, but also by forming public policy networks with other local actors (elected officials, representatives of para-public bodies such as chambers of commerce and industry in France or development agencies in Great Britain),[16] with a view to negotiating terms of redistribution with the states and the Commission. Although it should be kept in perspective, the partnership principle, imposed by the Commission for the scheduling and implementation of structural funding, in the fishing sector, resulted in a more effective engagement of local actors in the dynamic of regional programmes and the consolidation of their expertise. Admittedly, the institutionalisation of partnerships has not occurred in exactly the same way in the various national territories. In France, the decentralised state continues to make those actively involved in developing the fishing sector work around it, and supplies them with a framework for cooperative management.[17] That does not mean, however, that in France structural funding has reinforced the state's domination over local management. Confirming Patrice Duran's analysis, the example of Brittany shows, rather, that the regional prefecture and the regional fisheries administration act as stimulus and arbitrate among the diversity of those leading local projects and the fragmentation of their interests. As we saw earlier, in 1998 and in 1999, Agenda 2000 led the fishing industry and French-Cornish elected officials, grouped around the association Pesca Cornouailles and the Quimper Chamber of Commerce and Industry, to lobby the regional prefect for cantons which were eligible under the terms of the new objective 2 not to be solely restricted to coastal regions. The regional prefect's action was to listen to these grievances but also to allow the Cornish actors, through negotiation, to voice their own interests in relation to those of other local territories, such as the Lorient region.[18] In Great Britain, structural funding transfers to the fishing sector encouraged, much more clearly than in France, what some have called the emergence of 'local governance'.[19] Local development agencies were created, encouraging a bottom-up implementation of structural programmes by networks of actors made up of both central and regional administrations, fishing-related professions and also environmental protection bodies. In Scotland, between 1994 and 1999, the implementation of the PESCA programme in the Highlands and Islands region, for example, was entrusted to six local development agencies (Local Enterprises Companies) which themselves created six groups of local actors (Local Pesca Groups).[20] This institutionalised networking in turn reinforced the Scottish actors' representational weight with the Commission, during the process of defining which zones were eligible in terms of Agenda 2000.[21] In Spain, the programming of structural funding in the fishing sector remains a compromise between the autonomous Communities and the central state, the latter being always the representative spokesperson to the Commission for negotiating budgets; and they also participate in co-financing projects. On the other hand, the implementation of structural policies is the sole responsibility of autonomous communities, with the exception of a few actions – such as assistance to establish joint enterprises or compensations to fishermen affected by the non-renewal of fishing agreements – which are managed directly from Madrid.[22] The networks of local actors involved in the implementation of fishing-related structural funding, are not necessarily the same from one autonomous community to another, sometimes being solely confined to the autonomous community officials or, on the contrary, closely involving fishing professionals and local elected officials. In Spain, however, a large number of regional fishing actors in all autonomous communities have integrated the importance of the Community dimension in their political dealings with the state. In Galicia, a region which between 1994 and 1999 benefited from over one-third of funding allocated to fisheries structural programmes coming under objective 1, and which was due to receive 40 per cent of the 2000–2006 scheduled funding, Community funds fostered a feeling among officials and professionals alike, of independence vis-à-vis the Spanish state, which, locally, helped legitimate both the autonomous process and European integration.

The action of structural funding in the fishing sector leads directly to an exploration of the link between territorial redistribution and the process of legitimating the EU's polity. Transfers granted by the Community budget through structural programmes – including in those 'cohesion' countries who benefit most from it (Greece, Portugal, Ireland and Spain) – are not seen by fishing professionals as the manifestation of a supranational welfare state which could provide an equally powerful demonstration of solidarity on a European level. Structural funding is seen by politico-administrative and private actors in a much more utilitarian manner, as the product of an intergovernmental compromise which serves the interests of the territory by encouraging economic development and greater political autonomy with regard to the central state. In this sense, although the redistributive action of structural funding encourages the legitimisation of the process of European integration, it is a matter of what Fritz Scharpf would call 'legitimisation by outputs'[23] based on the interest of each territory rather than on the perception of a collective European identity. That does not prevent the European Commission from seeking to exploit this legitimisation by outputs politically by highlighting the action of structural funding in infranational territories. This is expressed in a number of speeches and practices emanating from commissioners and civil servants. There is the recurrent assertion of partnership in the form of support to any autonomisation of local actors in relation to

the states in the management of territories. The almost systematic financial support of social change is another Commission practice that fishing
professionals have assimilated as 'normal'. In April 1998, Emma Bonino,
commissioner in charge of fishing within the Santer Commission, for
example advanced the argument that retraining French, Irish and British
fishermen affected by the ban on driftnets, was not a problem since 'we
have the means to help them [...] structural funding can intervene'.[24] Her
successor within the Prodi Commission, Franz Fischler, used almost the
same terms in 1999 when he called for an FIFG intervention to assist
Spanish and Portuguese fishermen whose activity was brought to a halt by
the non-renewal of the fishing agreement with Morocco. Finally, the
Commission attempts to develop a policy in line with a general publicity
doctrine, which is aimed at raising awareness of the redistributive action
of structural funding among the beneficiaries and, more generally, citizens
in territories. A Commission regulation of May 2000 gives detailed
instructions to national managing bodies about how billboards must indi-
cate the precise source of European funding for all infrastructural work
co-funded by the FIFG.[25] But this attempt at legitimating the EU through
the action of structural funding has serious limitations. First of all, structural funds' complicated procedures of programming and implementation, and particularly the delays in disbursement, continue to stoke
the hostility of fishing actors towards the EU's excessive bureaucratisation
and technocratisation. The systematic practice of co-financing means,
moreover, that the European share of funds allocated to projects is often
difficult to measure by fishing professionals. More fundamentally,
European fishermen do not all attach the same legitimating value to structural aid, depending on the scale of the latter, on their particular economic
situation, and also on the national political culture in which they have
been socialised. Strong differences exist between France, Ireland and Italy
on the one hand, where public aid to fishing has always represented a high
per centage of the sector's added value, and the Netherlands and Denmark
on the other, where it is comparatively low.[26] Although national, regional
and local aid to fishing is subject to the Commission's control under the
terms of the competition policy, the injection of public capital in France,
as in Italy, is a fundamental component of the corporatist compromise
between the industry and the political authorities established following
the end of the Second World War. In France, the diesel fuel price rises
during 2000 inevitably led fishermen to protest and threaten to blockade
the ports in pursuance of their claim to public aid from the state. While
invoking the limitations imposed by Community law, the state responded
in their favour, albeit in total disregard for the rules of European competition policy: in addition to a total tax exemption on fuel, it granted a
temporary exemption from social charges worth 235 million fr. Since
decentralisation, the French regions have likewise often subsidised partic-

ular types of fishing vessels or activities, sometimes in total contradiction to the priorities set by the European Union's regional policy.[27] In the response by the Union des Armateurs à la Pêche de France (UAPF, Union of French Fishing Shipowners) to the Commission's questionnaire on CFP reform in 2002, it was said, in highly revealing language, that the 'over-haul, modernisations and *a fortiori* replacements ' of fishing vessels 'cannot take place without contributions from public finances'.[28] The French shipowning businesses also set out their expectations *vis-à-vis* European redistribution within the framework of a general demand for public assistance, without which, for them, there could be no legitimate public policy. In other countries, such as the United Kingdom for example, the legitimating impact of European redistribution is not neces-sarily the same as it is in France, in that the state is not as used to granting direct aid to fishermen. These examples demonstrate once again the need to take into account a differentiated acceptance of Community public policies as well as the national polities in which the social actors have been socialised.

Distribution through support to markets

The establishment of a Community price support mechanism to fishing and aquaculture products, which is part of the framework of the common organisation of markets,[29] is likewise part of a distributive compromise established at the European level. Although this mechanism was inspired in 1970 by existing models in the agricultural sector, it was also a projec-tion of a system of price compensation from public finances established by the French state in the early 1960s to assist its industrial shipowning busi-nesses. Initially limited to three sensitive products – tuna, cod and sardine – the French system was applied in general to all industrial species after a price collapse in 1964. In parallel, from 1965 onwards, it had also led to the creation of the first regional fund for the organisation of markets (FROM) which inspired the Commission in its proposal to create producers' organisations (POs), to which management of Community assistance mechanisms was delegated.[30] The French industry representa-tives, particularly Jacques Huret from Boulogne, president of the Union interfédérale des armateurs à la pêche and founder of FROM Nord, had a great deal of influence on the Commission's choices. At the time they found support among French officials, particularly Raymond Simonnet, who was charged with devising the new CFP with the Mansholt Commission (see Chapter 1).[31]

Price support mechanisms in the fishing sector are similar to those which apply to some agricultural products in the framework of the CAP. Subsidies charged to the Community budget, and more precisely to the EAGGF's Guarantee section, which funds, within certain limits, the with-

drawal of species unsold on the market as well as deferment measures –
such as stocking and processing – with a view to putting them back on the
market when there is an eventual upturn in demand. They apply when the
price of products sold on the market is lower than a withdrawal price. The
latter is established in relation to a guide price fixed by the fishery ministers annually for each product, based on price averages over the course of
the three previous years in a range of representative ports. One species,
tuna, also benefits from a specific compensatory indemnity paid to
producers as soon as a fall in prices affects the Community market.
Although the withdrawal of fishing products cost the EU budget only
€11 million in 1998, an amount well below the 1,262 million support
granted to arable crops and the 313 million granted to wine-producing,
they still represented regular transfers from the Community budget to
European fishermen.[32]

   Withdrawals are managed by producers' organisations (POs), privately
constituted institutions fostered by the EU whose functions are recognised
by national administrations. Based on the principle of voluntary membership of dues-paying fishermen, some 169 POs were existent within the EU
in 1999, most usually constituted according to geographical criteria or,
more rarely, around a species, such as tuna.[33] Fishermen's PO membership levels are generally higher in the North than in the South of the EU
(France included). In 1994, the twenty-nine French POs thus represented
35 per cent of fishing vessels and 68 per cent of production in terms of
value.[34] On the contrary, in the United Kingdom, where the first PO – The
Fish Producers' Organisation (FPO), which still exists – was not created
until 1973, the nineteen POs registered in 1996 included the vast majority of fishermen, fishing vessels and catches.[35] The same is true with the
Danish POs, whose members represented 60 to 65 per cent of catches in
2000. Although the POs implement the withdrawal mechanisms locally,
they are also supposed to monitor the application of trading standards
and conservation of the resource, notably through the management of
quotas. As we saw in the previous chapter, national differences linked to
the varying relationships of fishermen to the resource, but also to the
state, mean that these tasks are not carried out in the same way from one
country to another. Although the Danish POs have long-established catch
plans which their members do in fact respect, such a practice has always
seemed more difficult to implement in France where the POs are faced
with a less collectively disciplined membership. The POs' scope of action
remains largely national, or even local. There is no really transnational
PO, although thirty of them have grouped together within the European
Association of Producers' Organisations (EAPO), which acts as the representative voice to the Commission at the European level. Similarly, there
have recently been some attempts at collaboration between the POs of
several countries with the objective of organising sales of product coming

from the same fishery. The Danish Association of producers' organisations maintains, for example, a trilateral cooperation with German and Dutch POs for managing sales of shrimps from the Dutch Inner Sea.[36] In France, the POs grouped within the Fédération des organisations de producteurs de la pêche artisanale (FEDOPA) likewise created a computerised information exchange network on sales with Belgian, British and Irish POs – Eurofish – to try to regulate the market for species fished in the Atlantic. Finally, transnationalisation of POs occurs indirectly, through the phenomenon of quota-hopping, by encouraging, for example, Dutch fishermen exploiting fishing vessels under British flags to create their own structure in Great Britain (see Chapter 5).

Community price support policy contributes to funding the revenues of European fishermen. However, the latter are even less conscious of the effects of transnational distribution than they are of structural funding. The amounts committed are certainly lower, and do not really mobilise networks of local actors. In addition, they are intended to fund stocks rather than infrastructures, which to some extent symbolises the ineffectiveness of the CFP. PO leaders, however, have a more positive attitude than their members do towards the EU. Although they do not view the mechanisms of assistance as the manifestation of European solidarity, they still view financial transfers from the EU as an interest that encourages not only economic development, but also the institutional autonomy of fishermen with regard to administrations. Evidence of this can be seen in their responses to the Commission's 1998 questionnaire on the future reform of the CFP, when participating European PO leaders all called for intervention mechanisms to continue, with the exception of one Spanish organisation which claimed it was ready for total liberalisation of the market.[37] Similarly, starting in 1997, PO leaders worked with the Commission on reform of intervention mechanisms and the role of their organisations. This reform was in line with the process of amending public policies, which often takes place at Community level. DG Fish officials began in December 1997 by submitting a communication with no legally binding implications to the Council and the European Parliament on the future of the market of fisheries products in the EU intending to gather responses from the industry and national administrations.[38] Aiming to reform the COM as a whole – including the regime for exchanges with non-member countries (see Chapter 7) – this document highlighted a DG Fish priority with regard to the CFP and another more general Commission priority with regard to Community policies. The DG Fish' priority was to bring the market more into line with the resource, by requiring that in future all the POs regulate catches through restrictive planning measures, in order to avoid the destruction of fish as far as was possible. The Commission's general concern was to make savings in the EU budget by encouraging a reduction in subsidies to definitive withdrawals. Following the Commission's formal tabling of a reform proposal in March 1999, nine months of intergovernmental negotiation were needed within the Council of Fishery Ministers and its subsidiary organs for new rules on the COM to be adopted.[39] Given that the effects of COM's distributive functions on the interests of European professionals vary in scale depending on the particular fisheries concerned, the structure of the markets and the type of regulation that the POs were able to exercise, the national administrations took varying positions during the negotiation (Table 4.3). Faced with national POs, which had integrated the practice of catch plans, the German and Dutch administrations, for example, supported the Commission's policy of reducing levels of assistance to definitive withdrawals. On the other hand, administrations in countries where the mechanisms of withdrawal were used more, such as France, the United Kingdom and Ireland, argued for a more limited reduction in levels of intervention and for supplementary aid to adapt the POs to the tasks proposed. Although PO leaders in these latter countries accepted the fact that the EU provided a real financial support to the sector, which necessitated playing the game in terms of reform, they were not really however in a position to deliver this reformist message to their members.[40] In a country like France, which benefits most from EU price support, the generally critical attitude of PO members with regards to the COM shows that the financial transfers granted by the EU have not created legitimacy in favour of a distributive European policy.

European fishermen benefit from distributive and redistributive transfers coming from the EU budget through structural funds and the price support mechanism for fisheries products. Although modest in relation to those paid to farmers, these transfers are not perceived by fishing professionals as the manifestation of solidarity operating at a European level. Admittedly, European distribution and redistribution are not necessarily synonymous with a reduction in individual inequalities. In the case of structural funding, the professional actors who are locally the best organised, and particularly the industrial shipowners, often demonstrate a capacity to take maximum advantage of Community subsidies to which the territory in which they are established can lay claim. Although it is only the perception of an interest that leads these latter actors to legitimate the CFP and, more generally, the EU's polity, the situation is different for the great majority of fishermen. Although European distribution and redistribution are part of their 'social security', the latter in no way perceive them as elements of a social policy driven by an embryonic European welfare state.

Table 4.3 Totals of assistance given by the EU, by country under the common organisation of markets between 1988 and 1998 (in thousands of euros)

	1988	1989	1990	1991	1992	1993	1994	1995	1996	1997	1998
Belgium	76	306	351	176	132	375	82	300	200	200	100
Denmark	1,546	1,598	1,157	1,523	1,407	3,508	5,426	5,900	8,400	3,400	1,800
Germany	488	267	271	101	2009	309	398	300	300	0	0
Greece	337	429	594	771	740	855	1056	900	0	0	100
Spain	19,384	8,679	8,872	11,254	11,468	8,332	7,977	3,100	200	5,955	200
France	18,221	6,123	7,314	6,789	9,852	9,190	11,237	10,000	6,530	5,500	3,000
Ireland	978	915	1,161	1,133	1,880	2,585	2,178	3,100	3,030	1,400	1,500
Italy	2,786	2,282	1,658	1,894	1,371	1,293	696	700	0	0	0
The Netherlands	65	280	103	13	29	82	35	200	100	100	100
Austria	0	0	0	0	0	0	0	0	0	0	0
Portugal	474	728	710	818	1,596	1,829	2,120	1,600	1,000	1,500	900
Finland	0	0	0	0	0	0	0	0	0	0	0
Sweden	0	0	0	0	0	0	0	200	2,340	500	400
The UK	2,690	2,389	1,406	1,682	1,591	2,041	1,835	1,800	3,100	3,100	2,700
Total EU	46,915	23,996	23,597	26,154	32,075	30,399	33,040	28,100	25,316	21,809	10,907

Source: European Commission, DG Fish

Notes

1   Giandomenico Majone, *Regulating Europe*, London, Routledge, 1996 p. 79.
2   *Ibid.*, p. 52.
3   Olivier Guyader, *Manuel d'économie des pêches*, DG XIV contract, Rennes, Oïkos Environnement-Ressources, part IV, typescript, 1997, p. 56.
4   Bino Olivi, *L'Europe difficile. Histoire politique de la Communauté européenne*, Paris, Gallimard, coll. Folio, 1998.
5   Guyader, *Manuel d'économie des pêches,* p. 59.
6   One of the Commission's proposals, which was not taken up by the European Council of Edinburgh, was to suggest the creation of an objective 6, specific to fishing.
7   European Parlement, *Le rôle de la pêche, de l'aquaculture et des cultures marines en tant que factors de développement régional des régions maritimes de l'UE*, Brussels, Direction générale des études, 1998.
8   See Regulation 1263/1999 relating to the FIFG, *OJEC*, L 161, 26 June 1999.
9   'Fonds européens: la Cornouaille à cran', *Ouest-France*, 30 September 1999.
10 See Regulation 2792/1999 CE, *OJEC*, L 337, 30 December 1999.
11 For a critical analysis of structural funding actions, see Jeffrey J. Anderson, 'Les fonds structurels: tremplin ou pierre d'achoppement pour la dimension sociale européenne', in Stephan Leibfried and Paul Pierson (eds), *Politiques sociales européennes entre intégration et fragmentation*, Paris, L'Harmattan, 1998, pp. 139–178.
12 Danièle Schirman-Duclos and Frédéric Laforge, *La France et la mer*, Paris, PUF, 1999, p. 98.
13 For a critique concurring with this point, see Majone, *Regulating Europe*; Anderson, 'Les fond structurels'.
14 Le Marin, 28 May 1999.
15 See Clare Coffey and David Baldock, *European Funding for Fisheries Development. An Environmental Appraisal*, London, IEEP, 1998.
16 Patrick Le Galès and Mark Thatcher (eds), *Les networks de politique publique*, Paris, L'Harmattan, 1995.
17 Patrice Duran, 'Le partenariat dans la gestion des fonds structurels: la situation française', *Pôle Sud*, 8, May 1998, pp. 114–139.
18 Interviews with Mme Mercier, Rennes, 27 September 1999, and M. Dusart, Rennes, 28 September 1999.
19 Andy Smith, *L'Europe politique*.
20 Coffey and Baldock, *European Funding*, p. 49.
21 'Start Lobbying for EU Cash', *Fishing News*, 27 March 1998.
22 Pedro Arruza Beti, *Ponencia la nueva programación estructural 2000–2006 del sector de la Pesca*, Madrid, Ministerio de Medio Ambiante, typescript, 2000.
23 Fritz Scharpf, *Gouverner l'Europe*, Paris, Presses de Sciences Po, 2000.
24 *Le Figaro*, 7 April 1998.
25 Commission Ruling 1159/2000, *OJEC*, L 130, 31 May 2000.
26 European Commission, *8th survey on State Aid in the European Union*, Brussels, COM (2000) 205 final, 11 April 2000.
27 Interview with Bruno Guillaumie, CEASM, Paris, 7 September 2000.

28   UAPF, in 'Réponse an questionnaire de la Commision sur la politique commune de la pêche après 2002', *La pêche maritime*, May–June–July 1998, p. 329.

29   COM also comprises arrangements on exchanges with third countries, which will be discussed in Chapter 7.

30   IFREMER, *Les organisations de producteurs des pêches maritimes française. Situation et typologie*, Direction des resources vivantes, October 1995.

31   Huret, *Le livre de bord*.

32   The Court of Auditors of the EC 'Annual Report 1998', *OJEC*, 3 December 1999, p. 28.

33   In 1999, only Finland had no producers organisations.

34   IFREMER, *Organisations de producteurs des pêches maritimes française*, p. 28.

35   John Goodlad, 'Sectoral Quota Management: Fisheries Management by Fish Producer Organizations', in Gray, *Politics of Fishing*, pp. 146–160.

36   See website (www.dfpo.dk).

37   European Commission, *8th Survey on State Aid*, p. 15.

38   European Commission, *The Future of the Market for Fishing Product in the European Union: Responsibility, Partnership, Competitiveness*, communication to the Council and the European Parliament, Burssells, COM (97) 19 final, 16 December 1997.

39   Regulation 104/2000 of 17 December 1999 dealing with the common organisation of markets in the fishing and aquaculture sector, *OJEC*, L 17, 21 January 2000.

40   Interviews with Jean-Pierre Plormel, Concarneau, 22 July 1998 ; and Maurice Benoish, Paris, 8 February 2000.

5

The territorial legacy versus a market rationale

From its very inception, the inter-territorial compromise that determined the elaboration of the CFP entered into partial contradiction with the priority that European governments had assigned to creating a common market. From the mid-1980s, the project for an internal market, initiated with the Commission's 1985 White Paper, was a factor in making these contradictions more apparent. In the name of the free circulation of capital (Article 294 EC) and the freedom of establishment (Article 43 EC), shipowners in some EU countries found they could use the situation to buy fishing vessels in other EU countries and could consequently use quotas that were originally allocated to national fishermen. British fishermen denounced these effects on 'their' fishermen's communities as 'quota-hopping'. This phenomenon, peculiar to the fishing sector, illustrates the dialectic that can pit territorial rationale against market rationale in the European political arena. The present chapter starts by showing how the market norm, and, more generally, globalisation, influenced changes in the professional practices of European fishermen. It then goes on to analyse the rise and development of the phenomenon of quota-hopping, practised by new transnationalised actors who, while defying state sovereignty, did not however necessarily constrain governments to relinquish using restrictive laws to protect their territories.

The deterritorialisation of professional practices

In a context of well-established globalisation of trade in fishing products, the European rules on the free circulation of goods, people, services and capital have encouraged a deterritorialisation of professional practices in the industrial and semi-industrial fishing sector within the EU. This process can be observed in landing practices, crew recruitment and in the formation of companies' capital.

Although a majority of European high-sea fishermen continued to sell their product exclusively in their ship's port of registry, or at least in the flag state they sailed under, the free circulation of goods increasingly encouraged them to relocate their sales to other EU countries in response to market prices. The pelagic trawler-owners of Saint-Jean-de-Luz, in the French Basque country, thus sell part of their catches in the Spanish Basque port of Pasajes, where they are bought by local fish wholesalers at prices higher than those offered in France. In 1998 Henri Pivert, a shipowner in Saint-Jean-de-Luz and president of the Bayonne local fishing committee, expressed, even as he tried to refute it, the contradiction which faced fishermen of the French Basque Country by selling their fish in Spain: 'I'm primarily a businessman. I cannot allow myself the financially suicidal policy of staying in Saint-Jean. But that doesn't necessarily stop me looking for solutions to improve the situation locally'.[1]

Although they were selling a seasonal product in small quantities, the albacore tuna fishermen of Newlyn in English Cornwall had likewise taken to selling part of their catches, destined mainly for canning, in the French ports of south Brittany. Some Cornish shipowners even chose to become members of French producers' organisations to improve their access to marketing circuits. Sometimes the deterritorialisation of sales also occurs in European states that are not EU members. Scottish shipowners do not hesitate to sell their product in Norwegian ports when the price is right there.

Changes in some landing practices are part of a similar deterritorialising trend of the activity. In order to reduce the costs of returning a ship to its port of registry between two trips, semi-industrial French shipowning businesses operating in the British and Irish EEZ land their catches directly at 'advanced bases' located in the Welsh, Scottish and Irish ports. Fish and shellfish are then transported, mainly by lorry, to auctions in Boulogne and Brittany. These deterritorialised practices demonstrate how European high-sea fishermen are inevitably subject to the move toward liberalised economies, which leads them to prefer the market to the territory.[2] In the fishing sector, however, many actors are highly conscious of the implications of the development of deterritorialisation. It is still accompanied, in particular among those who practise coastal fishing, by strong fears as to the future of local infrastructures (the auctions), labour markets (dockers, cooperatives, processing industries), but also of the local fishing communities.

Industrial fishing fleets operating outside EU waters have, for several decades now, employed sailors originating from non-member countries. For instance, the Concarneau shipowning businesses, specialising in fishing tropical tuna off the coasts of west Africa and in the Indian Ocean, have employed African and Malagasy sailors since the 1960s. The fishing agreements made by the EU with some non-member countries, such as the African-Caribbean-Pacific states (ACP) signatories to the Lomé convention, even laid an obligation on European shipowners to employ a percentage of local sailors in return for granting fishing licences (see Chapter 7). As for the EU–Morocco agreement, in force from 1995 to 1999, it stipulated that any European (in practice, Spanish or Portuguese) ship authorised to fish in Moroccan waters should, depending on its tonnage, have from one to six Moroccan sailors aboard. Some European shipowners have sometimes seen this obligation as a constraint, although it had been conceived by the services of the Commission as a developmental measure. Others have, on the contrary, found it economically advantageous for their businesses, given the reduced labour costs in the countries concerned. According to a report made by the International Transport Federation in March 1998, a Malagasy sailor working on a European tuna-boat earned on average €1.50 a day with a bonus of €0.30 per tonne of fish caught: which was equivalent to an average salary of €380 to 460 for a two-month voyage, obviously a great deal less than that paid to Breton or Galician sailors.[3]

The deterritorialisation of employment is of little concern, for the moment, to the small-scale and industrial high-sea shipowners that operate in EU waters. The latter continue in effect to recruit most of their crews in the ship's home country, even home region. A limited trend toward labour relocation has also become evident since the 1990s. This may become more marked in future, not so much as a consequence of future EU enlargements than as the result of the problems of finding young recruits – including in those 'sanctuary' regions such as Brittany or the Spanish Basque Country – who are willing to work in a profession that is dangerous and involves unsocial hours. The French shipowners Petrel, a subsidiary of the Intermarché retail chain, chose to employ several Portuguese sailors in 1998 to work on trawlers operating off the coasts of Scotland. CGT and CFDT union members' fears about Petrel's employing Portuguese sailors were linked to the potential disappearance of 'the fishing culture [. . .] of France'.[4] This formulation undoubtedly expresses the fear that the free circulation of labour will gradually put an end to fishermen being based in their home ports.

Thirdly, European shipowners have become increasingly aware that from the late 1980s onwards the removal of obstacles to the free circulation of capital could have consequences for investment in their sector. Unlike the industrial shipowning businesses operating outside EU waters – such as the Concarneau tuna shipowners or the Pescanova shipowning business in Vigo – companies practising middle-water fishing off the Community fishing zone have long relied on strictly national capital. This situation has changed to the extent that shipowning business groups, in particular the Dutch and the Spanish, have taken advantage of their financial capacity to buy up companies in other member states. The example of south-east Brittany is interesting in this respect. In 1991, the biggest semi-industrial enterprises in Concarneau, the Dhellemmes shipowning business, came under the control of the Dutch group Jaczon. In 1994, it was the turn of the Jego-Quere shipowning business, the main operator in semi-industrial Lorient-based fishing, to be bought up by the Spanish group Pescanova. In both cases, the foreign shareholders made a commitment to continue ships landing their catches in the ports of Concarneau and Lorient, and indeed to promote new equipment and products there. The takeover of shipowning businesses by foreigners was felt by Breton fishermen to be 'a factor in local disintegration',[5] arousing its share of fears and social mobilisations. For example, after having granted a degree of autonomy to Jego-Quere's Lorient-based management, from 1996 the Spanish company Pescanova sought to impose more centralised management from its headquarters in Vigo. Breaking with local working customs, it demanded that skippers of Lorient-based ships inform them of their fishing plans. The refusal of one of them got him sacked, which led to thirty-nine days of strikes by crews in May 1997. This incident reveals the sailors' suspicions about the consequences of the Europeanisation of business capital in fishing enterprises.

Quotas in the grips of free circulation

Destabilisation was all the more strongly expressed when the TAC and quota system, symbolic of the CFP's inter-territorial compromise, was called into question. In the early 1980s, Spanish shipowners began to export and register fishing vessels in the United Kingdom in order to circumvent the limited access to EC waters imposed upon them by the agreement of 15 April 1980 between their country and Brussels. The fisheries administration of the United Kingdom gave licences to these foreign investors at that time. Relocating registration of some Spanish ships to the United Kingdom was nothing unusual, moreover, since Dutch shipowners had done likewise earlier in Germany.[6]

Following Spain's entry into the EC on 1 January, 1986, a further threshold was crossed. With the Act of Accession strictly limiting Spanish ships' access to Community waters for a transitional period of sixteen years, Spanish shipowners decided to buy ships and fishing licences in the United Kingdom – in Cornwall in particular – and Ireland, to exploit them under the British and Irish flags as apparently authorised by the Treaty of Rome. To the extent that ownership of a fishing vessel implies the right to use the quotas allocated to the state flag under which the ship sails, English and Irish fishermen's organisations soon made their hostility felt. It was within the National Federation of Fishermen's Organizations (NFFO) that the term *quota-hopping* was then coined. This is a far from neutral term since it refers to the pillage by 'outside' fishermen of fish stocks that were seen as part of the national heritage. In the United Kingdom, NFFO's opposition to quota-hopping gradually increased as it realised that Spanish shipowners were landing almost none of their catches in the United Kingdom, and that Dutch shipowners were, in turn, buying up vessels to increase their fishing capacity in the North Sea. Over the 1990s, alarm spread through the French and Belgian professional organisations. Just as their British and Irish counterparts had been, French fishermen were faced with Spanish and, to a lesser degree, Dutch shipowners in the Nord-Pas-de-Calais region, who were looking for new ways to exploit ships in France due to the financial problems besetting the industrial and smaller-scale fishing fleets.[7]

Faced with the mobilisation of national organisations of shipowners and fishermen which were quick to resort to the bellicose rhetoric of 'invasion',[8] the British, Irish and French Fisheries ministers decided, in the late 1980s, to put quota-hopping onto the EU political agenda. The immediate debate targeted Spanish far more than Dutch investors, giving the strong impression that the dynamism of entrepreneurs originating from a southern European country ran counter to the prevailing representation of the economic leadership in Europe. However, the number of ships listed by the French fisheries administration under the administrative term 'Franco-Spanish' (and not French, financed by Spanish capital), or by MAFF as Anglo-Spanish, suggests that the economic effects of the phenomenon should first of all be put into perspective. In 1998, there were 57 of these ships out of a total of 6,496 in France and around 80 out of a total of 8,482 in the United Kingdom. To take another indicator, in 1997 Franco-Spanish ships represented barely 2.5 per cent of the French fishing fleet's total motor power. This is a small percentage, even if it matched the reduction effort demanded at that very time by the European Commission from French fishermen under MAGP, which fuelled a sense of injustice among the latter. It was not possible to establish the levy raised on the quotas – the main criticism of the CFP rules – with any degree of precision. In 1996, the Major government's minister for fishing, Tony Baldry, nonetheless maintained in Brussels that 150 quota-hopping Spanish and Dutch ships were tapping 44 per cent of the British TAC of hake, 40 per cent of that of plaice, 34 per cent of sardine, 29 per cent of monkfish and 17 per cent of sole.[9] On the French side, the fisheries administration never supplied exact figures on the actual use of quotas by ships financed with European capital.

The phenomenon of quota-hopping warrants analysis in terms of its economic and institutional foundations. This involves considering a series of factors: the compartmentalisation of national fishing markets, the social representations that fishermen have of their activity, the national process of implementing the CFP and, finally, the protection that Community law offers to economic actors.

Although fishing products circulate freely between EU countries, markets still continue to be specialised by territory and to obtain differing revenues for national fishermen. Compared to the average of EU markets, those of Spain and the Netherlands offer national fishing fleets high take-up rates for their catches. Due to a high consumption rate, Spain has the highest internal demand in terms of volume. This is expressed in the high prices available to Spanish professionals who specialise in catching fresh fish such as hake, angler fish and anchovy in Community waters for immediate consumption. In a different way, the Netherlands has a national market for the export of frozen products, which likewise ensures comfortable revenues for a fleet of modern trawlers specialising in fishing and on-board packaging of pelagic species such as herring, mackerel or horse mackerel. The prices that national shipowners can obtain on the Spanish and Dutch markets have a consequence. The latter, including those who own only one or two ships, as is often the case in Galicia, have enough liquid assets to be able to invest in new equipment. Once the MAGPs had strictly limited the construction of any new ships to avoid increasing fishing fleets' capacity, and given the existence of a second-hand market in countries such as France and Great Britain, the choice of Spanish or Dutch shipowners naturally inclined to the second option. Of course, exploiting ships under British or French flags procured greater access to the resource and sometimes also enabled them to profit from less restrictive management rules. This last remark applies to Dutch fishermen who are subject, domestically, to the system of *Biesheuvel* groups (see Chapter 2), which makes it more difficult to exceed annual quotas than other national systems. Quota-hopping is thus for the most part a micro-economic phenomenon that exploits the legal framework of the internal European market. It is not, however, as some professional organisations sometimes tend to believe, the result of wilful institutional policies on the part of Spanish or Dutch governments seeking to monopolise eventually European high-sea fishing.

Secondly, explanations of quota-hopping must take into account the social representations that shipowners and fishermen, and, more generally, social actors from 'buyer' countries have of the occupation of high-sea fishermen and its future in Europe. This second factor refers us back to what some writers call the cognitive dimension of social action, which involves consideration of images, beliefs and representations to understand actors' motivations.[10] The example of Galicia is interesting in this respect. In this region, for a long time one of the poorest in Spain, fishing is an activity perceived as part of the modernisation process that occurred following the end of the Franco regime. In 1997, 120,000 jobs were linked to fishing, making Galicia the EU region most economically and socially dependent on this activity. In some areas of west Galicia, 43 per cent of the local population still derive their livelihood from fishing. This does not mean that Galician fishing has not had to deal with economic changes since Spain's entry into the EU, which have taken their toll in terms of social costs. The exit plan for fleets imposed by the EU on ships called *Gran Sol* (i.e. on the trawlers and longliners operating in Community waters) incurred job losses between 1990 and 1996. Unlike the situation in English Cornwall and French Finistère, however, fishing is not associated with economic crisis in the representations of fishermen and of Galician social actors (journalists, bankers, elected politicians, annd so on). Since Spain's membership of the CFP, Galicia has not experienced any sharp falls in the price of fish leading to forced sales of ships, as was the case in Brittany in 1993–94. The few social mobilisations that had an impact in the Galician ports since the early 1990s had to do with the conditions of renewal and application of the EU–Morocco fishing agreement, on which 1,400 sailors' jobs were dependent. The prevailing impression amongst Galician fishermen is thus that the profession remains profitable and has a future. This is an explanatory factor in the propensity of the Galician shipowners of the *Gran Sol* fleet, and also investors outside the fishing sector, to invest capital in ships available in Great Britain and France. Similarly, Galician sailors, who for several years had worked on trawlers fishing in distant waters, were quick to convert the capital accumulated into British or French high-sea vessels.[11] This confidence in the future also explains why, as was the case in the Netherlands, Galician commercial banks were willing to support the investment projects of quota-hoppers. The Galician example thus argues in favour of taking social representations into account when analysing the economic choices of fishing actors.

Thirdly, we have stressed the fact that Community policies are not so much implemented as interpreted in different ways in national and local territories, which remain the product of specific histories between companies, markets and governments.[12] Quota-hopping fuels these differences in national interpretation. Comparison of how MAGP rules were applied in Spain and the United Kingdom supplies another pertinent illustration here. Subject to pressures from autonomous governments, in particular those of Galicia, and Andalusia and the Basque Country, and professional organisations such as the Federación Nacional de Cofradías de Pescadores, as soon as Spain entered the EU, Felipe Gonzalez' socialist government had established a plan to decommission the oldest fishing ships with a view to topping up European subsidies with national aids. This had a significant impact on the crews of the *Gran Sol* fleet, which fell from 300 Spanish ships in 1986, to 210 in 1997. Because of the Thatcher and Major governments' policy of budgetary restraint, a British plan to decommission ships could not be implemented on the same terms and timescale in the United Kingdom. In the absence of supplementary national aid, British shipowners wanting to abandon their activity were thus tempted to sell their ships and licences to the highest bidders on the second-hand market. Adding subsidies for decommissioning ships to their own capital raised on the market, Spanish shipowners, in particular the Galicians, were ideal customers for British vendors. This example is a perfect illustration of how a general objective assigned to a Community policy – in this case, reducing the capacity of fishing fleets with a view to preserving the resource – can, through the diversity of its national inter-pretations, provoke unexpected effects such as quota-hopping.

Finally, quota-hopping cannot be understood without considering the resources that Community law offers economic actors to defend their interests. Community law is the outcome of a process that is as much judi-cial as it is legislative.[13] It has been constructed around defending the free circulation of goods, people, capital and services within the EU. When in 1988 the Thatcher government sought to modify national law on ship registration (the Merchant Shipping Act), by imposing a nationality condition on shipowners, the Spanish quota-hoppers realised that their best bet was invocation of Community law. With help from their lawyers, they lodged complaints for infringement of the free exercise of their professional activity with the Commission and national courts, knowing that the latter would not fail to refer the case to the CJEC as was provided for in the Treaties. We concur with studies that have described the European Commission as a 'multi-organisation' composed of various segments expressing a plurality of ideas and interests.[14] Bearing this in mind, it is not surprising that quota-hopping gave rise to sometimes contradictory stances within the Commission. Drafted by DG Fish offi-cials, the communication of 19 July 1989 on 'a Community framework for access to fishing quotas' revealed a desire to restrict the phenomenon, in order not to jeopardise the inter-territorial compromise that formed the basis of the CFP. It stated that 'recourse to the facility of granting national flag and/or licences to obtain exploitation of fishing quotas [...] is perceived by the local communities of fishermen as an injustice', and that its spread could 'substantially modify the socio-economic equilibrium in some coastal regions'.[15] But this position did not prevent the Commission's Legal Service from bringing an action before the CJEC some weeks later, on 4 August 1989, against the United Kingdom's government for the breaches of the Merchant Shipping Act in respect of European rules regulating the free circulation of capital and the freedom of establishment.[16] In line with what Nicolas Jabko has also shown, this decision proves that, despite the divisions among Directorates General, the respect for market rule is the norm that always ends up prevailing in the positions taken by the Commission.[17] In a way, the sensitivity of the DG Fish officials to British and French fishermen's fears of quota-hopping cannot withstand the fact that this practice conforms to the rationale of the internal market.[18] This validity in respect of market rules is equally present at the CJEC, which, since 1952, has assiduously applied itself to constructing a European legal order based on the progressive removal of all national obstacles to the free circulation of goods, people, services and capital. Referred by the British courts, the Community judges logically ruled that decreeing a condition of nationality, residence or domicile to registering a fishing ship in a member state amounted to a violation of Community law. In several rulings, including the four *Factortame* rulings,[19] they did however consider that the flag state could require shipowners to prove a 'real economic link ' between its business and the national territory. Following the first *Factortame* judgment issued in July 1991, the British government embarked on a procedural battle to avoid paying £80,000 (€125,000) in damages to the Spanish owners of fishing vessels which the Merchant Shipping Act had banned from all activity in 1989 and 1990. In October 1999, the House of Lords decided, in the last resort, that the government should pay this compensation. Following the example of numerous European economic actors, the quota-hoppers realised it was in their interest to use Community law to counter possible restrictions that states might seek to impose on the Europeanisation of the activity of shipowner and fisherman.

The states faced with new economic actors

Quota-hopping enables us to observe the emergence of new European fishing actors for whom business must be deterritorialised and who are prompt to resort to the rules of the internal market to circumvent state sovereignty.[20] The managers of Spanish-financed companies established in Great Britain and France illustrate this new actor's profile in a total break from the traditional image of the shipowner solidly anchored to his port. Their task is transnational by nature, since it consists in putting Spanish investors in touch with British and French sellers, and managing relations between these same investors and the French and British administrations. In Charente and French Basque Country, this new occupation appeared on the institutional fishing scene in the late 1980s. One example is Elian Castaing, who came from a La Rochelle family that had been forced to divest itself of a semi-industrial shipowning business and who turned to representing Spanish shipowners in France. His task was in fact twofold. It involved finding fishing vessels on the French second-hand market for Galician buyers, and providing administrative and accounting management for companies registered in France with headquarters based in La Rochelle, but whose ships, crewed by a majority of Galician sailors, made almost no landings in France. Jean-Marie Zarza is another example of these new economic actors who the Spanish investors' growing interest in French high-sea ships has fostered. Originally from the French Basque Country, Jean-Marie Zarza moved abroad for several years, first to Venezuela where he ran a fishing business, then to the United States. With the international experience thus acquired, he formed the French-registered company Pronaval in Hendaye, which, in 1998, was managing the interests of fourteen companies, financed with Spanish capital. It owned sixteen high-sea fishing vessels from which 80 per cent of sales were made in Spain and 20 per cent in France. For these new European fishing actors, seeking profit through maximum exploitation of the rules of the internal market is the priority that directs the activity. Thus, in their rationale the issue of allegiance to a territory or a community of fishermen is of little importance. If Franco-Spanish shipowners sell most of their product in Spanish ports, it is because they obtain higher prices offered from the fish wholesalers there. When they sell to the flag state, likewise it is market considerations that are paramount. For example, the French port of La Rochelle, located midway between the fishing sites of the ships (Scotland and Ireland) and the main point of sale (Spain), enabled shipowning businesses affiliated to Pronaval to market species which sell better on the French than on the Spanish market.[21] This commercial rationale led to practices of loss leadership pricing in some ports, such as La Rochelle, that would seek to attract landings from quota-hoppers. The shipowners will, for their part, play on this to obtain the cheapest possible landing costs in exchange. The strictly commercial rationale that drives the quota-hoppers has its counterpart in the flexibility they demonstrate as far as social security schemes for crews are concerned. The Anglo-Spanish or Franco-Spanish shipowning businesses employ sailors who, for the most part, are Spanish nationals and live in Spain. Although some lawyers might see a contradiction with European regulations on 'the coordination of national health insurance schemes',[22] these sailors are registered by the shipowning businesses sometimes with the French or British social security system, sometimes with the Spanish system. In 1998, for instance, Pronaval employed 160 sailors, of whom 70 were Spanish, 50 Portuguese and 40 were French. Some of the Spanish sailors were affiliated to the Établissement national des invalides de la marine (ENIM), which is the French health insurance fund for sailors, whereas the others were affiliated to the Instituto Social de la Marina (ISM), which is the Spanish equivalent. For the manager of the shipowning business, the choice of health insurance system was not a matter of allegiance to a territorial health insurance but more a matter of business management. Pronaval paid contributions into the ENIM for all its Spanish employees living less than two hours from the French border, judging the standard of medical services in France to be higher than those in Spain. For sailors living in Galicia, however, Pronaval paid contributions to the ISM, which had the advantage of being slightly less expensive for the shipowner. This growing leeway of choice for shipowners with regard to the states and national laws in managing health insurance is not insignificant in the fishing domain, since it is in direct conflict with the link between the activity and the territory. European integration is considered positively by quota-hoppers in so far it increases their businesses' room for manoeuvre. As was underlined by the manager of Pronaval: 'I don't make the rules of the European market, but I exploit them as far as Community law allows'.[23]

State sovereignty is not dead

In the states concerned, quota-hopping has fuelled political mobilisations and provoked responses from governments in the form of reactive national policies. These developments show that the EU states have not relinquished their capacity to protect their national economies when confronted with economic actors' strategies of finding new support from the rules of the internal market.

In the United Kingdom, it is no coincidence that political movements opposed to the overall project of European integration have made quota-hopping a hobbyhorse in their crusade against Brussels since the 1990s.[24] This is the case with the Referendum Party and the Campaign for an Independent Britain movement, created in 1996 by personalities from various political parties to defend the supremacy of British law in the face of 'attacks' by Community law. A pamphlet drafted by Austin Mitchell, Labour MP for the English port of Grimsby and a prominent figure in the Save Britain's Fish campaign, thus used quota-hopping to denounce the EU's damaging effect on state sovereignty. With a large dollop of romanticism, Austin Mitchell invited the 'nation of fishermen' to 'save Britain's fish' by withdrawing from the EU, as, if they didn't, others would grab their quotas.[25] The association Austin Mitchell made between fishing and state sovereignty shows once again the need to take into account the social representations of actors when analysing a public policy such as fishing. Austin Mitchell's 'seafaring' nationalism in effect relies on a cognitive triptych that is expressed in almost the same terms by some French professionals: the past strength of the national fleet, the suffering of fisherman for the nation's well-being, and finally the alienation of fisherman by bureaucrats.

On the occasion of legislative elections and the signing of the Treaty of Amsterdam in 1997, the Conservative Party's 'Eurosceptics' would likewise choose to make quota-hopping central to their anti-European arguments. Benefiting from a relative majority in the House of Commons, Prime Minister Major was forced to take their arguments seriously, to the point of committing to refuse any agreement on the Treaty of Amsterdam unless it contained a protocol restricting the freedom of investment by non-nationals in the fishing sector.[26] The proposed draft did not appear in the final conclusions of the intergovernmental conference charged with revising the treaties for two reasons. The first was the Spanish government's firm intention to contest any conditions based on territorial criteria at the CJEC. The second was the victory of Tony Blair, in the

May 1997 elections, to whom it fell to be the final signatory to the Treaty of Amsterdam. The new prime minister was certainly keen to break with the image of a Great Britain fixated on symbolic oppositions to the EU in sectors such as fishing. Nonetheless, he could not sign the Treaty of Amsterdam either if it gave the impression of giving up on any resolution of a problem that had been popularised mainly by the Conservatives. The political tack he took thus revolved around an exchange of letters with the Commission's president, Jacques Santer, in June 1997, concerning conditions for implementing the 'real economic link', defined by the CJEC, between any ship sailing under a British flag and the communities of British fishermen. On the basis of the response delivered by the Commission, the United Kingdom's Fisheries administration decided that from 1 January 1999, it would only deliver fishing licences to ships respecting one of the four following conditions: at least 50 per cent of catches of species under quota-being landed in a British port; half the crew had to be resident in a coastal zone of Great Britain; a certain amount of expenditure on fitting up the ship had to be spent in Great Britain; any other proof supplied by the shipowner as to a real economic link. The Anglo-Spanish or Anglo-Dutch shipowning businesses could no longer merely have their ships drop anchor in British ports once a year for a technically obligatory visit. They would henceforth have to negotiate the terms of an imposed allegiance with the administration and the port communities. However, this proved to be quite a flexible negotiation in Great Britain, given the British administration's liberal consensus on economic matters. In 1999, some Dutch quota-hoppers supplied evidence – that would have been accepted with difficulty in France – of their real economic link with the British territory by, for instance, handing back unused quotas to British producers' organisations.

In France, quota-hopping was never exploited in the electoral arena by political movements opposed to the EU. Demands and mobilisations were confined to professional circles. The repeated concerns of the UAPF and the main fishermen's unions did, however, lead the socialist minister for Agriculture and Fishing, Louis Le Pensec, who was an MP from Brittany and a former Minister for the Sea, to decree a series of conditions for exploiting ships financed with European capital. The framework law on maritime fishing and marine cultures of 18 November 1997 stipulated that from 1 January 1999 'a fishing vessel sailing under the French flag is only authorised to fish on national quotas [...] when there is a real economic link with the territory of the French Republic and it is run and controlled from a stable establishment located on French territory'.[27] The criteria defining a real economic link, very similar to those introduced by the British administration, were detailed in a circular of 31 August 1998. Relations between the administration and the quota hoppers are more conflictual in France than in Great Britain. This is due no doubt to the

Fisheries administration's less positive attitude to economic liberalism. In July 1999, the latter banned eight Franco-Spanish ships registered in La Rochelle from fishing species under quota because they were landing their catches in Galicia and were linked to a company which had its headquarters in France. To control the activity of Dutch quota-hoppers who had bought fishing ships in Flemish ports without landing fish there, in February 1999 the Belgian Ministry of Agriculture likewise demanded proof of a real economic link.[28] But as in the British case, the Belgian administration was very flexible in its implementation of criteria due to its greater openness to economic liberalism.

Although the effects might vary from one national context to another, the decreeing of reactive national policies to quota-hopping is a good demonstration of how states have not lost all their means of protecting their territories and the interests of their fishermen, and also of those employed in the docks, auctions and naval shipyards. They are nonetheless obliged to negotiate with new economic actors who may at any time oppose them through the legitimacy of European economic law. The Spanish quota-hoppers who were banned by the French administration from fishing species under quota in July 1999 thus demanded that the Commission institute procedures for non-compliance with criteria on the real economic link. In future, the obligation imposed on ships by the French maritime labour Code to have aboard a captain and a first mate of French nationality, on the grounds that the latter have responsibilities relating to order and public safety – such as registering birth, marriage or death – could likewise be the object of complaint by quota-hoppers at the CJEC for infringement of the principle of the free circulation of labour. [29]

Quota-hopping well illustrates how the EU constitutes a polity in which the states are faced with actors and organisations that have the resources to satisfy their economic interests beyond the principle of territorial sovereignty.[30] In such a polity, neither governments nor non-governmental actors have the monopoly on setting the political agenda. Public policies are defined through a constant process of interaction, negotiation and compromise. Beyond the opposition between an inter-state EU and a supranational EU, quota-hopping confirms that neither the logic of territory nor that of the market completely dominates the EU. The two coexist in a constant 'state of balance'.[31] Secondly, it is quite obvious that the logic of the European market challenges the social order inherited from the welfare state. In relying on the rules of free circulation, the quota-hoppers are, in effect, able to move their activities from one territory to another, thus creating social uncertainty. Finally, quota-hopping shows that, in the EU, economic and social actors increasingly escape the monopoly of *any one* authority that could protect the values of equity and justice beyond the functioning of the market. National administrations have few resources to control the quota-hoppers who 'play' with the social rules of several member states. The dynamics of transnationalised economies are thus accompanied by a diffusion of responsibilities, which, in turn, blurs the exercise of political control.[32]

Notes

1 *Le Marin*, 23 October 1998, p. 26.
2 Pierre de Senarclens, *Mondialisation, souvererainté et theories de relations internationales*, Paris, Armand Colin, 1998.
3 *Le Marin*, 20 November 1998.
4 *Ouest-France*, 4 March 1998.
5 Jean-René Couliou, *La pêche bretonne. Les ports de Bretagne sud face à leur avenir*, Rennes, Presses universitaires de Rennes, 1997, p. 333.
6 Annie Cudennec, 'La stabilité relative d'activités de pêche: mythe ou realité? La question du *quota hopping*', *Espaces et resources maritimes*, 10, 1996, pp. 204–236.
7 See the interview with the Lorientais shipowner Patrick Le Bronze, 'Pourquoi j'ai vendu ...' à *France-Éco-Pêche*, July–August 1996.
8 See for example the terms used by Alain Parrès, president of the CNPMEM, in his report *Affirmer la place des pêches maritimes françaises face aux defis mondiaux*, Paris, September 1997, p. 202.
9 France-Éco-Pêche, July–August 1996.
10 Pierre Muller, Yves Surel, *L'analyse de politiques publiques*, Paris, Montchrestien, coll. 'Clefs', 1998; for a particular application to fishing see Jan Kooinman, 'Experiences and Opportunities: A Governance Analysis of Europe's Fisheries', in Jan Kooinman (ed.), *Creative Governance: Opportunities for Fisheries in Europe*, Aldershot, Ashgate, 1999.
11 Interview with Jacobo Fontán Dominguez, Vigo, 19 October 1997.
12 Smith, *L'Europe politique*.
13 See Stephan Leibfried and Paul Pierson (eds), *Politiques sociales européennes. Entre intégration et fragmentation*, Paris, L'Harmattan, 1998; and also Renaud Dehousse, 'L'Europe par le droit', *Critique internationale*, 2, February 1999, pp. 133–150.
14 Laura Cram, 'The European Commission as a Multi-Organisation: Social Policy and IT Policy in the EU', *Journal of European Public Policy*, 1 (1), 1994, pp. 195–218.
15 Cudennec, 'La stabilité', p. 213.
16 Judgment of the Court of 4 October 1991. *Commission of the European Communities* v. *United Kingdom of Great Britain and Northern Ireland* (case C-246/89).
17 Nicolas Jabko, 'In the Name of the Market: How the European Commission Paved the Way for Monetary Union', *Journal of European Public Policy*, 6 (3), 1999, pp. 456–474.
18 Evidence of this is supplied by the section on quota-hopping in the general evaluation report on the CFP drafted in December 1991 by the Commission for the attention of the Council of the European Parliament.
19 Cases C-213/89, C-221/89, C-46/93 et C-48/93; see also cases *Agegate* C-

3/87 and *Jaderow* C-216/87.

20 Justin Greenwood, *Representing Interests in the European Union*, Basingstoke, Macmillan, 1997.

21 Interview by Jean-Marie Zarza in *France-Éco-Pêche*, July–August 1996.

22 Gwenaële Proutière-Maulion and Patrick Chaumette, 'Un virus dans la politique commune des pêches: le phenomenon du *quota hopping?*', *Espaces et resources maritimes*, 11, 1997, pp. 215–237.

23 Interview with Jean-Marie Zarza, Hendaye, 15 July 1998.

24 See Jacques Leruez, 'Le Royaume-Uni après les elections de mai 1997', *Les Études du CERI*, 38, 1998.

25 Austin Mitchell, *The Common Fisheries Policy: End or Mend?*, London, Campaign for an Independent Britain, 1996.

26 Interview with Tony Baldry, Minister of State for Agriculture, Fisheries and Food for the Major government, London, 3 July 1997.

27 *JORF* (laws and decrees), 19 November 1997.

28 *Le Moniteur belge*, 12 February 1999.

29 Michel Morin, 'La condition de nationalité du capitaine de navire français', *Annuaire de droit maritime et océanique*, 1999.

30 See Gary Marks, Liesbet Hooghe, Kermit Blank, 'European Integration from the 1980s: State-Centric vs. Multi-Level Governance', *Journal of Common Market Studies*, 34 (3), pp. 341–378; and also Bertrand Badie, *Un monde sans souvereraineté. Les États entre ruse et responsabilité*, Paris, Fayard, 1999.

31 Markus Jachtenfuchs, 'Theoretical Perspectives on European Governance', *European Law Journal*, 1 (2), 1995, pp. 115–133.

32 Jürgen Habermas, *Après l'Etat-nation. Une nouvelle constellation politique*, Paris, Fayard, 2000.

6

The new environmental order: the European Union bans driftnets

There is a plethora of books on international relations and international political economy dealing with 'globalisation' or 'global governance'.[1] All of them attempt to show how a number of global norms, such as the market economy, human rights or ecological safety, are now imposed on the ensemble of states and defy their sovereignty.[2] They rarely analyse, however, the way in which these global standards encounter the local territories in which most political mediations continue to operate. The EU's territorial diversity provides a particular case that enables us to comprehend this phenomenon, which has sometimes been described as 'glocalisation'[3] or 'globalisation of the local level'.[4] This chapter examines the process by which one global environmental norm, the protection of dolphins, led the EU to ban the technique of fishing with driftnets in 1998. It first recaps the conditions under which the environment emerged as a legitimate dimension of the CFP. It then analyses the political context in which some Spanish fishermen came to exploit this global environmental norm to defend their interests. The third section examines how the protection of dolphins came to acquire the status of global norm. This is followed, finally, by an analysis of the conditions under which an objective alliance between environmentalist NGOS, some Spanish fishermen and EU institutions came about, along with their effects on groups of French, Irish and British fishermen.

The environment as a dimension of the Common Fisheries Policy

Maintaining that there is a close relationship between fishing and the environment is a truism. The state of the natural habitat inevitably affects fisheries resources and, reciprocally, fishing activity has an influence on the marine environment of which the dwindling of stocks is an immediate expression. The transnational community of fishing biologists that developed in 1902 around the ICES initially pursued a priority objective which was to prevent overfishing from diminishing fish stocks. It was, however, little concerned with the issue of preventing pollution risks, no more than were the national administrations that supported it. Convened in Washington in 1926, the International Conference to limit the discharge of oil at sea concluded in a crushing failure, due to a lack of signatory states. It was not until the London convention of 12 May 1954 that the first international regulations for the prevention of pollution of the sea by oil were enacted.[5] Similarly, for a long time marine fishing biologists and governments were unconcerned about the impact of fishing techniques on the life of marine mammals. There was virtually only the problem of protecting whales, which in 1946 led to the creation of the International Whaling Commission and brought together nineteen governments with the aim of regulating whaling. This situation evolved, however, in the late 1960s, as debate on the relationship between the sea and ecology began to emerge in industrialised societies. In effect, a series of serious incidents of accidental pollution, such as the oil slick in 1967 that resulted from the wreck of the petrol tanker *Torrey Canyon* off the Breton coast or, in 1971, the discharge of methylmercury into the Japanese bay of Minamata, demonstrated the threats that industrial economic developments could represent for the sea and coastal settlements. Also, environmentalist NGOs such as Greenpeace began to denounce the dangers of certain fishing techniques to marine ecosystems. The result was the gradual formation of what Bertrand Badie calls a worldwide 'community of responsibility'[6] calling for an approach to fishing that paid greater respect to environmental standards, through campaigns in the press, recourse to scientific expertise and appeals to consumer pressure.

It was at this time that the environment became a specific issue on the EU agenda. The first institutional expression of this new policy was the approval, in 1973, of an 'Environment Action Programme' aimed at preventing and reducing pollution in member states and encouraging EU presence in international institutions. A series of economic factors explains this evolution. In addition to the governments of the nine states' growing awareness that environmental deterioration called for a necessarily transnational response, it coincided with the growing power of ecological movements expressing post-industrial values in several EU countries such as Germany and the Netherlands. In addition, industrialists in these same countries began to express the fear that, if national legislation on the environment were not harmonised, the high standards their governments held them to could eventually compromise the competitiveness of their export products.[7] Within the European Commission, an Environment Directorate General was created in the 1970s. It quickly established itself as a forum for exchange in which officials and experts from new national environmental administrations exchanged ideas and strategies with scientists and NGO representatives with a view to spurring on governments reputed to be lukewarm.[8] Increasing the number of initia-

tives, as per the model described by Laura Cram as 'intentional oppor-
tunism',[9] the Environment DG was instrumental in bringing the
environment into the field of legitimate Community policies. At the
signing of the Single European Act in February 1986, it insisted that a
clause on the environment be included in the Treaty of Rome, in order
that action would be based in a specific legal foundation. While accepting
this formal recognition of environmental policy, a majority of governments demanded in exchange that unanimity remained the rule for
decision-taking within the Council of Ministers. It was not until the
implementation of the Maastricht Treaty, in November 1993, that a
movement in favour of qualified majority and a close association with the
European Parliament developed, which continued with the signing of the
Treaty of Amsterdam in October 1997. Wanting to increase its influence
through new common policies, starting in June 1979 the European
Parliament, elected by universal suffrage, supported the emergence of a
European policy for the environment. As we have already pointed out,
from June 1984 onwards the increased representation of ecological parties
in Strasbourg encouraged this support, although the Green MPs had never
unanimously agreed on priorities for a European policy on the environment.[10] Faced with Commission officials and European parliamentarians
who sought to legitimise their political entrepreneurship through
exchange with the social actors,[11] the environmentalist NGOs realised the
value of an institutional presence in Brussels, opening offices there in the
late 1980s.

DG Fish officials, and particularly the biologists in charge of the policy
for conservation of stocks, did not wait for NGOs to become sensitised to
a global environmentalist discourse. The work of the ICES, FAO and the
OECD, as well as that of scientific colloquia, had long since familiarised
them with new global standards such as sustainable development and the
precautionary principle. This was all the more the case as maritime activities had on occasion been at the origin of the very definition of these
standards. The first forum that sanctioned the precautionary principle in
international law took place in 1987 at the Second International
Conference on the Protection of the North Sea, five years before the 1992
Rio summit.[12]

Over the 1990s, and often in advance of shipowners' and fishermen's
organisations, the seafood-processing industries likewise became aware
that their presence on the markets was becoming increasingly dependent
on respecting new global environmental standards. An illustration of this
was the multinational Unilever's invitation to the WWF in 1997 to create
the 'Marine Stewardship Council', charged with issuing ecolabels to
marine products caught in accordance with methods 'respecting sustainable use of marine resources'.[13] One of the largest multinational
corporations buying frozen white fish, Unilever intended to safeguard its

market share with this initiative in response to consumers' ecological sensitivity. This private sector initiative met with some reserve from the European Commission, which considered it a rival to its own projects for ecolabelling, supposed to represent a priority for the new European environmental policy.[14]

It was in this context of growing legitimation of the environmental dimension within the EU that in 1990, conflict between the albacore tuna fishermen in the north-east Atlantic broke out over the use of driftnets.

Occupational conflicts, nationality conflicts

French and Spanish sailors along the Atlantic coast have fished for albacore tuna (or white tuna) since at least the eighteenth century. It is a seasonal activity that takes place between May and October and consists of following the shoals of tuna moving from the Azores to Ireland. In France in the mid-nineteenth century an albacore tuna fishery 'underwent a boom in the Bay of Biscay, thanks to the development of the canned foodstuff industry'.[15] On the eve of the First World War, the French tuna fleet comprised around 700 sailing boats using dragnets. In 1949, a new technique originating in the United States was introduced to Saint-Jean-de-Luz, in the French Basque Country. This was pole-and-line fishing, or fishing with live bait, which led to the installation of fish-wells on board ships.[16] This technique was taken up from 1951 onwards by Spanish Basque fishermen from the border province of Guipuzcoa and by Breton fishermen. In 1967, the total production of French and Spanish fishing fleets of liners and pole-and-line vessels amounted to 48,000 tonnes. But, while the Spanish fishing fleets' landings remained fairly stable, those of French pole-and-line vessels started to decline in the mid-1960s, followed by those of surface liners in the early 1970s.[17] The French decline was the result of both a change in fishing techniques and the social context. As far as fishing techniques were concerned, from the 1960s onwards French fishermen of the Atlantic began to equip predominantly with trawlers which were no longer convertible into liners or pole-and-line vessels in the albacore tuna season. This was a major difference from Spain where ships fish for anchovies using purse seines in the Bay of Biscay continued converting to pole-and-line vessels or liners for tuna during the summer. Secondly, in the 1970s French crews began 'to appreciate the improvement of living conditions on trawlers, in particular the shortening of the time spent at sea'. Moreover, fishing for albacore tuna with surface lines and pole-and-lines, which involved longer trips, seemed 'to give an impression of outmoded practice', gradually leading men to leave the occupation.[18] In 1986, albacore tuna fishing in France involved only a few liners on the verge of abandoning their activity, while the number of ships using the same technique has hardly altered since the 1960s in the Spanish provinces of the Basque Country and Galicia.

The gradual abandonment of albacore tuna fishing led the technicians at IFREMER, driven by a modernist engineering vision, to propose, in 1986, to a ship from Yeu Island, in Vendée, and to a ship from Saint-Guenole, in Brittany, that they try out driftnets in the hope of achieving much higher yields than those attainable through using surface lines and pole-and-line. The driftnet technique is as ancient as it is simple. It consists in letting drift a net, maintained by floats on the surface and held down by weights below, in which fish are caught. The living resources directorate at IFREMER welcomed this project, since albacore tuna was not a stock at risk of depopulation. The tests carried out by IFREMER soon proved conclusive, arousing growing interest among shipowners. In 1987, a French fishing fleet of twenty ships (of which five were on Yeu Island) generally exceeding 18 metres, equipped themselves with driftnets for seasonal albacore tuna fishing. The fleet grew to thirty-eight ships in 1990 and sixty-four in 1994. The main attraction was economic. Given the demand from canneries, the turnover from a three-week voyage proved profitable. Moreover, this form of fishing, which is practised beyond the 200-mile limit, avoided the fierce competition operating on other fisheries, particularly over hake, in the Bay of Biscay.

It was with a similar view to avoiding competition over hake in southwest England that in 1990–91 some Irish and Cornish fleet-owners decided to equip with driftnets to catch albacore tuna in the Bay of Biscay, despite the distance from fishing sites.[19] In 1993, eight Irish ships and six Cornish ships were practising this form of fishing.[20] The new albacore fishing fleet grew until 1992 without the Commission and the European Fisheries Ministers passing any kind of regulation on the use of nets of up to 6 or 7 kilometres long.

However, concern was soon felt among Spanish fishermen, in particular among Basque pole-and-line fishermen, whose 200 ships listed in 1994 now had to share the albacore tuna stock with fishing fleets practising a different occupation. In a sector of activity where the sense of belonging to a common public space was weak, occupational conflict soon came to be expressed as a conflict of nationality. This example, incidentally, also argues for an empirical sociology of the European public space that would take into account social practices in particular sectors.[21] The conflict was stoked by vested interests but also by different social beliefs. For the Basque fishermen began to fear becoming gradually excluded by 'bigger' and increasingly 'modern' ships from a fishery that had strong historical and ideological significance for them. So it was not surprising that the Basque leaders of the opposition to driftnets in the province of Guipuzcoa should sometimes be close to radical nationalist parties such as Herri Batasuna. Estebán Olaizola Elizazu, president of the San Pedro *cofradía* in Hondarribia, thus developed a classic theme of identity-based regionalism, according to which 'small communities' should resist the extremes of modernity of those 'bigger' than they, lest they lose their specificity.[22] The fear of being excluded by 'the French' was reinforced by the fact that in 1975 IFREMER, along with their promotion of driftnets, had encouraged shipowners in French Basque ports such as Hendaye and Saint-Jean-de-Luz to develop the technique of pelagic trawling. Now, intensive use of these bottom nets in the coastal zones of South Gascony coincided with a reduction in stocks of some species, such as red sea-bream, which was particularly prized by Spanish Basque fishermen. The second reason for the Spanish fear was social. In the 1990s, Basque and Galician liners caught, on average, 0.5 tonne of tuna per fishing day, and the pole-and-line vessels from 1 to 1.5 tonnes. In comparison, the French and Irish netters had yields of 1.5 to 2 tonnes. Moreover, the Spanish ships continued to employ crews of from ten to fifteen men on average, whereas the netters of Yeu Island and Douarnenez employed only five to six men.[23] Hence the doubtless overly simplistic calculation which nonetheless featured in the minds of Spanish fishermen, that the productivity gain of ships equipped with driftnets, if used systematically by their own fishing fleets, would encourage a reduction in crew numbers and a rise in unemployment in the ports. A third explanatory factor for the protesting attitude of Spanish liners and pole-and-line vessels was the fear that driftnet-caught tuna imports into the Spanish market encouraged lower prices for line-caught tuna which was bought at higher prices by fish wholesalers. This was the root of the conflict, even if was never made explicit, and although the modest tonnages of French, Irish and British exports of albacore tuna to the Spanish market were not, objectively speaking, justified.

Conversely, albacore tuna very quickly came to be considered by French, Irish and British netters as a profitable fishery. On Yeu Island, for example, the annual production of albacore tuna fished with driftnets grew from 125 tonnes in 1987 to 2,000 tonnes in 1993, the seaman's share of fish landed being considered at the reasonably decent sum of €1,928 for a three-week voyage in 1997.[24] For Yeu Island ship-owners, who had built up family businesses around albacore tuna fishing, this profitability also symbolised the integration of an island micro-territory into a modern fishing system.[25]

Over the course of the summer of 1990, the first incidents took place at sea in the Bay of Biscay. Spanish pole-and-line vessels and liners took to task, and damaged the nets of, French, British and Irish fishermen. Repeated with a greater or lesser violence every summer, the altercations reached their height in July 1994 when *La Gabrielle*, a ship from Yeu Island, was rammed by Spanish tuna-boats, then captured and towed to the Galician port of Burela. The Spanish, French and British governments sent no less than six of their national navy ships to the fishing zones, which over the summer of 1994 amounted to one of the biggest marine law enforcement operations since the creation of the CFP. The conflict was taken to intergovernmental level, with the Spanish fisheries administration on the one side, the French, British and Irish on the other, initiating an institutional dialogue with a view to defusing the violence between professionals. Despite these efforts of inter-state dialogue, the Spanish liners and pole-and-line vessels maintained their determination to get driftnets banned. In this they benefited from an exceptional source of support, in that their demands became part of a global debate on the protection of dolphins.

The protection of dolphins: a legitimate global norm

Many analyses dealing with public European policies neglect to contextualise them in terms of more global configurations of actors and ideas. What analysts call the 'Europeanisation' of public policies is often simply the manifestation of processes, debates and policy decisions which occur on a much wider scale.[26] Whereas driftnets had been a source of endless conflict between European fishermen operating in the North Sea since the mid-nineteenth century, the contemporary debate on their banning originated in the United States. It began in the early 1980s, orchestrated by environmentalist NGOs, such as the Earth Island Institute and Greenpeace,[27] which were engaged in campaigns to ban the long nets used by the Japanese, Korean and Taiwanese for fishing in the north Pacific. The main criticism advanced by these NGOs was the equipment's non-selectivity, resulting in substantial by-catches of marine mammals – dolphins – and seabirds. Continuing its 'strategy of dramatising problems',[28] Greenpeace embarked on a series of commando actions in the north Pacific. In 1983, the Greenpeace ship *Rainbow Warrior* prevented Japanese boats from setting their nets. It was easy for the ecological organisation to forge an alliance with Canadian and American fishermen who were quick to support any action aiming to reduce the activity of Asian ships on stocks.[29] The combined campaigns of environmentalist NGOs, fishermen and American scientists (particularly researchers at the National Marine Fisheries Service) against driftnets led the United States Congress to legislate. In 1987 the Driftnet Impact Monitoring, Assessment and Control Act was passed, limiting the use of driftnets in the American EEZ to those no longer than 1.5 miles (approximately 2.5 km), thus excluding Asian ships using long nets. In 1988, the 1972 law on the protection of marine mammals, the Marine Mammal Protection Act of 1972 (MMPA) was amended. The new drafting required that henceforth tuna-boats, whether using driftnets or purse seine nets, comply with specific standards for the protection of dolphins and submit to monitoring by observers. In the tradition of extra-territorial trade laws, the text likewise authorised the US federal administration to decree an import embargo on all products coming from a third country which did not conform to criteria laid down by the US legislation.

For environmental and wildlife NGOs, the adoption of these legislative measures confirmed the value of pursuing an active campaign in the United States. From 1989, they chose to concentrate on the protection of dolphins, knowing that the fate of an animal fetishised in popular imagery could not fail to affect the American citizen–consumer. Media campaigns accused American tuna canners of selling tuna caught with nets that killed dolphins. Anxious to retain market share, the latter responded to the accusations by sticking 'dolphin safe' labels on their cans. The ecolabel, which was made official in 1990, was reserved for product coming from ships using neither driftnets over 2.5 km long nor purse seines. The following year, the US administration implemented the trading embargo provided for in the MMPA against Mexican tuna fishermen operating in the east Pacific. The latter considered this to be a disguised form of protectionism and asked their government to refer this to GATT. In September 1991, a first panel concluded that the United States was in violation of Mexico's trading rights by imposing production regulations external to it.[30] The GATT condemnation of the United States was upheld by a second panel, in May 1994. But despite these two decisions the American Administration refused to lift the embargo. This political choice was dictated less by the vague attempts at protectionism by American tuna fishers' organisations than by the legitimacy conferred by the image of threatened dolphins within American society.

The NGOs then took their demands to the international level. In the late 1980s, Greenpeace decided to replicate its actions undertaken in the north Pacific in other zones. Its divers revealed that dolphins, as well as whales and sharks, were being caught by driftnets in the Tasmanian Sea.[31] A media campaign stated that 5,000 to 6,000 dolphins were caught each year. Substantiated or not, these figures could not fail to have an impact on Australian and New Zealand society, where environmentalist NGOs in general and Greenpeace in particular[32] had a militant base. In November 1989 in Wellington, the governments of the South Pacific also finalised an agreement restricting driftnets to 2.5 km in the zone. At the same time, the Greenpeace International office decided to move into international organisations. Failing to mobilise the FAO as it had hoped to do, in November 1989 Greenpeace gambled on the United Nations General Assembly (UNGA) by tabling a memorandum there against the use of driftnets on the high seas.[33] Greenpeace's ability to project itself transnationally is evidence of its resources in terms of expertise. It would, however, be vain to consider that the NGO's transnationality led it to dispense with any state intermediaries. On the contrary, transnationality is only effective due to strong governmental support. At the 44th session of UNGA, Greenpeace's demands for the banning of driftnets were in effect echoed by American government representatives who, in agreement with several other national delegations (including Australian, Canadian, Fijian), stressed the dangers of the technique. Conversely, the Japanese delegation, a country in which shipowners are the main users of big driftnets in the Pacific, merely proposed a periodic examination of the effect of driftnets on marine fauna, in addition to cooperation aimed at eliminating a number of particularly negative effects.[34] Adopted on 22 December 1989, resolution 44/225 was inspired more by the first than by the second proposition. It called for imposing moratoria 'on all large-scale pelagic driftnet fishing by 30 June 1992, with the understanding that such a measure will not be imposed on a region or, if implemented, can be lifted, should effective conservation and management measures be taken based upon statistically sound analysis'. Thanks to the translation effort of environmentalist NGOs, this text received international publicity 'that might be the envy of many resolutions adopted in analogous circumstances by the United Nations' General Assembly'.[35] ENGOs presented the resolution as a pure and simple ban on driftnets, while the moratorium targeted only the 'large-scale' nets, without at any point actually defining criteria for them.

The alliance between NGOs, fishermen and Community institutions

This United Nations' General Assembly resolution had immediate institutional consequences for the EU. In February 1990, the commissioner in charge of fisheries, Manuel Marin, proposed that Community ships be banned any fishing activity which involved one or more driftnets of a total length greater than 2.5 km. This measure was exactly in line with that featured in the US legislation and in the convention signed by the South Pacific States. In December 1991, Manuel Marin spoke of defending driftnets as 'fighting a losing battle. Being right or wrong about the effects of French albacore tuna fishing on marine mammals no longer matters [...]. We shall see whether the French representatives will take the political risk of having the finger pointed at them by the global community. As far as I'm concerned, I simply acknowledge that there is now a general feeling in terms of public opinion and I do not want to put the reputation of European fishing at risk over thirty boats which use driftnets'.[36] The European commissioner's position should not be seen simply as a rhetorical formula leading him to defend the interests of fishermen of his native country. It instead reveals his conviction that Community policy will inevitably align with a global norm that constitutes a legitimate cause. This belief in an inescapable global ethic was also expressed in the positions of the European Parliament, which approved the Commission's proposition in September 1991. But the debate became less unanimous when it reached the Council of Fisheries Ministers. Strong opposition was expressed by the French, Irish and British ministers, and also the Italians whose fishermen used large-scale driftnets to catch swordfish in the Mediterranean.

The mechanism of qualified majority, however, enabled the Council of Ministers to approve the Commission's proposition in October 1991, making 2.5 km the maximum permissible driftnet length in the Community, except in the Baltic Sea. At the request of the French delegation who firmly opposed this decision, dispensation was given to albacore ships who had been fishing in the North-East Atlantic during the previous two years to continue to use driftnets no longer than 5 km until 31 December 1993.[37] This new European regulation was a formidable political lever for Greenpeace and animal welfare associations such as Eurogroup for Animal Welfare or Birdlife International, which were committed to a global battle for a complete ban on driftnets. From summer 1990, a Greenpeace ship was present in the Bay of Biscay to observe dolphins caught by European albacore ships. Press releases talked about 'walls of death' and called on the support of militant ecologists in the EU States. Greenpeace could count on an alliance with the Spanish liners and pole-and-line vessels. This Spanish group could appreciate the tactical advantage of espousing the cause of dolphins, although in fact it had no compassion for the fate of these marine mammals. Basque and Galician owner-skippers joined Greenpeace.[38] Local NGOs were created with a view to relay the action undertaken to a global level. This was the case of *Itsas Geroa* ('the future of the sea' in Basque). Created on the French side of the border, this NGO had 300 French and Spanish members in 1998, a majority of which were liners and pole-and-line fishermen from the Spanish province of Guipuzcoa. Although the representativeness of *Itsas Geroa* in the institutional landscape of French and Spanish fishing had always been weak, its alliance with Greenpeace, combined with the defence of 'small' fishermen against 'the potential for a few fleet-owners to get rich',[39] did get it a hearing by the European Commission.

In April 1994, the Commission took a further step which may be considered an illustration of the 'dependency' stressed by some EU institutionalist analyses.[40] Flushing out a position that the passing of time would have made inevitable, commissioner Paleokrassas, who was in charge of both fishing and the environment, called for a total ban on driftnets in all Community waters from 1 July 1998. The European Parliament supported this proposal by a very large majority in September 1994. In a study published some months earlier, IFREMER researchers concluded, however, that driftnets did not significantly reduced dolphin numbers in the north-east Atlantic.[41] It is here that the limitations of any explanatory schema of EU policy-making that systematises the influence of experts on the making of common policies become apparent. Faced with the triangular alliance among environmentalist NGOs, certain Spanish fishermen, the Commission and the European Parliament, the French, Irish and British albacore tuna fishers, as well as their governments, were helpless. As for the professionals targeted, they had to adapt their businesses to the 2.5 km ruling applicable as of 1 January 1994. In Cornwall some shipowners were driven to abandon fishing for albacore, gauging that the maximum size imposed on nets made them no longer profitable.[42] Although the new Community ruling involved a 30 per cent reduction in tonnage in 1994, French enterprises cushioned the fall in yield by making various savings and trying to improve the technical quality of their equipment in collaboration with IFREMER.[43] The violence of the summer of 1994 (see pp. 000) likewise led them to formulate two demands. The first concerned strict control of the use of driftnets (elimination of spare nets on board, introduction of a licensing scheme) in the belief that anticipating the Commission's regulatory methods would be the best way to protect their working tools. In May 1995, special fishing permits administered by the CNPMEM were established in France, strictly limiting the number of ships authorised to fish. The second demand, unsurprisingly, concerned financial aid to help businesses adapt, granted by the French fisheries administration in line with the well-established clientelistic compromise: subsidies for social peace.

For governments, the Community regulation likewise brought about two short-term reactions. The first was to increase the amount of scientific expertise available as a way to postpone the ban. In November 1994, French researchers at IFREMER published a report demonstrating that adopting the 2.5 km norm did not prevent French albacore tuna boats from operating a profitable activity. At MAFF'S request, during the summer of 1995, it was then the turn of British biologists to conduct an observation campaign aboard Cornish tuna-boats, which concluded that there was a degree of dolphin by-catches, without, however, saying it was a danger to the species. Another response from governments was to anticipate the decision to ban by obtaining EU financing for plans to cease activity. This was the choice of the Italian government. In April 1997, the Council of EU Ministers agreed to fund 50 per cent of a national plan to cease activity by 600 swordfish fishermen in the Mezzogiorno whose fisheries had seen their profitability seriously compromised by the adoption of the 2.5 km regulation. From 1994 to 1997, the proposal for a complete ban on driftnets was a recurrent feature of every Council of Fisheries Ministers, without any decision being taken. The cumulative votes of France, Ireland, Great Britain and Italy, to which were added those of Denmark, then Sweden and Finland, keen to see a specific treatment for the salmon and sea trout fisheries in the Baltic Sea, constituting a minority blockage with delaying effects. Moreover, over the course of 1995 and 1996, since the French held the Council presidency, Italian and Irish did not encourage activation of the dossier. This proves that presidency of the EU Council, which is on a six-month rotation, offers governments and administrations leeway with respect to Community negotiations that should not be underestimated.[44]

The European Union votes for the ban: the local level in action

The election of the Blair government, in May 1997, relaunched the debate on driftnets within the EU Council. Bearing in mind the British presidency of the first six months of 1998, the minister for Agriculture, Jack Cunningham, and his deputy for Fishing, Eliott Morley, announced their intention to get them banned. They were thereby manifesting support for the demands of British environmental and wildlife defence organisations, such as the Royal Society for the Prevention of Cruelty to Animals and the Royal Society for the Protection of Birds (which had a million members in 1999), which were Labour Party supporters.[45] This was a significant difference from the case of the Cornish fishermen who had never constituted a significant electoral base for the Labour Party.

In March 1998, a qualified majority developed within the Fishing Council with regards to the ban tabled by the British presidency. The exclusion of the Baltic Sea from the scope of the ban, despite scientific studies demonstrating by-catches of seals and seabirds by nets of up to 21 km long, was a purely political measure aimed at winning over the northern states to form a qualified majority within the Council. Some NGOs were prompt to support this exclusion, with tactics prevailing over ecological beliefs. The position of the association Birdlife International is highly revealing in this respect. An internal report stressed, in June 1998, that the NGO accepted the exclusion of the Baltic as a pragmatic approach that was essential to ensure the support of riparian states of this sea in favour of the ban. As a result, only the constraints of Community negotiation mattered. The Council of Fisheries Ministers finally passed the ban on driftnets on 8 June 1998.[46] This was a precedent in the history of the CFP, since it was the first time that the EU had banned the use of a particular fishing technique. Applicable from 1 January 2002, the measure was accompanied by a declaration from the Commission and the Council calling for the adoption of a plan to subsidise the reconversion of fishing fleets. Only the French and Irish governments voted against, the Italian delegation having chosen to abstain despite the solidarity shown by Italian professional associations towards their French, Irish and British counterparts. The result of a decision which went as high up as the Council's president, Romano Prodi, the Italian abstention was not unrelated to the United States' threat of embargo on Italian swordfish exports since 1996. It also attests to the political choice, some days after Italy qualified for the euro, not to compromise the European image of the government on an issue considered less important.

The decision to ban cannot be understood without returning to the position in which the local groups of fishermen concerned found themselves, from November 1997 to June 1998, faced with the global ecological norm in the specific EU context. In the Spanish Basque Country and Galicia, right from the outset the surface line and pole-and-line fishermen mobilised on a transnational political scale. The example of Basque fishermen from Guipuzcoa, led by their leader Estebán Olaizola Elizazu, is particularly interesting. Sometimes marginalised within organisations of Spanish fishermen for their attachment to traditional fishing techniques and by the Spanish government for their support to the Basque cause, these fishermen took their action beyond the Spanish borders from the start. Enlisting the help of Greenpeace, they sent petitions and moratoria to the DG Fish commissioner Bonino and the European Parliament in which they hammered home three points: the selective character of fishing with surface lines and with pole and line; the threat that driftnets posed to the employment of Spanish Basque sailors; the disproportionate enrichment of tuna shipowners using driftnets.[47] Added to these arguments was the threat that, in the absence of a total ban on driftnets, Galician fishermen would proceed to start using them. The transnational alliance with Greenpeace was turned to their advantage and exploited. At the initiative of the Basque NGO *Itsas Geroa* in April 1998, the ship *MV Greenpeace* sailed to several French and Spanish ports located between Galicia and Bordeaux to increase awareness of the ban on driftnets amongst small-scale local fishermen, environmental protection associations and, more generally, the public at large. In the French Basque Country, the port communities scarcely mobilised for the arrival of Greenpeace.[48] The Commission and the European Parliament were no less sensitive to the actions undertaken. Within commissioner Bonino's cabinet, *Itsas Geroa*'s petitions, preceding the decision of 8 June 1998, were considered as coming from 'communities of fishermen who are fighting to preserve responsible fishing and which have the close support of Greenpeace whose activists have mobilised across the whole of Europe'.[49] This incident displays a number of the specificities of interest representation within the EU. Deprived of direct relationship with the territories, the Commission's commissioners and officials tended to evaluate the legitimacy of their interlocutors by giving credit to those who were able to get their message across. Social actors with little legitimacy at local level thus have the potential to maximise the effectiveness of their protests by taking them to the Commission. The Spanish Basque fishermen learned this lesson well.

The French fishermen, on the other hand, limited representation of their interests to the national arena. On Yeu Island, for example, the local fisheries committee and local shipowners set out to defend driftnets as a priority within the CNPMEM, to the French Ministers for Agriculture and Fish, as well as to locally elected officials of the regional council of the Pays de la Loire, the National Assembly and the European Parliament. The pursuit of alliances with environmentalist NGOs who did not concur with Greenpeace's diagnosis on dolphin catches, likewise remained confined to the national context. Does the centralised state model of France explain why the Yeu Island fishermen should experience such problems in projecting their interests in the resolutely polycentric space that is the EU, unlike the Spanish Basque fishermen, used to a distribution of power between the central state and the autonomous communities? It is tempting, but hazardous, to reply in the affirmative since to do so would amount to confining the practices of social actors to political cultures conceived of as fixed collective heritages. This would underestimate the aptitude of individual actors to make changes in their practices through a political learning process. The debate on banning driftnets certainly went along with a reappraisal among French fishermen, albeit clearly too late to be effective, of representation practices which had hitherto remained exclusively national. In early 1998, the Yeu Island local committee began to consider the necessity of transnationalising mobilisation against the ban on driftnets, and took an initial step in that direction by meeting with the Italian swordfish fishermen who had accepted a plan of voluntary retraining. This initiative with the Italians netters shows the extent to which the emergence of a European scene of interest representation can be a factor in destabilising national guild-like institutions.[50] It was in effect by trading contacts between their supplier of nets and an equivalent Italian company, and not through the national administration or any professional organisations, that the Yeu Island fishermen organised a meeting in Sicily in February 1998. Likewise, the costs of the trip were not financed by the CNPMEM but by their own producers' organisation which sent, in addition to five representatives from Yeu Island, two other members who were joined by the French net manufacturer initiating the contact and a member of the CNPMEM.[51] This latter body, logically enough, did its utmost, in accordance with the French fisheries administration, to channel this transnational grassroots activism in order not to jeopardise the national corporatist model. At the end of the first Franco-Italian meeting, the CNPMEM in effect retook the initiative for the exchange with the Irish and British fishermen's organisations, with a view to discussing the creation of a European coordination to defend driftnets. Similarly, in March 1998, the CNPMEM president led a delegation of the European coordination to see the European Parliament's fishing commission. One can gauge here the difficult position in which the EU put representatives of the CNPMEM, the French fisheries administration and the Minister of Agriculture and Fishing office confronting a base that feels threatened. While orchestrating the campaign against the ban on driftnets, the former had to explain to the fishermen concerned the legitimacy of the global environmental norm, and also the nature of Community negotiation (such as majority voting), leaving the Community little hope of circumventing the obstacle. In advancing such arguments, they admitted to the very people who had mandated them at national level the limitations of their action and their legitimacy. The exercise of representation, the essential machinery of democracies, was clearly destabilised. This did not necessarily mean that French fishermen lost all confidence in a state that they still needed. They in effect continued to address the latter to negotiate the repercussions of the driftnet ban. The implementation of assistance for retraining, approved by the EU Council in October 1998, was thus negotiated with the French fisheries administration and the CNPMEM. Similarly, it was the state – via IFREMER – that the Yeu Island fishermen addressed to try out new fishing techniques that could replace driftnets as of 2002. The French fishermen's learning experience with Europe lay more in their aptitude to circumvent the limits that the state sometimes set on its own negotiating capacity by taking the transnational route. In September 1998, twenty-two shipowners from Yeu Island thus lodged an appeal with the EU Court of First Instance aimed at repealing the Council of Ministers' decision affecting them, after the French Minister of Agriculture had mentioned the futility of such a step on the part of the government. The appeal decision, which was judged nonadmissible by the Court in February 2000, came under the rational defence of interests. Knowing that the Community legal system had sometimes allowed fishermen (such as the quota hoppers) to protect their rights in the face of the States, Yeu Island's tuna fishers tried one last time to get a decision they considered unjust repealed through a channel that has become transnational.

This chapter is not about assessing whether the EU's ban on driftnets was the right response to the ecological necessity to protect dolphins. It is more of a reflection on how the protection of dolphins, as a legitimate global norm, came to bear on a conflict between European tuna fishermen that had origins linked to other causes. It also aimed to demystify the idea that a global norm would always be experienced in the territories as a constraint that would jeopardise the identity of actors. On the contrary, for the Basque and Galician fishermen using longlines and pole-and-line, the environmental norm represented an excellent means of defending economic and social interests. For other fishermen, in particular the Yeu Island netters in France, it was indeed experienced as an unjust effect of globalisation in the face of which their state declared itself powerless. The lesson that these social actors learned – that the future of their territory and their economy was henceforth more dependent on respecting global standards than on intergovernmental negotiation – was fundamental. In the specific

EU institutional context, the process that led to the ban on driftnets also reveals the destabilisation and the evolution of interest representation practices. The transnationalisation of these practices, materialised through the alliance of Spanish fishermen with the NGOs, the Commission and the European Parliament, does not mean the end of states and intergovernmental rationales. It is more indicative of the emergence of a political game which operates at multiple territorial levels (the EU, the state, the local level), the main contradiction being that if the exercise of interest representation is transnationalised, that of political representation remains, to a great extent, confined to the framework of states.

Notes

1 See for example R. Robertson, *Globalization: Social Theory and Global Culture*, London, Sage, 1992; Malcom Waters (ed.), *Globalization: Key Ideas*, London, Routledge, 1995; Olivier Dollfus, *La globalisation*, Paris, Presses de Sciences Po, 1997.

2 Susan Strange, *The Retreat of the State: The Diffusion of Power in World Economy*, Cambridge, Cambridge University Press, 1996.

3 R. Robertson, 'Glocalization: Time–Space and Homogeneity–Heterogeneity', in M. Featherstone, S. Lash and R. Robertson (eds), *Global Modernities*, London, Sage, 1995, pp. 1–24.

4 Bertrand Badie, *Un monde sans souveraineté. Les États entre ruse et responsabilité*, Paris, Fayard, 1999.

5 Jean-Pierre Beurier, 'Le droit international des pêches maritimes', *Droits maritimes*, vol. III, Lyon, Éditions Juris, 1998, pp. 17–18.

6 Badie, *'Une monde sans souveraineté.*

7 Elizabeth Bomberg, *Green Parties and Politics in the European Union*, London, Routledge, 1998; Susan Baker, Maria Kousis, Dick Richardson and Stephen Young (eds), *The Politics of Sustainable Development: Theory, Policy and Practice within the European Union*, London, Routledge, 1997.

8 Philippe Lequenne, *Dans les coulisses de Greenpeace*, Paris, L'Harmattan, 1997, p. 160.

9 Laura Cram, *Policy-Making in the European Union: Conceptual Lenses and the Integration Process*, London, Routledge, 1997.

10 Bomberg, *Green Parties*.

11 Sonia Mazey and Jeremy Richardson (eds), *Lobbying in the European Community*, Oxford, Oxford University Press, 1993.

12 Jean-Pierre Reveret, Jacques Weber, 'L'évolution de régimes internationaux de gestion pêche', in Olivier Godard (ed.), *Le principe de précaution dans la conduite d'affaires humaines*, Paris, MSH-INRA, 1997.

13 Marine Stewardship Council, *Principles and Criteria for Sustainable Fishing*, London, 1997.

14 Eva Eiderström, 'Ecolabels in EU Environmental Policy', Florence, *EUI Working Paper* 98/20, 1998. For a critical viewpoint, see Jonette N. Braathen, 'La mise en place de l'écolabellisation dans le secteur de la pêche. Les enjeux', *El Anzuelo*, 2, 1998.

15 Loïc Antoine, 'Quand la controverse tourne à l'impasse: la guerre du thon', *Natures-sciences-sociétés*, 3 (1), 1995, p. 8. I draw on this key article to summarise the causes of the conflict as well as on Michel Goujon, 'Captures accidentelles du filet maillant dérivant et dynamique de populations de dauphins au large du Baie de Biscay', *Les publications du laboratoire d'halieutique*, 15, ENSAR, Rennes, May 1996.

16 Michel Josié, Geneviève Ladouès, *Patron pêcheur*, Paris, Payot, coll. 'Récits de vie', 1997.

17 Antoine, 'Quand la controverse tourne'.

18 *Ibid.*, p. 9.

19 Interview with Mike Williams, Newlyn, 6 July 1998.

20 See M. Findlay and A.E. Searle, 'The North East Atlantic Albacore Fishery: A Cornish Crisis of Confidence', *Marine Policy*, 22 (2), pp. 95–108.

21 Andy Smith, 'L'espace publique européen: une vue trop aerienne', *Critique internationale*, 2, 1999, pp. 169–180.

22 Interview with Estebán Olaizola Elizazu in Hondarribia, 15 July 1998.

23 Antoine, 'Quand la controverse tourne', p. 13.

24 Quartier maritime de l'île de Yeu, *Monographie pêches maritimes 1997*, 1998.

25 Interviews with Bruno Girard and Bernard Groisard, shipowners on Yeu Island, 18 February 1998.

26 See Yves Meny, Pierre Muller and Jean-Louis Quermonne (eds), *Politiques publiques en Europe*, Paris, L'Harmattan, 1995.

27 Grant J. Hewison, 'The Role of Environmental Nongovernmental Organizations in Ocean Governance', *Ocean Yearbook*, vol. 12, 1996, pp. 32–51.

28 Lequenne, *Dans les coulisses,* p. 188.

29 Antoine, 'Quand la controverse tourne', p. 14.

30 Damien Gerardin, 'Trade and Environmental Protection in the Context of World Trade Rules: A View from the European Union', *European Foreign Affairs Review*, 2, 1997, pp. 33–61.

31 Greenpeace France, *Filets dérivants européens: bientôt l'interdiction*, type-script, 1998, pp. 1–2.

32 Lequenne, *Dans les coulisses*.

33 Michel Savini, 'La réglementation de la pêche en haute mer par l'Assemblée de Nations Unies (À propos de la resolution 44/125 sur les grands filets maillants dérivants)', *Annuaire français de droit international*, 1990, p. 780.

34 For more details, see Savini, 'La réglementation de la pêche'.

35 Savini, 'La réglementation de la pêche', p. 810.

36 Interview given to *France-Éco-Pêche*, September 1991, pp. 9–10.

37 Council regulation 345/92 of 27 January 1992, *OJEC*, L 42, 18 February 1992.

38 Interview with Estebán Olaizola Elizazu, Hondarribia, 15 July 1998.

39 Phrase taken from a letter sent by 'Itsas Geroa' to Commissioner Bonino 29 May 1998; source: interview with Robert Alvarez, Hendaye, 15 July 1998.

40 Paul Pierson, 'The Path to European Integration: A Historical Institutional Analysis', *Comparative Political Studies*, 29, 2 April 1996.

41 Michel Goujon *et al.*, *Approche de l'impact écologique de la pêcherie thonière au filet maillant dérivant en Atlantique du Nord-Est*, internal report by the Direction de Resources Vivantes, Brest, IFREMER, 1993.

42 Findley and Searle, 'North East Atlantic Albacore Fishery'.

43 Interview with Sebastien Chauvet, Yeu Island, 18 February 1998.

44 Emil Kirchner, *Decision-Making in the European Community: The Council Presidency and European Integration*, Manchester, Manchester University Press, 1992.

45 See *Memorandum on Animal Welfare to the United Kingdom of the Council of the European Union*, presented in November 1997 by the RSPCA, as the 'Eurogroup for Animal Welfare', of which it is an active member.

46 Council Regulation 1239/98 EC, 8 June 1998, *OJEC*, L 171, 17 June 1998.

47 Robert Alvarez, president of *Itsas Geroa*, sent me some copies of petitions addressed to Commissioner Bonino.

48 Jose Arocena, 'Greenpeace accueilli fraîchement à Saint-Jean-de-Luz', *Le Marin*, 24 April 1998.

49 Interview with Christian Rambaud, Brussels, 3 June 1998.

50 See Muller 'Introduction', in Muller *et al. Politiques publiques*.

51 Interviews with Sebastien Chauvet, Bruno Girard and Bernard Groisard, Yeu Island, 18 February 1998.

7

The European Union as an international actor

The EU's capacity to act on the international scene is not solely confined to common foreign and security policy. As has been pointed out by writers interested in the formulation of European external policy, the EC[1] was initially conceived as a 'civil power' able to negotiate with other international actors through diplomatic, economic and legal channels.[2] Since the 1970s, fishing is a sector for which the EC has been resourced by the states to negotiate the interests of European professions externally. Driven by a Commission seeking legitimacy, the communitarisation of the relationship with third countries was facilitated by the fact that the fisheries resource was a global environmental issue, that the international law of the sea called for a strengthening of Community interests in the face of the triumph of riparian rights, and that the supply of raw materials to European processing industries was largely dependent on trade with non-member countries. This chapter examines how an external EU policy in the fishing sector was formed, by examining the relations of autonomy and dependence of the Commission, the formal interlocutor of non-member countries, dealing with member states who were highly sensitive to professional interests. The conditions of emergence of the EU as an actor in the international arena are studied in terms of the three following areas: trade policy, fishing agreements with non-member countries and EU participation in regional fishing organisations (RFOs).

External trade policy: between openness and protectionism

The EU countries' trade deficit in fishing products is a longstanding and recurrent phenomenon. Arising from the European processing industry's strong demand for raw materials in the aftermath of the Second World War, this deficit doubled between 1989 and 1997. It was accompanied by a trade policy with respect to non-member countries which had always been more liberal than that governing trade in agricultural products within the framework of the CAP.

The dismantling of tax barriers

The common customs tariff (CCT) applicable to fishing products had been consolidated almost in its entirety at GATT during the Dillon Round negotiations in 1960–61. The reasons for this early consolidation were both political and economic. First of all, fishing products were used as bargaining chips by national administrations and Commission officials to refuse to consolidate, indeed to deconsolidate, agricultural products whose protection from external competition had always been *the* sensitive political issue. Moreover, from the 1950s onwards, the European processing and trading industries had had massive recourse to imports from non-member countries to compensate for the insufficient supply of fishing products from the common market (see Chapter 1). Grouped from 1958 within the Association of EU Fish Industries (AIPCEE-CEP), the major processing corporations such as Unilever, Pescanova and Trinity had always ensured that the EU tariff arrangement was as close as possible to GATT rules over the course of the various negotiating rounds (Kennedy Round in 1964–67, Tokyo Round in 1973–77, and Uruguay Round in 1986–93). Thus the quantitative restrictions on imports and measures having equivalent effect were largely absent from the CFP. Similarly, the range of protection instruments, allowing for a guaranteed preference for Community products over products from non-member countries, was in no way comparable in scale to that of the CAP.

Two-thirds of Community fishing product imports are, moreover, exempt from CCT either through trading agreements made by the EC with non-member countries or groups of non-member countries, or contractual or unilateral development aid measures. As far as trade agreements are concerned, in May 1992 the EC concluded an agreement with Norway, Iceland and Liechtenstein,[3] creating the EEA. The EEA extended the rules of the EU internal market to those three countries. For fishing products, which made up a substantial share of Norway and Iceland's export revenue, the EEA agreement provided for admissions of product on the common market at zero duty or at reduced duty. Although, in exchange, the Norwegian and Icelandic governments accepted a total suppression of customs duty and charges having equivalent effect on fisheries products coming from the EU, their higher level of exports clearly made them major beneficiaries of this agreement. In terms of development aid measures, the Lomé conventions, which since 1975 had regulated trade between the EU and 71 countries in the African, Caribbean and Pacific zone (ACP), likewise, Lomé convention II, signed in 1979, provided for access of ACP fishing products (raw and processed) to the EU that was completely exempt from customs duties, benefiting from the rule of origin.[4] The new EU–ACP partnership agreement signed on 23 June 2000 maintained this arrangement for access to the common market while requiring, in accordance with WTO's liberal philosophy, the gradual establishment of reciprocity on ACP markets. Exports of fish and shellfish from ACP countries to the EU benefited from an average growth rate of 17 per cent between 1976 and 1992, whilst the ACP share of total European imports tended, on the contrary, to decline.[5] Shrimp exports, for example, grew sharply through sales from Senegal, Mauritania and the Ivory Coast. But the Lomé conventions are of substantial benefit to EU industries based in the ACP countries. Canned tropical tuna from the Ivory Coast, Senegal and Madagascar is thus counted as ACP product exempt from customs duty on the common market. In fact, these products are produced by the big European canning groups, who are also the owners of industrial ship-owning businesses operating within the framework of agreements made by the EU (see pp. 000). The best example here is that of the Saupiquet company, based on the Ivory Coast. This concerned a development aid measure, unilateral this time, the generalised system of preferences (GSP) which was agreed in 1968 by UNCTAD (United Nations Conference on Trade and Development) and applies either to types of products, or to states (the least developed countries, drug GSP, Central America GSP). It likewise favoured the entry of marine products into the EU at very low, indeed nil, customs tax rates. The GSP sometimes gave rise to deflections of trade which were vociferously attacked by shipowners and European processors. Over the course of the 1990s, ships sailing under Asian national flags had thus taken to landing tuna in Latin American countries benefiting from the 'drug GSP' (Columbia, Ecuador), which was then re-exported with the indication of country of origin without customs duty to the EU.[6] The inspection services of the Commission and member states were all the more set on curbing these fraudulent practices as the governments of ACP countries saw them as a direct threat to what had been achieved with the Lomé convention.[7]

Whatever the EU's effort to dismantle tax barriers in the fishing domain, the economic actors and governments of non-member countries still do not perceive the CFP as being in complete accord with the rules of Word Trade Organisation (WTO). The public subsidies granted by the EU and its member states to fishermen are regularly denounced in the United States, Australia, Iceland and New Zealand as infringements of the principles of free trade. At the WTO meeting held in Seattle in November 1999, twenty-five countries suggested including a proposal to ban all public aid to the fishing sector in the final declaration project. Clearly aimed at the EU, this proposition received support from environmental NGOs, including Greenpeace and the WWF, who considered Community aid as an indirect inducement to overfishing.

Within the EU itself, external trade policy is the object of a constant pendulum swing between, on the one hand, actors demanding more border protection and, on the other, those insisting on the necessity to guarantee cheap imports for the processing industry. This debate is not a straightforward conflict between would-be protectionist countries and would-be free-traders. With the exception of Germany, which has a weak productive sector but powerful fish-processing industries, the main producer countries of marine products (Denmark, Spain, the United Kingdom, France, Italy and the Netherlands) are also the main processors and importers of third-country products. Thus, the divide between the demand for openness and the demand for greater protection is more inter-sectoral than interstate, as was shown by the consultation on reform of the CFP that the European Commission carried out in 1998. While the national organisations of shipowners and fishermen from countries such as Belgium, France, Spain, Ireland, Portugal and the United Kingdom crit-icised exemptions and reductions in customs duties, the business sector in these same countries was unanimously opposed to any additional protec-tive measures and called for more free trade.[8] That is why national ministers and fisheries administrations may perceive delegation of respon-sibilities in trading matters to the Commission as an advantage, since it concerns a dimension of the CFP in which, par excellence, interests of the various actors in the industry diverge within each state.

The producers/processors compromise
In terms of external trade policy, the Fisheries Directorate's approach has never been characterised by the categorical defence of either a total opening or a strict closing of borders. The DG-Fisheries has, on the contrary, always sought a form of tempered liberalism, which aims to reconcile both the interests of national associations of fishermen, and those of the processing industries grouped within the AIPCEE. This tempered liberalism was also the result of necessary bureaucratic compromises that the DG Fish must make within the Commission with, on the one hand, the Trade DG, which is very keen on respecting WTO rules and, on the other, the Development DG which is anxious to perpet-uate some of the dispensations applied to southern countries. The compromise is highly visible in the provisions of the new rule on the Common Organisation of the Market passed by the Council of Fisheries Ministers in December 1999 (see Chapter 4), which provided for both autonomous measures to dismantle tax barriers in accordance with the 'needs of the processing industry' and safeguard measures aimed at preventing disturbances in the functioning of the common market. As far as the first aspect is concerned, it is accepted that the fisheries ministers can fix autonomous tariff quotas and decide on total or partial suspen-sions of customs duties for some import products that are necessary to the processing industry. The Council of Fisheries Ministers of December 1999, for example, adopted autonomous suspensions of customs duties for the year 2000, applied to fifteen products particularly

prized by European processors, such as Pacific salmon. But establishing such a list was neither automatic nor consensual. It was the result of an intergovernmental negotiation that reflected opposing interests between processors and shipowners. For instance, in December 1999, the Italian agro-foodstuffs group Trinity Alimentari wanted tuna loins, imported at low prices from Central America, to benefit from a suspension of customs duties on entry to the EU. Faced with the mobilisation of its tuna-boats shipowners, the Spanish government strongly opposed this within the Council of Fisheries Ministers. The Spanish tuna fishermen had the willing support of French tuna fishermen who saw a risk of eventual exemption of tinned tuna from non-member countries in the suspension of customs duties on tuna loins. At the same time, the (French) National Union of Freezer-Tuna-Boat Owners (SNATC) was obliged to maintain a certain reserve on this matter, since 98 per cent of the capital of one of its main members, Saupiquet, was about to come under the control of the Italian company Trinity in January 2000. This shows the effects of the internationalisation of processing businesses' capital on the national rationales of interest representation. As far as the protective aspect is concerned, any serious disturbance possibly affecting the functioning of the common market might lead European fisheries ministers to suspend the autonomous tariff quotas, indeed to initiate safeguard measures. The application of this latter mechanism remains, however, highly unusual, since it obliges the Commission to conduct surveys and consult the contracting parties to the WTO. It is also not surprising that limited use of safeguard measures should, in the main producer countries that are Spain, France or the United Kingdom, be the object of criticism and some-times sharp protests by organisations of shipowners and fishermen. Justified by the facts or not, one of the fundamental demands of fishermen from south Brittany who in 1993–1994 formed the Comité de Survie, was an immediate halt to imports coming from third countries, particularly from Russia. The link between the exchange rate crisis their auctions were undergoing and the perception of a porosity of EU external borders appeared all the more to Breton fishermen to be the cause of their prob-lems since the Commission had refused to trigger safeguard measures, arguing that not all European markets were affected. But the EU's protec-tive trade measures may, conversely, enjoy strong legitimacy with fishermen, when they help to put a stop to unfair practices such as dumping. In April 1998, the Scottish and Irish salmon producers gave a very positive response to the Council of Ministers' decision to make defin-itive the Commission's anti-dumping measures against Norwegian exporters of farmed Atlantic salmon, who had violated a commitment to the minimum sale price of their product, an agreement made directly with the EU in 1997.

In the fishing sector, the EU's external trade policy thus has given rise to contrasting evaluations depending on the actors and the interests at stake. It is a model of compromise between acceptance of thoroughgoing liberalisation of exchange and a regulation of trade flows by a political authority, once the economic actors believe they are no longer enjoying fair competition conditions with respect to the rest of the world.

Negotiating access to the resource in third countries: the fishing agreements

Just as with trade, access to the resource raises the issue of the relationship between the EU and the rest of the world. In 2000, around 35 per cent of the world's ocean surfaces were made subject to the jurisdiction of states in application of rules of international law of the sea. Numerous zones, which had been freely exploitable by European fishermen up until the 1970s, were progressively removed from their free access. Since EU countries had lost their formal capacity to conclude agreements with third countries in application of Community law, fishing provided a test of the EU's capacity to represent collectively the interests of an economic sector on the international scene.[9]

The institutional diversity of agreements

The EU has developed its own diplomacy in the fishing sector since the Hague resolution of November 1976. For the Irish diplomat Eamonn Gallagher, the first Fisheries director-general at the Commission, as for his deputy Raymond Simonnet, the revitalisation of this external action began with the political realisation that any successful autonomisation of the CFP in relation to national policies called for the constitution of common arrangements with respect to third countries.[10] It was thus that responsibility fell to the Commission to conduct exploratory talks and negotiate fishing agreements with third countries on the basis of directives previously defined by the Council of Fisheries Ministers. The commissioner in charge of fishing is the political authority that represents the fifteen EU countries to third countries. Franz Fischler made several trips to Rabat between November 1999 and May 2000 to discuss with the Prime Minister and the Fisheries Minister the possible follow-up to the EU–Morocco fishing agreement, which was due to expire. A team of civil servants within the DG-Fisheries whom their colleagues nicknamed 'the diplomats' seconded the commissioner.[11] As representatives to administrations from non-member countries, these civil servants sometimes had intermediaries, in the form of a fisheries adviser, in the Commission's delegations established in non-member countries, as was the case with Morocco.[12] This European diplomacy in the fishing sector was established with the empiricism that characterises institutional creation within the EU. As a result, a discrepancy sometimes arises between the EU's declared ambitions in terms of fishing agreements and the quite finite resources at the DG-Fisheries' disposal. This discrepancy is often viewed negatively by the sector's economic actors.

As with other segments of the CFP, the European Parliament is simply consulted by the Council of Ministers in negotiations pertaining to fishing agreements, which are generally concluded on the basis of Articles 37 (ex-43) and 300 (ex-228) of the EU Treaty. For some agreements, such as those negotiated with Greenland, Mauritania and Morocco, the European Parliament, however, demanded to give an advisory opinion in line with the Council's decision, arguing this was required by Article 300, if it had significant budget implications for the EU.[13] Although this demand received the Council's assent for the fishing agreement with Morocco, it was rejected in all the other cases. When the European Parliament referred the 1996 agreement with Mauritania to it, the CJEC confirmed the legitimacy of the Council's restrictive attitude, judging that the financial compensation at stake was too low in relation to the total amount of funding allocated by the Community budget to the EU's external policy.[14] The European Parliament's fishing commission did not of course abandon its demand for a generalised consent procedure.[15]

At the end of 1985, the EU had signed no less than fourteen agreements with non-member states as varied as Canada, Guinea-Bissau, the Seychelles and Finland. The joining of Spain and Portugal on 1 January, 1986 marked a new stage in the development of Community fishing agreements. The shipowning businesses of these two countries were in effect used to operating in the waters of non-member countries thanks to a varied range of bilateral agreements. The latter had been brought within the scope of the Community either when they expired, or through integration into existing Community agreements. The EU thus integrated the bilateral fishing agreements made between the Spanish government and Morocco since 1977, but also those made with Mauritania, Angola and Mozambique. The same process was repeated in 1995 when Finland and Sweden joined, both of whom had likewise concluded numerous bilateral fishing agreements with their neighbours such as Estonia, Latvia, Lithuania and the Russian Federation.[16]

In 2000, twenty-five Community agreements were in force. With the exception of one Latin American country, Argentina, they concerned either non-member countries in northern Europe, or African and Indian Ocean States party to the Lomé convention. What are known as the 'Northern fishing agreements', concluded by the EU with non-member countries, were based, with the exception of Greenland, on a straightforward reciprocity of access to the resource in exchange for access to the resource. This was the case with agreements with Norway, the Faroe Islands, Iceland, Estonia, Latvia, Lithuania, Poland and Russia.[17] The agreements with the ACP countries, called the 'Southern agreements', almost always provided for financial compensation from the EU budget in exchange for access to the resource by Community ships. Some were restricted to the catching of tropical tuna alone (Gabon, Comores, Equatorial Guinea, Madagascar, São Tome and Príncipe, the Seychelles, Cape Verde, Ivory Coast and Mauritius). The others, called 'mixed agreements', dealt with the fishing of various species (Angola, Gambia, Guinea-Bissau, Guinea-Conakry, Mauritania, Mozambique, Senegal). The agreement with Argentina finally provided for access by Community ships to Argentine waters, in return for the creation of joint Euro-Argentine companies supported from the EU budget.

The interplay of interests within the European Union

Catch value and employment are indicators which make it easy to understand that the Community policy of fishing agreements does not represent the same interest for all shipowners and all EU national administrations. The agreements with the southern countries (ACP, Argentine and Morocco before it expired in November 1999) concerned, primarily, the Spanish shipowners for whom they provided 20 per cent of the annual value of catches in 1999.[18] Next to benefit from these southern agreements were the Portuguese, French and Dutch shipowners and, more marginally, the Italians and Greeks. If one takes into account annual catch averages, conversely, the agreements with the northern countries mainly concerned the interests of Danish, German and British shipowners.[19]

The economic impact of fishing agreements was felt in some local territories. In terms of added value and jobs, the island of Bornholm in Denmark and several Scottish ports in the region of Aberdeen are highly dependent on agreements made by the EU with Norway, the Faroe Islands, Greenland and Iceland. In the case of the Scottish ports, dependence was linked not only to the catches made by the port's ships in non-member countries' waters, but also to the landings of Norwegian or Icelandic ships operating in British waters in accordance with the reciprocity of access. The economic dependence of some Spanish and Portuguese ports on southern agreements is still more marked. This situation explains the problems experienced by Malaga and Barbate in Andalusia, Las Palmas in the Canaries, Vigo in Galicia, and Sesimbra and Olhão in Portugal, after the Moroccan government decided, in November 1999, not to renew the fishing agreement with the EU, which was due to expire. In the industrial and small-scale sectors, 415 Spanish ships, employing no less than 4,300 sailors, found themselves stuck in port. The non-renewal of the EU–Morocco agreement, which also affected between 20,000 and 25,000 related jobs onshore, posed a serious social problem in the Andalusian and Canary ports. In Andalusia, reconverting former sardine-fishing ships for other fishing grounds was not really feasible. Similarly, it seemed difficult to envisage onshore employment for sailors in that southern part of Spain where unemployment levels were much higher than the national average. It was no coincidence that it was in Barbate, in Andalusia, that in spring 2000 social movements of sailors called upon the EU to take a firmer line with the Moroccan government.[20] And this was despite an indemnity policy for shipowners and sailors financed from EU budgets and the Spanish state.

An illustration of the territorial dimension of fishing, the agreements bring us back to the representation of local and/or sectoral interests in the formulation of a segment of the CFP whose negotiation had been largely delegated to the Commission. They confirm the finding that the representation of these interests in the Community space continues to proceed mainly through national governments. With the exception of a limited number of industrial ships from Boulogne, Saint-Malo, Dieppe and Fécamp, on which the northern agreements conferred fishing rights (in particular in Norwegian waters), French interests that are the most dependent on EU contractual policy are those of freezer tuna-boat owners with their headquarters in the Breton port of Concarneau such as Saupiquet, the Compagnie bretonne de cargos frigorifiques (COBRECAF) and France-Thon.[21] The local foothold of these shipowning businesses should be put in perspective in that the origin of their capital is mainly international. Furthermore, the thirty big seine vessels belonging to these tuna-fishing concerns do not land their catches in Concarneau but directly on the Ivory Coast, or the Seychelles and Madagascar where the canneries are established. Tropical tuna fishing continues to be a component of Concarneau port identity. Twenty-five out of thirty-six ships run by the tuna-shipowners in early 2000 were registered in Concarneau,[22] the French sailors working aboard them are often from the Concarneau region, and the Concarneau shipyards specialised in building new vessels, such as the ship *Torrey Gullia* delivered in 1997 by the Piriou shipyard to the COBRECAF shipowners. Concarneau is also where the National Union of Freezer-Tuna-Boat Owners (SNATC) is based, which represents the interests of French companies to the French administration of fisheries, the European Commission, and regional fishing organisations such as the International Commission for the Conservation of Atlantic Tuna (ICCAT). Maintaining an active EU contractual policy with respect to ACP countries is essential for SNATC, partly because politically it provides a sense of security in terms of its members' access to the resource by linking fishing to development aid, and partly because it externalises most of the costs of access to the EU budget. The SNATC in effect prefers the tuna agreements financed by the EU to private agreements based solely on the purchase of licences by the shipowners, in line with the policy imposed by Ghana and the Sierra Leone governments. SNATC's interest is thus for the Commission to embark on as many exploratory talks as possible with the riparian African countries of the Atlantic (Ghana, Togo,

Sierra Leone), and even with some Pacific states (Kirabati, Papua New Guinea) and Latin America, with a view to concluding new tuna agreements.[23] The interests of Concarneau tunashipowners are represented to the EU by the Union of French Fishing Shipowners (UAPF),[24] by the CNPMEM, which included a commission on tropical tuna whose president was the CEO of a Concarneau shipowning business, and by the French administration of fisheries. This is clearly a matter of a state mode of interest representation that has proven efficacious for at least two reasons. First, SNATC is an organisation capable of generating its own expertise assisting the French administration of fisheries to respond to the Commission. Secondly, large-scale tropical tuna fishing is practised not only in France, but also in Spain and other EU countries, and for the Commission legitimated demands to formulate a European policy towards non-member countries.

This latter element marks a major difference with the position of Spanish industrial ship-owning businesses specialising in fishing cephalopods. Until 30 November 1999, their ships benefited fully from the EU–Morocco agreement. Operating from the Canaries port of Las Palmas, near Moroccan waters, the Spanish cephalopod-fishing vessels – often owned by Galician capital and employing Galician crews – caught, between 1995 and 1999, some 150,000 tonnes of cephalopods in Moroccan waters which were sold for the most part on the European and Asian (especially Japanese) markets. The Spanish owners of cephalopod vessels had been organised, since 1976, within the National Association of Cephalopod Freezers (ANACEF) established in Las Palmas. Although this association of industrial shipowners was well resourced in terms of expertise of its own, it had poorly anticipated the Moroccan government's decision not to renew the fishing agreement with the EU, officially to safeguard stocks but, in fact, for a series of other reasons. The main reason was the emergence of a powerful Moroccan deep-sea fishing industry close to royal power and the Moroccan army, determined to eliminate Spanish competition from the lucrative market for cephalopods. Following the example of the French tuna-boats, the ANACEF represented its interests at a European level, mainly through use of Spanish state channels. But the fact that, with the exception of Portuguese shipowners, and more marginally the Italians and Greeks, the EU–Morocco agreement concerned exclusively Spanish interests, was a disadvantage with Moroccan representatives who regularly pointed out to the Commission that this was not a European but a Spanish problem. What Anglo-American literature on the EU's external capacity sometimes calls the lack of *actorness* is illustrated here as a major constraint on the conduct of effective negotiation with a non-member country.[25]

European debates on agreements

Just as with external trade policy, EU contractual policy is not the result of straightforward technical exchanges between governmental and non-state actors of European fishing. On the contrary, the policy reveals the emergence of debates around the issue of budgetary and environmental costs.

Contrary to the northern agreements based on strict reciprocity in terms of access to the resource, with the notable exception of Greenland, the southern agreements provide for financial compensation. The latter is shared between shipowners, who pay charges to non-member states directly for issuing licences and for each tonne caught, and the EU budget. The share assumed by the latter is in no way comparable to the shipowners' share. Between 1993 and 1997, it represented 82.8 per cent of the total cost of agreements compared to only 17.2 per cent paid by the shipowning businesses.[26] Since this financial compensation represents between 30 and 35 per cent of the CFP annual total budget, approximately €260 million out of a total of 875 in 1999,[27] and primarily serves the interests of Spanish shipowners, followed more selectively by those of Portuguese, Italians, Dutch, French and Greek shipowners, their cost to the Community budget has prompted some intergovernmental debate. In October 1997, the Council of Fisheries Ministers asked the Commission for an expert report on the costs and benefits of fishing agreements with non-member countries. Contracted by the Commission in August 1999, IFREMER's report provided confirmation of the positions held by the main actors. Governments of countries whose fishing fleets benefited from privileged access to the waters of ACP countries and Argentina were naturally in favour of the EU budget's paying for the agreements. The Spanish Economic and Social Committee thus observed, in 1999, that 'Community budgets should convert the budget item for fishing agreements to current values in order to facilitate negotiations and maintain a policy of fishing relationships with non-member countries'. It added that 'the sector's financial participation should remain at its current level', i.e. without increasing the charge on shipowners.[28] The position of the Union of French Fishing Shipowners (UAPF) was identical to that of the Spanish professional organisations. It was in marked contrast to the approach of Irish, British and Swedish organisations, which regularly called for a reduction of the share of the CFP budget allocated to the southern agreements and for a gradual transfer of costs to shipowners.[29] As with structural funds, here one sees that once the issue of redistribution is raised, the territorial (or national) limitations of any expression of a legitimate solidarity within the EU become clear. These debates aroused fears in the main countries benefiting from the agreements, notably Spain, to the extent that some professional and political actors demanded the renationalisation of the contractual policy, which would lead to a resumption of responsibility for paying financial compensations from national budgets.[30] In a way, the existence of an EU external policy was perceived as less of a guarantee than national external policies would be because of the uncertainty hanging over its budgetary resources.

Between 1993 and 1997, non-member southern countries, as well as Greenland and Argentina, received an average of almost €217 million in return for granting fishing rights to Community fishing fleets. For some of these countries the financial contribution is far from insignificant relative to their total budgetary receipts: 13 per cent for São Tome and Príncipe, 15 per cent for Mauritania, nearly 30 per cent for Guinea-Bissau.[31] Although some agreements make explicit mention of the appropriation of funds to scientific and technical programmes, or training initiatives and study grants aiming to develop the national fishing sector, most of the compensations paid to non-member countries are not earmarked for specific uses. Another consequent budgetary debate within the EU concerns the actual use of funds by governments from non-member countries. The sharpest criticisms on this subject come from those governments (Ireland, Great Britain, Germany, Sweden and Denmark) whose fishing fleets benefit least from the agreements. The German, British and Dutch fisheries administrations thus reproached the EU–Morocco agreement, applicable over the period 1995–99, for payments made to the Moroccan state without any kind of guarantee of its appropriation for the development of a national fishing sector.

There is a second debate within the EU, this time around the cost of fishing agreements for the fishery resource. Unlike the preceding debate, this one is no longer intergovernmental, but rather due to non-state actors motivated by the defence of a global environmentalist ethic. Environmentalist NGOs, which have offices in Brussels, regularly accuse the Community agreements of exporting overfishing to developing countries. In March 1999, Greenpeace International published a highly critical report on the EU–Mauritania agreement in which they accused twenty-two EU industrial ships, Dutch ships in particular, of contributing to the deterioration of Mauritanian fisheries stocks, especially cephalopods and demersal fish.[32] In keeping with their protest strategy, in March 1999 the Greenpeace activists went so far as to blockade the port of Rotterdam to prevent a Dutch trawler from sailing for Mauritania.[33] Greenpeace intended this form of action to denounce the contradictions between the draconian objectives of reducing fishing fleets aimed at Community waters and the growth of the fishing effort in waters from non-member countries through incentives to relocate. This contradiction does indeed exist, as can be shown with the agreement that the EU concluded with Argentina. By financially supporting the creation of joint enterprises in Argentina, this agreement led to the transfer of Spanish freezer-trawlers with no concern for the burden this represented for the global fishing effort. A study published in spring 1999 by one of the European NGOs pointed out that 'the transfer of freezer-trawlers which process fish on board for direct re-export had contributed to the deterioration of Argentine hake stocks whilst exacerbating tensions with the coastal ships which constituted a significant source of revenues for [Argentine] ports such as Mar El Plata'.[34] This example allows us to measure the extent to which NGOs are actors in their own right in the CFP, with the positions they take having an influence on institutional debates. Taking on board the criticism of joint enterprises, the Commission proposed to the Council that they include consideration of a reduction of the fishing effort in the regulation on the new modalities of structural assistance, passed in December 1999. Similarly, the European Parliament's support to renewing the agreement with Morocco in October 1999 was hardly unanimous. Some European elected officials, particularly within the Greens group, pointed out the high cost of the agreement in force between 1995 and 1999, for the Community budget as well as for the fisheries resource.[35]

Power struggles for access to stocks
In so far as the growing shortage of the fishery resource and a chronic trading deficit places the EU in a position of demand, the economic and political actors from non-member countries are far from taking fishing agreements entirely for granted. Compensations from the Community budget and charges on European shipowners' licence fees, just like the obligation imposed on Community fishing fleets to land part of their catches in non-member countries or to employ local sailors, constitute undeniable short-term benefits for the economies of some countries.[36] It remains the case, however, that in countries where national economic actors are structured as interest groups, such as in Morocco, demands have emerged for a tough negotiating stance with the Europeans in one of the rare economic sectors where the balance of power is in their favour. When the Moroccan Fishing Minister Thami El-Khyari pointed out, in March 2000, that the only foreseeable alternative to the 1995 agreement with the EU was an agreement which no longer involved access to the resource, but the onshore processing of fishing products, he made quite clear his objective of exploiting a coveted natural resource to win market shares in the trade of processed products. The fishing agreements in this respect invalidate the often too hasty conclusion that globalisation has totally got the better of the sovereignty of southern states. Similarly, when in 1998 the Argentine Senate passed a series of laws banning fishing and reducing the fiscal advantages of European shipowners, this demonstrates the sovereignist concern for a tough negotiating stance over the terms of exchange with the EU. The strategic advantage of non-member countries is reinforced by the fact that the interests in fishing matters remain struc-

tured in a national framework within the EU. This has posed the repeated difficulty for the EU to link negotiation of fishing agreements to other elements of a global external policy. The demand of Spanish actors in 1999 to make the granting of new agricultural concessions to Morocco, within the framework of the partnership agreement concluded with the EU in 1996, subject to a renewal of the fishing agreement thus ended in failure. With the exception of the Portuguese government, no European government was ready to sacrifice the partnership agreement with Morocco on the altar of fishing. The sovereignist policies of some non-member countries, aiming to reduce European industrial fishing fleets' rights of access to their waters, have inevitable consequences for the general distribution of the fishing effort. European shipowning companies tend in effect to redirect their activities to waters of 'rentier states' which are more dependent on EU financial compensation.[37] Some Spanish cephalopod ships that were operating in Moroccan waters until November 1999, thus intend to use the EU–Mauritania agreement to re-locate further south, at a time of alarmist scientific assessments on the state of stocks of the Mauritanian EEZ. The sovereignist policies of non-member states likewise has an impact on the redistributive function which operates within the EU, in so far as it is up to the Community budget to assume the financing of ceasing activities and retraining shipowners and sailors.

Regulating access to the open sea: the European Community and the regional fishing organisations

The worrying state of many fisheries stocks, combined with the main global fishing fleets' excess exploitation capacity, has led experts and governments to seek compatibility between the regulations enforced in the EEZ and those applicable on the open sea. The RFOs are the vehicles for this cooperation. Although several RFOs were created at the turn of the century, most of them came into being over the last forty years with an increased involvement in managing the resource from the 1990s onwards. Within the RFOs, the interests of shipowners and European fishermen are formally represented by the Commission, which offers yet another oppor-tunity to examine the decision-making characteristics of a European external policy.

Multilateral fisheries diplomacy

In adhering in 1982 to the United Nations Convention on the Law of the Sea, the main maritime states intended to ensure a balance between the rights and obligations of coastal states and those fleets fishing on the high seas. Several international law conventions have been agreed which complement and specify this regulatory framework for the high seas: the agreement adopted in 1993 within the FAO on the respect, by ships fishing on the high seas, of international measures to preserve and manage the resource; next, the code of conduct for responsible fishing adopted by the 1995 FAO conference following the Cancun declaration of 1992; finally, the 1995 United Nations 'New York' agreement on the conservation and management of stocks whose movements occur as much inside as beyond EEZ's (straddling stocks) and of highly migratory fish stocks. These international legal instruments have sanctioned the role of RFOs in the implementation of multilateral fisheries diplomacy. In December 1999, there were thirty-five RFOs covering most of the planet's seas and oceans, of which thirty-two were performing resource management activities. Some were set up under the FAO, others were created independently of that organisation.[38]

> Of the former, a number are purely consultative and have no administrative organisation of their own, e.g. the Fishery Committee for the Eastern Central Atlantic (CECAF), while others have management powers and autonomous structures and budgets, e.g. the Indian Ocean Tuna Commission (IOTC). The majority have powers in relation to the conservation and management of resources. Some are concerned with all biological resources in the area for which they are responsible e.g. Northwest Atlantic Fisheries Organisation (NAFO). Others focus on a stock or group of stocks e.g. the International Convention for the Conservation of Atlantic Tuna (ICCAT). Their geographical area of competence may be limited to the high seas and the exclusive economic zones (EEZs) of coastal States on account of the biological unity of the stocks. Some organisations, such as the International Baltic Sea Fishing Convention (IBSFC) on the other hand, cover only zones coming under the jurisdiction of coastal States.[39]

In the 1990s, a policy was established within RFOs to strengthen their structures of decision-making autonomy relative to those of national fishing administrations. The Convention on Future Multilateral Cooperation in NAFO for example has an independent secretariat. Similarly, the General Fisheries Council for the Mediterranean (GFCM) has its own budget. Although the RFOs constitute original experiences of fishing regulation through international law, materialising through fishing quotas, catch plans and even inspection and monitoring programmes, their decision-making process is no less reliant on the intergovernmental. The implementation of regulatory measures continues to depend entirely on the good will of contracting states.[40] For a long time concentrated on the sole obligations of member states, the RFOs have however undergone an interesting development since the 1990s. They have begun to adopt measures intended 'to discourage the vessels of non-contracting parties (non-cooperating) from undermining the goals agreed to for the management of resources. [. . .]'. These measures targeted 'access to ports and the ban on landing of unlawful catches [by ships sailing under flags of convenience], as well as access to markets with the possibility of imposing trade sanctions on States which refuse to cooperate'.[41] In 1999, for example, ICCAT adopted a series of recommendations on the international trading of blue-fin tuna aimed at countering the practices tolerated by some (notably Asian) states who were not party to the convention. This is another manifestation of the gradual formation of a 'global community of responsibility'[42] around the protection of the fisheries resource, for which the FAO's code of conduct was a frame of reference. Beyond this debate relating to environmentalist ethics, the outflanking of the regulation outside the strict framework of member states was also devised to dissuade shipowners from switching their vessels to flags of non-member countries that were less scrupulous with regard to international law.

The Community speaks with one voice

In 1999, the EU was a member of ten RFOs and had observer status in two others (Table 7.1). Membership of a third of these RFOs had occurred over the course of the four previous years. The EU became a member of ICCAT in December 1997, leading British, Spanish, French, Italian and Portuguese governments to renounce formal membership status in the tuna organisation. The Europeanisation of representation within RFOs was often initially experienced as a loss of power by national administrations, which found themselves deprived of the right to commit the state's responsibility in an international zone. Some national administrations have as a result used subterfuge to circumvent, quite legally, the exclusive jurisdiction of the EU and retain a right to vote separately. This is the case with states owning overseas territories that were not part of the EU. A Danish civil servant is, for example, present at the NAFO on behalf of the Faroe Islands and Greenland, just as a British counterpart from the Overseas Department sits on the IOTC on behalf of the Chagos Islands and a French member of the Secretariat General for the Sea at ICCAT on behalf of Saint-Pierre-et-Miquelon. The EC's membership in the RFOs, however, obliges national fishing administrations to find a compromise among themselves in advance of negotiation with non-members. This coordination process in the end is a great deal like the negotiating mechanisms highlighted by studies on the external policy of federal states.[43] The necessary search for compromise is expressed by the systematic meeting of national administrations in a 'Community coordination' before and during any and all negotiation within RFOs. Analysts seeking to conceptualise the EU's external policy have used the notion of 'presence' in international relations by stressing that this notion was different from the capacity to take action of a state that reverts to a sovereign and unitary actor, according to a traditional definition.[44] There is indeed an EU 'presence' in the RFOs which maximises the interests of the European fishing industry by creating the perception among third parties of being a collective actor. At ICCAT, the EC – if only because it was perceived as the principal contributor to the organisation's budget – exercised more influence on decisions negotiated with the big tuna states such as Brazil, the United States or Japan than could have done the British, Spanish, French, Italian and Portuguese governments respectively. This maximisation of power through 'presence' explains how a professional organisation such as the UAPF consider it 'normal for the EU to be a member of international fishing commissions in its own right'.[45] The EC's membership as such in the RFOs is also perceived as a legal safeguard by EU professionals, since it brings about an integration of regulatory measures in Community law. Implementation thus becomes obligatory just as it is for measures governing the management of resources in Community waters. For their part, EU governments find membership of RFOs to be in the EC's interest for several reasons. The first is the funding of the contribution to RFOs out of the Community budget instead of out of national budgets. For example, a majority of EU governments want the Commission to take responsibility, on the basis of the Community budget, for the appropriation of resources – material (inspecting or monitoring ships) and human (inspectors, observers) – enabling the establishment of inspection and monitoring programmes within RFOs, which the Commission has refused. This controversy reminds us once again of the debate on the sharing out of costs arising from international commitments, which in the federal states pits the central government against federal entities.[46] Unlike the federal states, one must however acknowledge that the (federated) states retained strong pre-eminence in the EU by defining the share-out, since in this respect the autonomy of the centre (the Commission) is relative. The example of RFOs demonstrates that, in the conduct of an external policy, one characteristic of the EC lies in the limited autonomy of a central layer which is not composed of a government but of an agency able to negotiate only on the basis of the compromise drawn up by the various parties on the periphery.

J. Jupille and J. Caporaso have used four criteria to conceptualise the EC's capacity to act in international conferences on the environment: recognition, which indicates the acceptance of the EU/EC'S competence by others; authority, materialised through the possibility of exercising a legal competence; autonomy, linked to differentiation of the EC and its independence relative to other actors; and finally coherence, based on the expression of unified, consistent policy preferences toward the exterior.[47] Although these criteria tend to intersect, they are useful for showing the reality and limitations of the EC's external capacity in the fishing sector.

Table 7.1 Regional fishing bodies to which the EU is a contracting party or observer

	French acronym	English acronym	Community status
North-west Atlantic Fisheries Organisation	OPANO	NAFO	Member
Commission for the Conservation of Antarctic Marine Living Resources	CCAMLR	CCAMLR	Member
North-east Atlantic Fisheries Commission	CPANE	NEAFC	Member
Indian Ocean Tuna Commission	CTOI	IOTC	Member
International Baltic Sea Fishery Commission	CIPMB	IBSFC	Member
North Atlantic Salmon Conservation Organisation	OCSAN	NASCO	Member
International Convention for the Conservation of Tunas	CICTA	ICCAT	Member
General Fisheries Commission for the Mediterranean	CGPM	GFCM	Member
Fishery Committee for the Eastern-Central Atlantic	COPACE	CECAF	Member
Inter-American Tropical Tuna Commission	CIATT	IATTC	Observer
Indian Ocean Fishery Commission	CPOI	IOFC	Member
International Whaling Convention	CBI	IWC	Observer

Source: European Commission, *The European Community's Participation in regional fishing organisations*, communication to the Council and the European Parliament, 8 December 1999

With regard to the first criterion, the recognition of the EC by non-members is quite clearly apparent. Whether these are non-member countries signatory to fishing agreements or contracting parties to the RFOs, they consider the Commission to be the institution that should be addressed when negotiating a fishing issue with the EU. It is through Brussels that a non-member country, be it Norway, the ACP countries or Argentina, formally engages in negotiation with the EU. The criterion of authority resulting from the exercise of legal competence is equally a reality. The exclusive competence conferred by the treaties on the EC in the fishing domain, the obligation to implement Community law at national level and the judicial control operated by the CJEC are elements that attest to this authority of the EC. It is thus that Community law makes it no longer possible for the administrations of the fifteen to conclude bilateral fishing agreements with a non-member state. The only possible circumvention is the negotiation of private actors with non-member governments. Once one considers the criterion of autonomy, the EC's capacity to act on the international scene is clearly less evident. This is due to the fact that the Commission is not a government able to make commitments with respect to non-members in the name of the EU by removing itself from intergovernmental or interstate compromise. The mandates to negotiate fishing agreements and Community coordinations within RFOs are intergovernmental procedures that underscore the limits of the Commission's autonomy when dealing with third countries. Similarly, the still strong sectorisation of interests between national territories considerably hinders the emergence of the fourth criterion, which is the EC'S internal cohesion toward non-member countries. The actors from non-member countries know how to take tactical advantage of differences in national interests between shipowners, as was seen in the debate on the renewal of the EU–Morocco fishing agreement which expired in 1999. With the result that, although an EC presence on the international scene certainly exists in the fishing domain, the transformation of this presence into a genuine external policy remains an open question.[48]

Notes

1   Contrary to the preceding chapters, this chapter often refers to the European Community (EC) rather than to the European Union (EU) since, according to the treaties, the EC and not the EU has the international capacity to represent member states in fishing matters.

2   Karol Twitchett, *Europe and the World*, London, Europa, 1976, p. 8.

3   Initially, the agreement had been made between the EC and the ensemble of EFTA States. Switzerland did not ratify it following a negative referendum result. In addition, Austria, Sweden and Finland became EU members on 1 January 1995.

4   Jean-Jacques Gabas (ed.), *L'Union européenne et les pays ACP. Un espace de coopération à construire*, Paris, Karthala, 1999.
5   Thanks to Jean Coussy for information he supplied about this.
6   The promoters of 'Drug GSP' naively imagined that trade at very low or reduced customs rates on fishing products from Latin American countries would encourage the retraining of cocoa farmers to become fishing professionals. The results did not live up to expectations.
7   Parrès, *Affirmer la place*, p. 163.
8   European Commission, *Rapport au Conseil et au Parlement sur la politique commune de la pêche*.
9   Christopher Hill, 'The Capability–Expectations Gap, or Conceptualizing Europe's International Role', *Journal of Common Market Studies*, 31 (3), September 1993, pp. 305–328.
10 Interview with Raymond Simonnet, Brussels, 21 October 1999.
11 Interview with François Benda, Brussels, 20 October 1999.
12 See Michael Bruter, 'Diplomacy without a State: The External Delegations of the European Commission', *Journal of European Public Policy*, 6 (2), June 1999, p. 183–205.
13 See art. 300, § 3, al. 2 of the EC Treaty.
14 Case C-189/97, *European Parliament v. EU Council*.
15 European Parliament, *Accords bilateral et conventions internationales pêches*, t. I, Brussels, Direction generale d'Études, 1996.
16 Consejo Económico y Social, *La politique des accords de pêche de l'Union européenne*, Report 3/1999, Madrid, Colección Informes, 1999.
17 The funds granted to Greenland essentially amounted to indirect development aid, after the exit of this Danish territory from the EU.
18 IFREMER, *Evaluation of Fisheries Agreements Concluded by the European Community, Summary Report* sent to the European Commission, Brussels, typescript, August 1999.
19 IFREMER, *Evaluation of Fisheries Agreement*.
20 Interview with Edoardo O'Shea Tapia, Madrid, 26 April 2000.
21 In Finistère there is a fourth tuna-fishing business which is based not in Concarneau but in Plouhinec. This is the Comasud (ex-ACF) shipowning business bought in 1999 by the Intermarché group who owns four ships.
22 Three other ships were registered at Audierne, the dozen others were under foreign flags (including Seychelles, Mauritius, Saint-Vincent-et-Grenadines) to avoid the rigours of the MAGP.
23 Interview with Michel Dion, Concarneau, 4 February 2000.
24 Michel Dion, SNATC general representative, is also general representative of the UAPF.
25 Hill, 'Capability–Expecatations Gap'; and also Roy H. Ginsberg, 'Conceptualizing the European Union as an International Actor', *Journal of Common Market Studies*, 37 (3), September 1999, pp. 429–454.
26 IFREMER, *Evaluation of Fisheries Agreement*.
27 Brian O'Riordan, 'La pêche au-delà des eaux communautaires. Qui paye et qui beneficie?', *El Anzuelo*, March 1999, pp. 4–6.
28 Consejo Económico y Social, 'La politique des accords de pêche', p. 63.
29 European Commission, *Rapport au Conseil et au Parlement sur la politique*

commune de la pêche.

30 Carmen Fraga Estevez, *Report on the Common Fisheries Policy after the Year 2002*, European Parliament, Fishing Commission, 2 October 1997.

31 IFREMER, *Evaluation of Fisheries Agreements*, p. 20.

32 Greenpeace, *Study of Mauritanian Fisheries Development and the European/Mauritanian Fisheries Agreement*, March 1999.

33 *Agence Europe*, 2 April 1999.

34 O'Riordan, 'La pêche au-dela des eaux communautaires'.

35 Interview with Toufiq Jorio, Rabat, 28 April 2000.

36 IFREMER, *Evaluation of Fisheries Agreements*.

37 Yasuki Matsunaga, 'L'État rentier est-il réfractaire à la démocratie', *Critique internationale*, 8, July 2000, pp. 46–58.

38 European Commission, *Community Participation in Regional Fishing Organisations*, communication to the Council of the European Parliament, Brussels, 8 December 1999.

39 European Commission, *Rapport au Conseil et au Parlement sur la politique commune de la pêche.*

40 See Marie-Claude Smouts, *Les organisations internationales*, Paris, Armand Colin, 1995.

41 European Commission, *Rapport au Conseil et au Parlement sur la politique commune de la pêche*, pp. 8–9.

42 Badie, *Une monde saus souveraineté.*

43 Renaud Dehousse, *Fédéralisme et relations internationales*, Brussels, Bruylant, 1991.

44 David Allen and Michael Smith, 'Western Europe's Presence in the Contemporary International Arena', *Review of International Studies*, 16 (1), 1990, pp. 19–37; Hill, 'Capability–Expectations Gap'.

45 uapf, 'Réponse au questionnaire de la Commission sur la politique commune de la pêche après 2002', *La pêche maritime*, May–June–July 1998, p. 329.

46 Dehousse, *Fédéralisme.*

47 J. Jupille and J. Caporaso, 'States, Agency, and Rules: The EU in Global Environmental Politics', in Carolyn Rhodes (ed.), *The European Union in the World Community*, Boulder (Col.), Lynne Rienner, 1998.

48 Allen and Smith, 'Western Europe's Presence'.

Conclusion

In studying the mechanisms of the formulation and implementation of the Common Fisheries Policy (CFP), we have sought to understand the way in which the EU polity routinely brings into play actors, processes and public policies which can clearly no longer be embodied by the states alone. In line with the thinking of several analysts, such as Simon Hix or David Wincott, this book shares the view that study of the EU can no longer restrict itself solely to that of European integration focused around the question of intergovernmental regime or supranational polity. To understand the EU henceforth requires a grasp of the foundations and the issues at stake in a political dynamics that does not differ considerably from the workings of politics at the national level.[1]

The shift of public action from the national to the Community level brings us back to the problem, well known to scholars of the state, of political agenda-setting.[2] What numerous writers call, using a generic term, the Europeanisation of public action is in fact the result of an incremental process of 'institutional cobbling-together',[3] through which public policies conducted initially within the framework of states (organisation of the market, structural support, conservation of the resource, and so on) have gradually shifted to the European level. Consideration of the institutional context specific to the EU (such as enlargements for example) as well as that of the global context (the global debate on resource depletion, the recognition by international law of the principle of riparian rights) are crucial for explaining the shift of fisheries management from national agendas to the new European agenda. The transfer of public action of the state towards the EU has nonetheless only been possible because it has been driven by actors for whom the EU has gradually become a space of political mobilisation. The French associations of industrial shipowners thus played a major role in putting regulation of ships' access to fishing zones onto the EU agenda. Similarly, the alliance between the small-scale Spanish Basque tuna fishermen and the environmentalist NGOs contributed to getting the use of driftnets banned by the EU Council. The

CFP nonetheless also led to highlighting the existence of a European politico-administrative class, formed around the commissioner and civil servants of the directorate-general in charge of a sector, who increasingly set the terms of reference of the common management of public policies by relying on the combined power of expertise and the right to initiate legislation. The principles of managing the fishery resource, of which the Commission's Fisheries Directorate General would like to see itself as guardian, illustrate the emergence of this supranational entrepreneurship, which is an integral part of European politics.

Secondly, the CFP led us to examine the dynamics of actors and institutions, as well as interest representation in a polity that can effectively be characterised as 'multilevel governance'. It is clear that the term 'multi-level governance' is by no means a concept and much less a theory capable of explaining the production of policy at the European level. It is, more modestly, a metaphor illustrating the labyrinth of responsibilities between various levels of government (supranational, state, sub-national) and the overlapping of these levels by the political actors, which makes the modalities of allocating authority more fluid.[4] This book has been an opportunity to measure this fluidity through constant observation of the shared intervention of European, state and sub-national institutions in the regulation of a particular economic activity. In such a configuration, it becomes difficult to rank levels of authority. In particular, the state no longer has monopoly of it. Community institutions (the Commission, European Parliament, Court of Justice and the Court of Auditors) have a capacity to generate their own ideas and interests by using a certain number of resources: mobilisation of expertise, use of a budget, legal responsibilities recognised by a Treaty. The CFP shows nonetheless that, by virtue of the importance accorded to intergovernmental negotiation, states also remain actors that are no longer exclusive but still essential to EU political system. In some respects, one might even wonder if European negotiation does not enable certain national governmental agencies such as fisheries administrations, which are in a structurally weak position in national governmental hierarchies, to maximise their power by inserting themselves into functional networks at the European level.[5] The question is all the more pertinent since the management of European fisheries, contrary to that of currency or agriculture, rarely goes beyond the ministers and the sectoral administrations to involve heads of state and government within the European Council. States also derive power from their participation in the implementation of Community policies, which remain highly differentiated by territory. This fact requires us to take some distance from Pierre Muller's hypothesis that the EU is the locus of a reconstruction of a new legitimate political community that has replaced the nation-state.[6] This also holds true for sub-national institutions, which, as Patrick Le Galès has underlined in his research, are highly differenti-

ated from one territorial context to another.[7] The autonomy with respect
to the state that the autonomous Spanish communities have to implement
Community regulations on fishing is far greater than that of the French
regions. Similarly, the mechanical equation by to which the projection of
sub-national institutions in the Community polity is enough to enable
them automatically to achieve autonomy in relation to states must at all
costs be avoided. It is above all political autonomy negotiated beforehand
with the state within national constitutional frameworks that enables sub-
national institutions to Europeanise with greater or lesser success. This
book has also shown the need to study the conditions of interest representation in the EU polity. In the fishing sector, the professional actors
continue to express their demands mainly on a national scene of representation, i.e., to the states and the powerful national guild-like
organisations they have sometimes fostered, such as the CNPMEM in
France. The emergence of a CFP continues to contribute to destabilising
national corporatist systems through the potential that private actors have
to project themselves onto Community institutions and to form new
alliances. Professionals thus experience the transnationalisation of interest representation as a learning experience. The successful alliance formed
between the Spanish Basque fishermen, Greenpeace, the Commission and
the European Parliament to get driftnets banned, thus led French fishermen to want to do likewise by forming a transnational coalition of netters
that at one point challenged the corporatist relationship between the
French administration of fisheries and the CNPMEM. In terms of the
institutionalisation of interest representation, this book has also shown
that the Eurogroups formed in Brussels are not necessarily as powerful
lobbies as some studies on European interests representation unsubtly
tend to describe them.[8] Europêche, the European association of shipowners and fishermen, has only a very limited capacity to practise lobbying. It
owes its existence above all to the financial support and status as official
interlocutor that the European Commission grants it. Community institutions have in effect developed voluntaristic policies of support to the
transnationalisation of social actors whose goal is to consolidate their
own legitimacy with regard to national administrations. Commission and
European Parliament support to the institutionalisation of interest groups
at the European level is also a way of ensuring alliances through which to
reform common policies. In the 1990s, the Commission's policy of openness to the environmentalist NGOs in the fishing sector, which achieved
official representative status within the Advisory Committee on Fisheries
and Aquaculture, reflects this quest for new alliances aiming to counter-
balance the reputedly conservative positions of shipowners and fishermen
on resource conservation policy.

Thirdly, the CFP has provided an opportunity to reflect on political
modus operandi at European level. We first assessed the legitimacy

conflicts that continually pit two norms against one another: that of the sovereignty of territories and that of the construction of a market. Since the 1980s, the market norm has established itself more as a global frame of reference for European public action.[9] Just as for telecommunications and transport, the policy of the internal market has come to destabilise economic protectionism and the social order inherited from welfare states in the fishing sector. Quota-hopping well illustrates how European rules on the free circulation of people and capital has encouraged the emergence of new actors and new deterritorialised professional practices, the legitimacy of which was immediately contested by 'traditional' actors accustomed to having their activity protected by national borders. Although the states have not lost all capacity to oppose the effects of European market policy by passing national laws, they can now only act within the strict limitations of what is permitted under an essentially liberal European law. This book then showed how regulation, defined as a political authority's permanent and concentrated control of activities endowed with a particular social value for a community, has taken hold as a dominant mode of political action in the EU polity. Supplied by the Commission nearly always on the basis of expert conclusions, European regulation continues to be perceived by a majority of fishermen as technocratic and top-down, although it is subject to the intergovernmental filter of the Council of Ministers. Social actors all the more dispute the legitimacy of European regulation that implementation and monitoring is not carried out in the same way in all national territories, creating a problem of fairness. Moreover, the industry, which denounces the proliferation of European regulation as a mode of technocratic government, are also those who, paradoxically, demand from a Commission reputedly less sensitive to particular interests, that it ensure centralised control of implementation. How European control should be organised, however, is perceived very differently by the professional actors and by the Commission itself. The first still advocate the creation of European inspectors that are eventually bound to replace national inspectors whereas the second call more for a networking of national inspectors around common practices. There is consequently a gap between social actors who continue to conceive of European policy in terms of substituting European institutions for state institutions, and of Community and national officials who are already in the process of negotiating among themselves a 'multilevel' network. In this configuration, the Commission no longer derives its strength from the project of becoming the government of Europe, but from its capacity to make the different levels of government work together. Finally, this book has been an opportunity to show that, although regulation tends to impose itself as a dominant operational mode in EU polity, this does not mean that the distributive and redistributive mechanisms inspired by the welfare state model are completely absent and insignificant. Although on a scale which is incomparable to that which some states have accustomed them to, European fishermen benefit from transfers from the Community budget through the intermediary of structural funds and a price support policy. This embryonic European welfare state has consequences as to the mobilisation of fishermen, who not only dispute the effects of European regulations that affect their daily activity, but must negotiate with the states and the Commission the allocation of their 'share of the pie' from the EU budget. The relationship that social actors maintain with distribution and redistribution in the fishing sector is nonetheless disconnected from any feeling of belonging to a European political community.[10] The embryonic European welfare state to some extent falls short of manifesting a European solidarity that would contribute to legitimating the functioning of the political system.

Fourthly, this book has stressed the need to analyse the EU polity by taking into account the wider global scene. In an article in the *Journal of Common Market Studies*, Lykke Friis and Anna Murphy rightly insisted on the fact that most studies on EU governance confined themselves to the interrelationships between Community institutions and state (indeed substate) institutions and completely neglected the relationship to the outside.[11] More recently, Yves Surel also wondered to what extent what is called the Europeanisation of public policies no longer tallies, more generally, 'with the dynamics attached to the idea of globalisation'.[12] In the fishing sector, all the measures which have been adopted in matters of conservation of the resource or of trade policy at European level address global problems and are inspired by ideas or formulas which circulate at the global level. This explains how the experts who attend scientific forums and debates at international organisations have often played a determining role as transmitters of ideas in the making of the CFP. This book has also allowed us to show, as regards the controversy on the ban on driftnets, that European institutions are sensitive to global standards (such as the protection of dolphins) and that some social actors in the territories have understood this better than others. This finding led us to raise an issue which warrants further research on other case studies in the European context: the relationship between the norms arising from globalisation and the local territories.[13] In concluding this book, it seems important that global standards should not be considered only as external factors destabilising the identity of local territories, but also as instruments that can sometimes serve the interests of social groups. The exploitation by the Spanish Basque fishermen of the global debate on the ban on catching dolphins is an example that demonstrated how a professional community practicing 'traditional' fishing can find in globalisation a way to exclude other fishermen from the market, out of fear that their fishing techniques result in superior economic performances.

Globalisation has, in this case, served the strategy of competition conducted by one territorialised social group at the expense of another. This book finally has posed the problem of EU representation in relation to the rest of the world. 'Who speaks for Europe?' asked Sophie Meunier and Kalypso Nicolaïdis in an article on actors of the EU trade policy.[14] In the global negotiation on fishery resources as in the commercial domain, the Commission has established itself – not unproblematically – as a representative recognised by non-member countries. It derives its recognition from the delegation of authority that governments have accorded it, to negotiate agreements with non-member countries and even to sit on international organisations. The autonomy of the Commission on the global scene remains no less circumscribed by governments and private actors who have interests which are sectorised by territory, to such an extent that although the Commission ensures an EU presence in global negotiations on fishing, this presence does not suffice to prove the existence of a genuine external policy.

As to the future of the CFP itself, the Community ruling of December 1992 instituting a common arrangement for fishing and aquaculture contained the terms for a revision in 2002, confirming the particular relationship that European policy maintains with a Community timescale, a continuous and anticipatory creation.[15] On the basis of a proposal from the Commission, before 31 December 1992, the Council of Fisheries Ministers had to decide new adjustments to achieve in several domains, including the essential one of access to the resource. Whether this is within the Commission or the European Parliament, administrations or national professional organisations, day-to-day implementation of the CFP cannot take place without taking into account this '2002 deadline' which has, moreover, taken on symbolic value.

In keeping with its initial vocation, which is to mobilise expertise (a task which it has always performed better than management, as was revealed by the events leading to the resignation of the Santer commission in March 1999), the Commission anticipated the reform of the CFP by initiating a consultative exercise with professionals. The consultation conducted by the DG Fish has assumed classical procedural forms: a request for an opinion by the Advisory Committee on Fisheries which was provided in an intermediary report of June 1998, organisation of public meetings in the member states, and so on. The work of Commission officials likewise consisted in devising and sending out a questionnaire to a deliberately diverse sample of 347 addressees (fishermen's professional organisations, scientific bodies, environmentalist NGOs, etc.), 150 of which returned their reply to Brussels. Taking advantage of a exercise a priori driven by institutional deadlines, the DG Fish also asked these bodies to comment on certain segments of the CFP which were not formally targeted by the 2002 reform, such as the common organisation of markets and agreements with non-member countries. Globalising the issues in the way illustrates how a directorate-general of the Commission can steer the political agenda of institutional reforms. The practice has not, incidentally, escaped criticism by some professional organisations. Constrained by the EU to take a position in the debate on reform, national organisations of shipowners and fishermen have shown the extent to which access to the resource remained an essential issue for each and at the same time embodied different interests. The 2002 deadline has likewise contributed to fuelling a debate on the individual responsibility of fishermen with respect to the resource, yet without visible perspectives of reform in this domain. With the exception of Dutch fishermen who are already subject to them, and some representatives of industrial high-sea fishing (for example Galician), the eventual substitution of individual transferable quotas (ITQs) for TACs, marking the emergence of individual rights of ownership of the fishery resource, remains unacceptable to a majority of European fishermen. The principal argument against ITQs is that it favours concentration of the resource among big companies of shipowning business at the expense of small-scale enterprises. Although the argument is worth considering, it must be pointed out that it did not take ITQs to bring to light the phenomenon of concentration within the EU. Free circulation of capital fostered the emergence of big European industrial groups of shipowners (Pescanova in Spain, Jaczon in the Netherlands) in the 1980s that bought up companies in the various EU countries. A similar tendency towards concentration can be seen at national level in the deep-sea fishing sector (Intermarché in France, Stevenson in Great Britain). This is explained by the fact that, in an area requiring heavy investment, business competitiveness increasingly depends on the quest for economies of scale. The tendency towards concentration pose an essential political problem which is that of their compatibility with the image that European societies have of an occupation which was historically constructed around the figure of the artisan. This problem in turn induces a very open debate on the priority choices of the CFP after the reform. Will priority go to helping some EU countries preserve the historic model of small-scale fishing through better-resourced redistributive programmes (identity option)? Will it, on the contrary, encourage the advance towards concentration in the name of an imperative competitiveness, even if it means financing the social costs of transition (the liberal option)? Unless the CFP continues to pursue the two options simultaneously, a syncretic option in line with a European social model.

Notes

1   Simon Hix, *Political System of the European Union*; David Wincott, 'Institutional Interaction and European Integration: Towards an Everyday Critique of Liberal Intergovernmentalism', Journal of Common Market Studies, 33 (4), 1995, pp. 597–609.

2   Pierre Muller, 'Les mutations de politiques communautaires', *Pouvoirs*, 69, 1994, pp. 63–75 ; Guy B. Peters, 'Agenda-Setting in the European Community', *Journal of European Public Policy*, 1 (1), 1994, pp. 9–26.

3   Pierre Lascoumes, *L'éco-pouvoir. Environnements et politiques*, Paris, La Découverte, 1994.

4   Gary Marks *et al.*, *Governance in the European Union*, London, Sage, 1996.

5   See Andrew Moravcsik, 'Why the European Community Strengthens the State: Domestic Politics and International Cooperation', *Working Paper no. 52*, Cambridge (Mass.), Harvard University Center for European Studies, 1994.

6   Muller, 'Les mutations de politiques communautaires'.

7   Patrick Le Galès, 'Conclusion', in Patrick Le Galès and Christian Lequesne (eds), *Le paradoxe des régions en Europe*, Paris, La Découverte, 1997.

8   Mazey and Richardson, *Lobbying in the European Community*.

9   Neil Fligstein and Iona Mara-Drita, 'How to Make a Market: Reflections on the European Union's Single Market Program', *American Journal of Sociology*, 102, 1996, pp. 1–33.

10   See Jean Leca, 'Après-Maastricht, sur la prétendue resurgence du nationalisme', *Temoin*, 1, 1993, pp. 29–38.

11   Lykke Friis and Anna Murphy, 'The European Union and Central and Eastern Europe: governance and Boundaries', *Journal of Common Market Studies*, 37 (2), 1999, pp. 211–232.

12   Yves Surel, 'L'integration européenne vue par l'approche cognitive et normative de politiques publiques', *Revue française de science politique*, 50 (2), April 2000, pp. 235–254.

13   On the American case, see Cynthia Ghorra-Gobin, *Les États-Unis entre local et mondial*, Paris, Presses de Sciences Po, 2000.

14   Sophie Meunier and Kalypso Nicolaïdis, 'Who Speaks for Europe? The Delegation of Trade Authority in the EU', *Journal of Common Market Studies*, 37 (3), September 1999, pp. 477–501.

15   Marc Abelès, *En attente d'Europe*, Paris, Hachette, 1996, p. 3.

Appendix: list of persons interviewed

Fishermen and industry figures

Godfrey Adams, Fish Merchants' Association, Newlyn, 7 July 1998

Alain Baranger, regional fishing committee of Pays de la Loire, Saint-Gilles-Croix-de-Vie, 19 February 1998

Maurice Benoish, Coopération maritime, Paris, 8 February 2000

Axelle Bodsea, shipowners union, Concarneau, 4 February 2000

Elian Castaing, manager of shipowning businesses, La Rochelle, 20 February 2000

M. Chartron, regional fishing committee, Saint-Jean-of-Luz, 16 July 1998

Sebastien Chauvet, local fishing committee, Port-Joinville, 18 February 1998

Rene-Pierre Chevert, local fishing committee, Le Guilvinec, 23 July 1998

Vincent Cocozza, shipowner, Lorient, 4 February 2000

Michel Coenen, AICP, Brussels, 20 October 1999

Michel Dion, UAPF, Paris, 9 September 1998; SNATC, Concarneau, 4 February 2000

Albert Etien, local fishing committee, La Rochelle, 20 February 1998

Jacobo Fontan Rodriguez, ASPE, Vigo, 29 October 1997

Alain Furic, shipowner, fish wholesaler, Le Guilvinec, 24 July 1998

Bruno Girard, shipowner, Port-Joinville, 18 February 1998

Jose Manuel Gonzalez Gil de Barnabe, Federación of Cofradías, Madrid, 26 April 2000

Bernard Groisard, shipowner, Port-Joinville, 18 February 1998

Nick Guille, association of Guernsey fishermen, 2 July 1998

Beatrice Harmel, regional fishing committee, Cherbourg, 30 June 1998

Pascal Heid, FROM Sud-Ouest, La Rochelle, 20 February 1998

Alain Jade, shipowner, Le Guilvinec, 23 July 1998

Toufiq Jorio, shipowner, Association of Moroccan Cephalopod Trawlers, Casablanca, 28 April 2000

Dirk Langstraat, Produktschap Vis, The Hague, 2 April 1998

Dominique Lapart, owner-skipper, Plouhinec, 8 August 1997

Peter Merrien, owner-skipper, Guernsey, 1 July 1998

Bill Ogier, owner-skipper, Guernsey, 1 July 1998

Estebán Olaizola Elizazu, Cofradía, Hondarribia, 15 July 1998
Alain Parrès, UAPF, Paris, 9 February 1998; 28 February 2000
Henri Poisson, Comité national des pêches maritimes, Paris, 14 January 1998
Jean-Pierre Plormel, FROM Brittany, Concarneau, 22 July 1998
Jose Suarez-Llanos Rodriguez, Cooperative of fishing shipowners, Vigo, 30 October 1997
Jean-Pierre Salaün, local fishing committee, Concarneau, 4 February 2000
Alain Schlesser, Chamber of Commerce and Industry, Quimper, 21 July 1998
Elisabeth Stevenson, shipowner, Newlyn, 6 July 1998
Jaime Teredor Uranga, Cofradías de Guipuzcoa, San Sebastian, 26 July 1999
Mike Townsend, NFFO, Newlyn, 6 July 1998
Antonio Urruticoechea, CEAP, Madrid, 27 October 1997; 26 April 2000
Guy Vernaeve, Europêche, Brussels, 31 March 1999
Niels Wichmans, Danish Fishermen's Association, Copenhagen, 13 April 1999
Mike Williams, owner-skipper, Newlyn, 6 July 1998
Jean-Marie Zarza, shipowner, Hendaye, 15 July 1998

Politicians

Gerard d'Aboville, Member of European Parliament, Brussels, 7 October 1997
Tony Baldry, former Minister for Fishing, United Kingdom, London, 3 July 1997
Colin Breed, MP, House of Commons, London, 3 July 1997
Andrew George, MP, House of Commons London, 3 July 1997

Community officials

David Amstrong, DG Fish, Brussels, 19 March 1997
Armando Astudillo Gonzalez, DG Fish, Brussels, 13 February 1997
François Benda, DG Fish, Brussels, 20 October 1999
M. Cesari, DG Fish, Brussels, 20 October 1999
Jean-Claude Cueff, DG Fish, Brussels, 12 February 1997
Harm Koster, DG Fish, Brussels, 14 February 1997
Lambert Kraewinckels, Fisheries Committee, European Parliament, Luxembourg, 14 February 1997
Alain Laurec, DG Fish, Brussels, 5 June 1997
Michel Legougne, DG Fish, Brussels, 11 February 1997
Dominique Levieil, DG Fish, Brussels, 11 February 1997
Giovanni Mattiacci, delegation of the European Commission, Rabat, 27 April 2000
Louis Mordrel, former DG Fish official, Rennes, 28 September 1999
Christoph Nordmann, DG Fish, Brussels, 3 June 1998
Christian Rambaud, Emma Bonino's office, Brussels, 5 June 1997; 3 June 1998
Michael Shackleton, European Parliament, Brussels, 13 February 1997
Raymond Simonnet, former DG Fish official, Brussels, 21 October 1999

National and regional officials

Pedro Arruza Betti, secretary general of the Fisheries Administration, Madrid, 26 April 2000

Yves Auffret, Affaires maritimes, Concarneau, 23 July 1998; French fisheries administration, Paris, 9 February 2000

Didier Baudouin, Affaires maritimes, La Rochelle, 20 February 1998

Neil Cumberlidge, Fisheries Administration MAFF, London, 2 July 1997

Edwin J. Derriman, Cornwall Sea Fisheries Committee, Penzance, 6 July 1998

Jose Ricardo Diaz Presedo, Galician Minister for Fishing, Santiago-de-Compostela, 28 October 1998

M. Dusart, prefecture of the Brittany region, Rennes, 28 September 1999

S.G. Ellson, Fisheries Administration, MAFF, London, 8 July 1998

Philippe Forin, French fisheries administration, Paris, 9 February 2000

Pedro Gallache, secretariat-general of Fisheries administration, Madrid, 27 October 1997, 26 April 2000

Maria Gallego Castro, Galician Minister for Fishing, Santiago-de-Compostela, 28 October 1997

Antonio Garcia Elloriaga, secretariat-general of Fisheries administration, Madrid, 27 October 1997

Jean-Luc Lejeune, CROSS, Etel, 3 February 2000

Alberto Lopez Garcia-Asenjo, Spanish representation to the EU, Brussels, 11 February 1997; 21 October 1999

Cathy Mc Glynn, ministerial adviser, MAFF, London, 9 July 1998

Fernando Miranda of Larra y Lonis, secretariat-general of Fisheries administration, Madrid, 26 April 2000

Yves-Laurent Mahé, French Embassy in Casablanca, Morocco, 27 April 2000

Jean-Yves Mobe, Affaires maritimes, Lorient, 3 February 2000

Mme Mercier, prefecture of the Brittany region, Lorient, 27 September 1999

Michel Morin, Affaires maritimes, Saint-Nazaire, 12 March 1997

Edoardo O'Shea Tapia, secretariat-general of Fisheries administration, Madrid, 26 April 2000

Étienne of Poncins, French representation to the EU, Brussels, 19 March 1997

Ole Poulsen, Fisheries administration, Copenhagen, 12 April 1999

François Pujol, Affaires maritimes, Bayonne, 17 July 1998

P. Roos, Minister for Agriculture and Fishing, The Hague, 2 April 1998

Larbi Sbaï, Fisheries Minister, Rabat, 27 April 2000

Mogens Schou, Fisheries administration, Copenhagen, 12 April 1999

Dominique Sorain, French fisheries administration, Paris, 14 January 1998

Tim Render, United Kingdom representation to the EU, Brussels, 31 March 1999; 22 October 1999

Julien Turenne, French Fisheries Administration, Paris, 11 July 2000

Raynald Vallee, Affaires maritimes, Port-Joinville, 18 February 1998

Victor Vasquez Seija, Galician Minister for Fishing, Santiago-de-Compostela, 28 October 1997

Miguel Torre, Galician Galician Minister for Fishing, Santiago-de-Compostela, 28 October 1997

David Wallace, United Kingdom representation to the EU , Brussels, 11 February 1997

Scientists and experts

Jose Arocena, journalist, Guethary, 16 July 1998
Denis Bailly, OIKOS consultant, Rennes, 13 March 1997
Alain Biseau, IFREMER, Lorient, 10 April 1997
Jean-Rene Couliou, Université de Bretagne occidentale, Concarneau, 21 July 1998
Alberto Gonzalez-Garces Santiso, IEO, Vigo, 29 October 1997
Christopher Hopkins, CIEM, Copenhagen, 12 April 1999
John Horwood, CEFAS, Lowestoft, 4 July 1997
Hans Lassen, CIEM, Copenhagen, 12 April 1999
Donaïg Lebon Le Squer, IFREMER, Lorient, 10 April 1997
Phil Lockley, Fishing News, Penzance, 7 July 1998
Alain Maucorps, IFREMER, Nantes, 12 March 1997
Claude Merrien, IFREMER, Lorient, 10 April 1997
John Pope, CEFAS, Lowestoft, 4 July 1997
Carmen Porteiro, IEO, Vigo, 29 October 1997
Jean-Luc Prat, Université de Bretagne occidentale, Brest, 14 March 1997
Jean-Paul Troadec, ORSTOM, Brest, 14 March 1997
Jacques Weber, CIRAD, Nogent-sur-Marne, 20 June 1997

Non-governmental organisations

Robert Alvarez, Itsas Geroa, Hendaye, 15 July 1998
Judie Cator, WWF European Policy Office, Brussels, 31 March 1999
Euan Dunn, Birdlife International, 13 April 1999
Bruno Guillaumie, CEASM, Paris, 7 September 2000
Tony Long, WWF European Policy Office, Brussels, 31 March 1999
Peter Scott, Marine Stewardship Council, London, 9 July 1997
David Wilkins, Eurogroup for Animal Welfare, Brussels, 31 March 1999

Select bibliography

On European Union policy-making

Abélès, Marc, *En attente d'Europe*, Paris, Hachette, 1996.

Claeys, Paul-Henri *et al.* (eds), *Lobbyisme, pluralisme et intégration européenne*, Bruxelles, Presses inter-universitaires européennes, 1998.

Costa, Olivier, *La délibération au Parlement européen*, Brussels, Éditions de l'ULB, 'Études européennes', 2001.

Cram, Laura, *Policy-Making in the European Union: Conceptual Lenses and the Integration Process*, London, Routledge, 1997.

Greenwood, Justin, *Representing Interests in the European Union*, Basingstoke, Macmillan, 1997.

Greenwood, Justin and Aspinwall, Mark (eds), *Collective Action in the European Union*, London, Sage, 1998.

Hill, Christopher, 'The Capability–Expectations Gap, or Conceptualizing Europe's International Role', *Journal of Common Market Studies*, 31 (3), September 1993, pp. 305–328.

Hix, Simon, *The Political System of the European Union*, London, Macmillan, 1999.

Le Galès, Patrick and Lequesne, Christian (eds), *Regions in Europe*, London, Routledge, 1998.

Leibfried, Stephan and Pierson, Paul (eds), *Politiques sociales européennes entre intégration et fragmentation*, Paris, L'Harmattan, 1998.

Mény, Yves, Muller, Pierre and Quermonne, Jean-Louis (eds), *Politiques publiques en Europe*, Paris, L'Harmattan, 1995.

Majone, Giandomenico, *La Communauté européenne. Un État régulateur*, Paris, Montchrestien, 'Clefs', 1996.

Moravcsik, Andrew, *The Choice for Europe*, Ithaca and London, Cornell University Press, 1998.

Muller, Pierre and Surel, Yves, *L'analyse des politiques publiques*, Paris, Montchrestien, 'Clefs', 1998.

Neunreither, Karlheintz and Wiener, Antje (eds), *European Integration after Amsterdam. Institutional Dynamics and Prospects for Democracy*, Oxford, Oxford University Press, 1999.

'Penser l'Europe', *Cultures et conflits*, 38, winter 1997.

Quermonne, Jean-Louis, *Le système politique de l'Union européenne*, Paris, Montchrestien, 'Clefs', 1999.

Rosamond, Ben, *Theories of Integration*, Basingstoke, Macmillan, 2000.

Sandholtz, Wayne and Stone, Alec (eds), *European Integration and Supranational Governance*, Oxford, Oxford University Press, 1998.

Scharpf, Fritz, *Gouverner l'Europe*, Paris, Presses de Sciences Po, 2000.

Wallace, Helen and Wallace, William (eds), *Policy-Making in the European Union*, Oxford, Oxford University Press, 2000.

Numerous articles can also be consulted in journals dealing with European issues, in particular *Politique européenne*, *Journal of Common Market Studies*, *Journal of European Public Policy*, *European Union Politics*.

On the Common Fisheries Policy

Couliou, Jean-René, *La pêche bretonne: Les ports de Bretagne sud face à leur avenir*, Rennes, Presses Universitaires de Rennes, 1997.

Crean, Kevin and David, Symes (eds), *Fisheries Management in Crisis: A Social Science Perspective*, Oxford, Fishing News Books, 1996.

Fraga Estévez, Carmen, *Rapport sur la politique commune de la pêche après 2002*, Brussels, European Parliament, 1997.

Gray, Tim S. (ed.), *The Politics of Fishing*, Basingstoke, Macmillan, 1998.

Holden, Mike, *The Common Fisheries Policy*, Oxford, Fishing News Books, 1994.

Huret, Jacques, *Le livre de bord*, Paris, UAPF, 1990.

Kooinman, Jan (ed.), *Creative Governance: Opportunities for Fisheries in Europe*, Aldershot, Ashgate, 1999.

Leigh, Michael, *European Integration and the Common Fisheries Policy*, London, Croom Helm, 1983.

Lequesne, Christian, 'Quand l'Union européenne gouverne les poissons. Pourquoi une politique commune de la pêche?', *Les études du CERI*, 61, December 1999.

Parlement européen, *Manuel de la politique commune des pêches*, Brussels, Direction générale des études, 1996.

Parrès, Alain, *Affirmer la place des pêches maritimes françaises face aux défis mondiaux*, rapport au Comité économique et social, Paris, 1997.

Proutière-Maulion, Gwenaële, *La politique communautaire de réduction de l'effort de pêche*, Paris, L'Harmattan, 1998.

Schirman-Duclos, Danièle and Laforge, Frédéric, *La France et la mer*, Paris, PUF, 1999.

Shackleton, Michael, *The Politics of Fishing in Britain and France*, Aldershot, Gower, 1986.

Simon, Philippe, *Les pêches maritimes françaises*, Paris, PUF, 'Que sais-je?', 2000.

Symes, David (ed.), *Alternative Management Systems for Fisheries*, Oxford, Fishing News Books, 1999.

Articles about the Common Fisheries Policy are often published in scientific journals, including *Marine Policy*, *l'Annuaire français de droit maritime et océanique*, *Espaces et resources maritimes*. Likewise, the trade press is a source of information by which to gauge national positions on the CFP: *Fishing News* in Great Britain, *Le Marin* in France, *Industrias pesqueras* and *Europa Azul* in Spain.

Name Index